SAVING OURSELVES FROM BIG CAR

SAVING OURSELVES FROM

BIG CAR

GREED

DAVID OBST

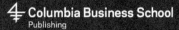

Columbia Business School
Publishing

Columbia University Press
Publishers Since 1893
New York   Chichester, West Sussex
cup.columbia.edu

Library of Congress Cataloging-in-Publication Data
Names: Obst, David author
Title: Saving ourselves from big car / David Obst.
Description: New York : Columbia University Press, [2025] |
Includes bibliographical references and index.
Identifiers: LCCN 2025000709 | ISBN 9780231210423 hardback |
ISBN 9780231558419 ebook
Subjects: LCSH: Automobile industry and trade—
Environmental aspects | Traffic fatalities |
Automobile industry and trade—Social aspects
Classification: LCC HD9710.A2 O27 2025 |
DDC 338.4/7629222—dc23/eng/20250606
LC record available at https://lccn.loc.gov/2025000709

Printed in the United States of America

Cover design: Irene Hoffman Design
Cover images: Adobe Stock

GPSR Authorized Representative: Easy Access System Europe,
Mustamäe tee 50, 10621 Tallinn, Estonia, gpsr.requests@easproject.com

CONTENTS

PREFACE

Big Car is not just an existential crisis facing humanity. It's a living threat that kills hundreds of thousands of our species every year. It has done so for well over one hundred years, and this brutal carnage shows no signs of abating.

If you think I'm just being dramatic, read on . . .

SAVING OURSELVES FROM BIG CAR

INTRODUCTION

The first book I worked on was *In the Name of Profit: Profiles in Corporate Irresponsibility.* The book consisted of profiles of men (it was the early 1970s, and they were all men) working in large corporations, and how they chose profit over the public good. The book wasn't about the companies they worked for but about the men and their actions. There was a common thread of human behavior in these profiles—the human willingness to commit malfeasance to make extra money. Corporate America was littered with well-barbered, expensively dressed men who were moral cripples. *The Wall Street Journal* wasn't a big fan of the book, but the reading public helped make the book a success.

Streetwise is also a book about people in corporations—let's call it the "Big Car" conglomerate—who rationalize truth for the sanctity of profit. By Big Car, I mean the myriad companies—including the auto, oil, insurance, media, tire, and concrete industries—that, working in concert, have had a vast influence on how we all live. Through this combined economic and social power, Big Car affects—and will continue to affect—all our lives. We will look at its constituent industries in turn. You'll also see how the influence of Big Car has put our world in a very precarious situation.

The book's salient point is that corporate responsibility doesn't take place in a void. Some men and women have made (and continue to make) decisions for their companies solely in the name of profit. Sometimes they're aware of the cost to their fellow humans, but they certainly don't seem to be aware—or to care—that their decisions are threatening our very existence.

Throughout the book I will show the staggering price we've paid to Big Car. A short list includes the following:

- Over one and one-third million humans are killed yearly because of Big Car.
- Car accidents are responsible for well over one-third of all accidental deaths in America.
- The number of people killed by cars in the last century—more than 60 million—is equal to the number of fatalities caused by World War II.
- In 2023, U.S. Secretary of Transportation Pete Buttigieg promised that his department was taking critical steps to help reverse the devastating trend of road deaths. Instead, the rate of carnage on our roads continued to rise—by another ten thousand Americans per year.
- In the 2020 presidential election, Big Car outspent environmental advocacy groups by an astonishing thirteen-to-one margin. Big Car has spent almost $400 million on campaign donations and lobbying efforts to help elect candidates favorable to their interests.
- According to the American Automobile Association, the average annual cost in the first five years of new-car ownership is now over $12,000 a year. That's equal to more than 15 percent of the median household income of the average American. We own 223 million personal vehicles, and we spend trillions of

dollars to take care of them. We spend less than $80 billion on all public transportation.[1]

- For half a century, Big Car knew that lead additives in gasoline killed people. They covered it up, and countless multitudes died.

- Seat belts that could have saved tens of thousands of lives a year were not installed in cars for almost half a century after they were developed.

- Shatterproof glass and countless other ways of protecting drivers were withheld from buyers to ensure that Big Car's profit margins remained robust.

- Big Car knew that their products were causing climate change but hid that information for decades. Instead, knowing what the long-term effects would be on the planet, they spent hundreds of millions of dollars funding politicians who called climate change a hoax.

And there is so much more. In this book, I will explore in detail how the executives who profited from selling lies and death to Americans did it. It's not a pretty picture, but it's one we should all know.

I will show how deep and pervasive the Big Car myth has been on the human psyche. We have worshiped at the altar of "easy mobility" for over a century. Unfortunately, we no longer can afford to do so. It will destroy our health and, ultimately, our ability to live on this planet.

I don't think of the car as a villain. Like you, I use my car almost every day. However, I now understand the price we're all paying for it. It's much too high. If we don't stop Big Car, Big Car will destroy us.

We still have time to break the stranglehold. Excellent, innovative models for doing so are being tested all over the globe.

When certain models are shown to be effective, we can emulate them in our own travel spaces.

At the beginning of the last century, transportation faced a similar crisis. The sheer number of horses needed for transportation made living in cities intolerable. Just as the car replaced the horse, we must replace Big Car.

We're a pretty intelligent species. Working together, we'll find new solutions for human mobility and make transportation safer, cheaper, and easier—and, most importantly, something that won't eventually end our time on earth.

I hope you enjoy reading this book as much as I've enjoyed writing it.

1

LEAD HERRING (PART ONE)

Matthew and Dora (not their real names) sat down to an ample serving of bacon and eggs that Dora had placed on the table. They were eating well these days, and why not? Matthew had just started work at the new Ethyl Corporation at a higher salary than he had ever expected. Ethyl Corporation was a newly formed partnership between General Motors (GM) and Standard Oil to produce an anti-knock car additive.

That morning, as he entered the sprawling building that housed the company, his shop steward approached him. "You're going to work in the mixing room today," he said.

As Matthew walked down to the tetraethyl lead additive floor, one of his coworkers gave him a sad smile and said, "Good luck with the loony gas." Another shook his head and asked if Matthew knew any good undertakers. Matthew's new job was to help mix the unique additive that Ethyl Corporation had developed for gasoline engines.

For the first few hours, Matthew felt fine. He didn't care that neither GM nor Standard had any real expertise in the field. This was 1924, and the internal combustion engine now dominated American roads, having driven steam and electric engines out of the marketplace.

The problem with the new engines was getting the combustion of the gasoline inside the engine right. Cars would often backfire, and the constant knocking and pinging of the engine did not make for a nice, relaxing ride.

Ethyl Corporation had recently solved this problem. Their new additive made the engine purr. They couldn't make it fast enough to keep up with demand.

Just before lunch, Matt noticed insects on the factory walls. A couple of hours later, he swatted at them as they swarmed over him. But there were no insects in the factory.

As his hallucinations increased, the shop foreman decided to send him home. Dora was surprised to see him back so early. She asked him what was wrong, but he just kept pacing the floor, swatting at the imaginary insects. After a few hours, she no longer knew what to do. She went into their small bedroom and got into bed, hoping that Matthew would wear himself out eventually. A short time later, she was awakened by screaming from the street. She hurried into the living room, but Matthew wasn't there. She rushed out to the landing of their fifth-story apartment and looked down. There was her husband, splattered dead on the street.

When doctors examined his body, they found strange beads of gas foaming out of his body tissue. Even hours after his death, these bubbles continued to form. They concluded that poor Matthew had died of plumbism, better known simply as lead poisoning.

Lead is poisonous because our body confuses lead with calcium. It quickly reaches the brain, and the result is similar to rabies: you become disoriented, hallucinate, and often die.

At Matthew's funeral, Dora found out that five other people he worked with had also recently died, and that dozens of others were now incapacitated. What Matthew and the others who had been working at Ethyl Corporation were mixing wasn't just some kind of phenomenal wonder cure for cars: it was poison.

Because of the number of fatalities at the plant, newspapers began running stories, which forced the company to hold a hearing to find out what was happening. To counter those who would impede Big Car's enormous profits, Ethyl Corporation brought in one of the great villains of twentieth-century science, Robert Kehoe, to testify.

Kehoe was well respected in his field. He'd been hired for a whopping one hundred thousand dollars a year ($1.8 million today) to be the primary medical advocate on the efficacy of the lead additive. Almost all the research that had been done on the effects of the additive on humans had taken place in his well-funded labs.[1]

Kehoe confidently told the examiners that although the research he'd conducted in his labs was highly confidential, it had shown there was no correlation between any of the health problems in the plant and its product. He had already arranged to install several enormous fans in the workplace as a precautionary measure. He further stated that lead in humans was normal and not in the least harmful.[2]

For the next fifty years, this titanic conflict of interest continued. The same people who made the product also oversaw safety testing of the product. I'll get back to this story later in the book, but suffice to say that the number of deaths and injuries is staggering.[3]

Welcome to the world of Big Car.

2

WHAT IS "BIG CAR"?

Less than 130 years ago, humans were offered a Faustian bargain. Would they sacrifice millions of their species over the years in exchange for improved mobility? Of course they said yes, and what we're calling Big Car made this deal possible. It radically transformed how humans lived. It allowed them to shrink the world, and made travel, shopping, and almost everything else much easier to do. It has come, however, at a staggering price.

Big Car is an international collaboration of industries that have banded together over the last century to make immense fortunes for its constituent corporations.

The combined wealth of this collaboration is more significant than all sovereign nations except the United States and China. Big Car's control of how we travel has profoundly impacted how we all live, eat, travel, and view the modern world. Big Car is as powerful as most nation-states.

THE AUTO INDUSTRY

The prominent first part of this group is the automobile industry. These are the companies who make the cars. Automobile producers are the highest-valued manufacturing entity in our economy. The number of Americans dependent on this business is staggering. One out of every six people in the United States makes a living by manufacturing, distributing, or servicing our cars. A full one-quarter of America's retail trade is car-based. Almost one-fifth of American steel production and nearly three-fifths of its rubber goes into the Big Car business. It is also the nation's largest consumer of machine tools.[1]

The core of Big Car is the automobile industry. We will go into much detail, looking at how this industry, which is less than 150 years old, grew into the behemoth it has become today. In the United States, the industry is concentrated in four major firms—General Motors (GM), Ford, Chrysler, and American Motors Corporation (AMC)—and one dominant manufacturer of commercial vehicles, The International Harvester Company.

OTHER HEAVY INDUSTRY: STEEL, TIRES, AND MACHINE TOOLS

To make a car, you need steel. Big Car was thrilled to add America's steel mills to the team. The United States is now the world's third-largest producer of raw steel. (China and Japan outproduce us.) The steel industry employs several hundred thousand people in its mills and foundries. If you have an extra $100 billion or more that you want to spend, you can buy up all 100 million tons of steel that will be produced next year.

You also couldn't have Big Car without the tire industry.

Early tires were simply bands of leather attached to a wooden wheel. The tradesman who would do this for you was called a wheelwright. He was the person who made wheels for carts.[2]

John Boyd Dunlop, a Scotsman who moved to Ireland in 1887, couldn't stand the constant headaches his poor little ten-year-old was getting from riding his tricycle over unpaved roads, so he invented an inflatable rubber tire to put on his son's bike. Others saw this, and soon, putting pressurized air into a wheel became the only way to roll.

The Northern Bank of Ireland put Mr. Dunlop's face on the ten-pound banknote for his achievement.[3]

As Big Car prospered, so did the tire industry. Working together, they continued to develop better and more comfortable rides for automobile users. In 1935, the tire business consolidated into the leading players: B. F. Goodrich, U.S. Rubber (which changed its name to the much cooler Uniroyal), Goodyear, and Firestone. Each ranked among the top ten corporate powerhouses in America. All except Uniroyal were based in Akron, Ohio, which was soon called "the Rubber Capital of the World."[4]

In 1968, the American tire industry got terrible news when *Consumer Reports* magazine announced that there was a new tire in town. A French company, Michelin, had developed a radial-ply tire. It doubled the life of a tire. It improved steering and made cars much easier to handle. It also got you more miles to the gallon. And you wouldn't have a blowout if you used Michelin tires. Blowouts were a terrible experience for even the most experienced drivers and often resulted in calamitous mishaps and death.

Two years later, radial tires were on the Ford Continental; the rest was history for poor Akron. Most of the big tire companies went into bankruptcy. Big Car didn't care; it simply moved on to the new dominant players in the field. There are nearly three billion tires produced each year on our planet in some 450 tire factories around the world.[5]

Americans use many tires. They also throw about a quarter of a billion of them away each year. These become fire hazards, although they make great vacation homes for mosquitoes. They are also a significant source of microplastic pollution—just another "thank you" from Big Car.

You can't make a car without machine tools. Machine tools, quite logically, are machines that help people make things. They can do what human muscles can't accomplish. Big Car is partially responsible for developing the ability to manufacture a car with various tools. These tools were also one of the primary reasons we won the Second World War. We were able to triple our production of machine tools relative to our enemies; it's said that the war was won as much by machine shops as by machine guns.[6]

The manufacturers of these tools make buckets of money. It helps that every time there's a change in design, there often must be a change in the corresponding machine tools. One of the principal strategies employed by American automobile manufacturers is "planned obsolescence." The idea is simple. Every year they make some changes to the design of each of their models. Since no self-respecting American wants to be seen in last year's car, the idea works brilliantly. It means that smaller manufacturers of cars can't compete because they can't afford to buy new machine tools each year.

Alas, like so many other things, America is no longer in the top tier of machine tool manufacturers. Yet once again, Big Car has simply made new friends in that industry.

THE INSURANCE INDUSTRY

Another happy member of Big Car is the automobile insurance market. In the United States alone, over $300 billion is spent annually on car insurance. That's more than $1,000 per driver, per year.[7]

Until the 1930s, there was no such thing as car insurance. But the increased speeds of cars and their nasty tendencies to crash into people and things meant that drivers started to need protection from the consequences of what cars can do.

Insurance providers now offer this protection in exchange for a premium paid by the driver. To get the cheapest rate on your car insurance, it's best to be a female driver, aged 60–69, living in Ohio. The worst rate is for teenagers in Pennsylvania.

The largest private passenger vehicle insurers in the United States are State Farm, Geico, Progressive, and Allstate.

These companies, over the years, have come up with ingenious ways of getting our money. First, new drivers pay much more than experienced drivers. Married drivers pay less than singles. That's because statistics show that married drivers have fewer crashes.[8]

If you've had an accident, your premium jumps by about 30 percent, half of what you'll have to pay if you get a DUI on your record. Insurance costs more in cities than it does in rural areas, and finally, to rub it in, drivers with poor credit scores pay way more on their premium costs.

Here's a further example of how Big Car and insurance work together. GM and the fine people who insure their cars decided to place tracking devices into new cars. Called the "Smart Driver Program," it was part of a database called OnStar. When you purchased a new car from GM, part of the avalanche of paperwork presented to the buyer was a form asking your permission to let GM pass along all your driving data to your insurance company.

Customers, unless they read the agreement carefully, had no idea that dealers had now connected their new cars to their insurers. Not only did the sale of this information make countless dollars for GM, but it also allowed insurers to increase premiums on the car's owners—often causing insurance premiums to sky-rocket by as much as 50 percent.

Even though GM had made a promise to the Federal Trade Commission to always notify its customers if it would be selling any data collected from their cars, new buyers had no idea why suddenly their insurance costs were increasing so rapidly.

The premiums were increasing because the insurance compa-nies were able to use the data from the cars to show that drivers had been speeding, braking suddenly, or otherwise driving in a way that increased risks.

This increase in so-called risks (the insurance company had no context to accurately measure them) meant that insurance premi-ums could be raised.

The result was that, once again Big Car was able to get its hands into our pocketbooks.[9]

ADVERTISING, MEDIA, AND ENTERTAINMENT

Yet another happy member of the Big Car family is the atten-tion theft market—more commonly known as the advertising business.

Ever since people came out of caves, they have been trying to sell each other stuff. The Egyptians used to put papyrus up on walls to attract buyers. Advertising as we know it was started by Thomas Barratt, an English businessman who owned a soap company. He is widely regarded as "the father of modern adver-tising." In the nineteenth century, Mr. Barratt made a soap called

Pears. Clever Tom came up with the catchphrase "Good morn-ing. Have you used Pears soap?" For some reason, everyone loved asking each other this question, and it was still going strong well into the twentieth century.[10]

Big Car saw how the tobacco industry used ads to create wonderfully positive associations for their product: nobody in any radio, print, or TV ad ever looked unhappy while they were killing themselves smoking. The same became true for auto ads.

An alien from another planet watching car ads would think that only one car at a time uses the roads on Earth. Watch an ad and you'll see a handsome, smiling couple zooming along city streets or mountain roads without another car in sight. Just like real life, right?

The dirty little secret about advertising is that most studies have found that advertising has a negative return on investment of more than 80 percent. Of course, this hasn't deterred Big Car from spending billions of dollars in magazines, newspapers, radio, TV, and now the Internet to make folks think they aren't living the good life if they aren't driving.

This leads to yet another willing partner of Big Car: mass media. Let's start with newspapers.

A full-page ad in the *Los Angeles Times* costs $25,000. An obituary costs a couple of hundred bucks. Do you think the editors of significant newspapers are more interested in the corporations that pay them hundreds of thousands a year, or in a low-income family that lost a loved one in a car crash?

Newspapers do cover the transportation business, but typi-cally not with an investigative slant. Instead, most papers' arti-cles are about either how well or how terribly the business side of car companies is doing. However, not a day goes by that you can't see pages and pages of ads depicting the car companies' wonderful products.

The movie business also has a long and willing history of making cars look good, often making them the costars of their films.

Without his Aston Martin, James Bond was helpless. In both *Le Mans* and *Bullitt*, Steve McQueen placed the cameras in such a way that the audience felt like they were inside the cars. Very cool. *The French Connection* depicted how a great car chase could take place in New York City. Countless other films, all the way back to the turn of the century's *Keystone Cops*, have shown the hilarity of a good car chase. W. C. Fields and the Three Stooges also used the car to get a good laugh. The tradition continues, from *Smokey and the Bandit* to *The Blues Brothers* to *Ford v Ferrari*. Speeding autos are a staple of cinematic entertainment.

Several cars have even starred as themselves. For example, *The Love Bug* made the Volkswagen Beetle a star—who could ever forget Herbie? The Disney company, in collaboration with Pixar Animation Studios, produced the 2006 blockbuster animated film (and, eventually, multimedia franchise) *Cars*, which anthropomorphizes the automobile into someone you'd like to hang out with.

Nor was television immune to Big Car's charms. In the 1960s, we were treated to what many call the worst sitcom ever made, *My Mother, the Car*. Several years later it was followed by *Car 54, Where Are You?* Then came *CHiPs*, the *Dukes of Hazzard*, *Knight Rider*, and countless others, with the auto playing a strong character in the stories.

Television news is also not immune to Big Car. "If it drives, go live" is the motto of many TV news desks. Nothing builds up an audience like a good car chase—it's such an easy thing for people to watch. There are the "bad guys"—criminals driving like maniacs through city streets—and the law enforcement "good guys" chasing them. No self-respecting metropolitan news desk would be without a helicopter, gassed up and ready to go in pursuit of a fleeing car being hotly pursued by the police or highway patrol. And who could ever forget O. J. Simpson's famous Bronco?

Such chases have, of course, spilled over to online computer gaming. Often nihilistically violent, these games allow players to disregard any sense of common decency and drive like maniacs. The most popular product in this genre is *Grand Theft Auto*, one of the largest-selling video games in history with over 45 million willing customers (and counting).

GASOLINE PRODUCERS

Now let's look at the assistant board chair of Big Car—the petroleum industry.

Gasoline is just a mixture of gobs of different hydrocarbons. Carbon emissions result from these hydrocarbons going through your car and out your muffler. Unfortunately, they account for about 30 percent of the energy-related carbon footprint of our great nation. These hydrocarbons and our current atmospheric conditions don't mix well. The result is the so-called "greenhouse effect." If this level of carbon emission proceeds for another decade or so, we will surely pay the price in terms of human suffering.[11]

Of course, it's not just America that contributes to rising emissions. Worldwide, about seven liters of gas are burnt for every 100km driven by non-Americans. The increasing sale of electric cars is not yet doing much good, especially since Big Car keeps making its products bigger and heavier. (Remember the Hummer?) The result is that gasoline combustion and carbon dioxide emissions per mile are simply not going down.[12]

One of Big Car's other favorite pastimes is simply ignoring the law. You stand a far greater certainty of being arrested and doing jail time for shoplifting than you do for despoiling our environment.

In 2024, General Motors paid a \$145 million penalty and forfeited hundreds of millions of dollars to the government when federal investigators found that GM's 2012–2018 cars emitted 10 percent more CO_2 than the company had reported. The forfeiture program that GM has had to pay into is usually used by the government as a means of confiscating income from terrorists, drug kingpins, and other criminals. Yet no single individual at General Motors has been arrested or personally held responsible for GM's malfeasance The good news is that General Motors continues to be a major funder for Safe Kids Worldwide, a program to ensure child automobile safety through education.

In addition, in July 2024, Marathon Oil agreed to pay \$241,000,000 to the Environmental Protection Agency (EPA), because it had unlawfully emitted methane gas, and other pollutants into the atmosphere in a clear violation of the Clean Air Act. Methane, the main ingredient in natural gas, is a much worse pollutant than even carbon dioxide, and the EPA has been desperately attempting to curtail its being pumped into our skies. According to the EPA, the amount of methane that this one oil company was spewing into the environment was equivalent to over four hundred thousand extra cars being on the road. Yet Marathon Oil announced that the deal would not have any adverse effect on its recent sale for seventeen billion dollars by Conoco-Philips.

It is equally unlikely that anyone at the company will be held liable for this "victimless crime."[13]

Also, there is the problem that electric cars still pollute. They don't have tailpipe emissions, but producing and transporting them creates almost 42 million tons of carbon dioxide emissions. Yes, it's only half as bad as gas cars, but it's still highly polluting, and the energy for charging electric cars doesn't just grow on trees.[14]

The central challenge for gasoline providers has always been to find the right mix of gasoline and compression. This is how a car's octane rating is determined. Octanes are just another family of hydrocarbons in gasoline. They're the "black sheep" of this chemical family: if you don't get the mix correct in your car, your vehicle will behave horribly. Who wants to drive down a busy street with your car knocking, making you very conspicuous (and not in a good way)? All gas today has octane ratings. This is simply the measure of how well your car and the gasoline will get along.

Early drivers had to carry their gasoline with them in giant, bulky cans. By the 1920s, gasoline-filling stations began to appear. Soon they were everywhere, all with gigantic storage bins built cleverly underground. Gas stations, each with multiple pumps, became gold mines for their owners.

The early gas station business was cutthroat. Everyone was selling the exact same product. The only way to get customers to come to your station was to sell your gas at a lower price than the station down the road. High-traffic roads became the natural home for the stations that survived. Massive billboards called out to passing motorists, advertising the low prices at the upcoming station.

Today in the United States there are over one hundred and twenty-five thousand gas stations, and it remains just as much a cutthroat business as it was in its early days.

Later in the book, we'll examine in more detail the staggering cost of public health and environmental degradation provided by our friends in the gasoline industry.

LOBBYISTS—AND OUR FRIENDS IN POLITICS

One last prominent—and perhaps the most crucial—member of the Big Car community is the United States Government, its regulatory agencies, and the lobbyists who serve them.

In the 2022 Congressional races, 96 percent of the seats were won by the candidate who spent the most money. Transportation lobbyists gave more than $68 million in contributions to members of Congress. About 70 percent went to Republicans. During the last presidential cycle, transportation lobbyists contributed nearly $100 million.

In 2023, Big Car spent $120 million lobbying Washington. It is naïve to imagine that the U.S. Congress will ever enact policies that cut into fossil-fuel profits.

Senator Charles Schumer of New York was the largest recipient, bringing in a tidy $650,000 from Big Car.[15]

Here's a short list of the largest donors:[16]

Koch Industries $11,290,000
Occidental Petroleum $10,474,000
ConocoPhillips $8,690,000
ExxonMobil $7,740,000
Chevron Corp $6,820,00
Shell $6,680,000

The combined lobbying, political contributions, and advertising efforts of trade groups opposed to climate change legislation meant that they could outspend climate advocacy groups by a 13-to-1 ratio. Again, most of these funds were contributed to Republican candidates.[17]

A perfect example of the power Big Car has in Congress was shown in a House bill passed recently in Congress that would require the federal government to increase fossil fuel development on public lands every time it taps into the Strategic Petroleum Reserve. The bill was introduced by House Energy and Commerce chairwoman Cathy McMorris, a Republican from Washington State. The fact that Representative McMorris received almost $400,000 from the oil and gas industry during her last midterm election tells the whole story.[18]

The American Petroleum Institute is a trade association for Big Car. It represents hundreds of corporations involved in the petroleum industry. For most of its history, it was fiercely dedicated to supporting climate change deniers. It was the mouthpiece for Big Car's denial machine. For years, with the help of conservative media and countless bloggers, the American Petroleum Institute was able to confuse the issue of global warming. Perhaps more important, it could protect its clients from any form of climate legislation that would have cost them money.

Another principal lobbyist is the National Auto Dealers Association. This American trade organization represents nearly 16,500 franchised new car and truck dealerships and spent $3 million on lobbying in 2023.[19]

Big Car knew that their product would be harmful to the environment. They've known it for over forty years. In 1980, the American Petroleum Institute informed its members exactly what the impact of climate change would be. They rightly concluded that "globally catastrophic effects" would occur.

But Big Car is no friend to our planet. They lied to the public about climate change for the next four decades. The four largest publicly traded oil and gas companies, ExxonMobil, Royal Dutch Shell, Chevron, and BP, spent over $1 billion of their shareholders' funds lobbying over three years to prevent a worldwide solution to climate change—the Paris Agreement—from being accepted.[20]

Like Ethyl Corporation, these companies have long known the scientific facts about how devastating their product is for humans. Yet, in the name of profit, they hid these facts from public discussion. More than 40 years ago, the scientists for Exxon prepared a report about the hideous effects their product would cause to humanity. The report remained hidden until 2023 when it was finally revealed. They knew the price we'd pay for using their products for three generations of humans. They didn't care if their quarterly earnings grew. I'm sure a special circle in hell is reserved for those folks.[21]

In my lifetime, a president of the United States told his many followers that trees cause more pollution than automobiles. Ronald Reagan proudly stated that approximately 80 percent of our air pollution stems from hydrocarbons released by vegetation. He chastised environmentalists for going overboard in trying to set and enforce laws against manufactured pollution.[22]

The 1998 Kyoto Protocol treaty was a plan for countries to try to reduce global warming by cutting fossil fuel emissions. The idea was that the whole world would finally work together to reduce the effects of greenhouse gases on the environment. Ninety-one countries signed it. When it came time for the United States to ratify the agreement, the top polluters in America—Conoco, Exxon, and others—took off the gloves. Big Car sympathizers put together a well-financed campaign to convince the American public and members of Congress that the facts being presented were "fake science"—even though their own people had given them the same information. As a result, the Kyoto Protocol's acceptance by the United States was defeated in the Senate by a 98–0 vote. Not a single senator was willing to vote against Big Car. In a clear-cut breach of the social contract essential to ensure overall social benefits for us all, the country that accounts for well over 5 billion metric tons of carbon dioxide a year. It also voted *not* to ratify the Protocol.[23]

We were the only major country to do so. Al Gore said that by subverting this vote, Big Car had committed the most serious crime of the post–World War II era.

Thanks to Big Car working with the American Petroleum Institute, the Koch brothers' money, and a myriad of fraudulent think tanks, climate science denial has remained a dominant force in both the United States and the rest of the world. Many of the people who helped organize the tobacco industry's big lie moved into cushy jobs working for Big Car. The extraordinary damage being done to the environment due to carbon emissions continues apace.

Climate denial also became political. Under the presidency of Ronald Reagan, drastic cuts were made in funding environmental research. CO_2 monitoring virtually stopped. Reagan's Secretary of Energy went public with the statement, "This administration knows there is no real global warming problem."[24]

Things went from bad to worse. The tremendous amount of money given to Republicans has resulted in every single Republican candidate in the 2016 election primary debates denying that climate change even existed. Senate and House leaders in their party echoed this sentiment.

Well into Donald Trump's administration, the denial continued. Trump claimed to be convinced that the Chinese had invented the climate change issue because they believed it would hurt American business. During his campaign, he called global warming a hoax.[25]

Big Car, with its immense wealth and influence, was able to forestall any meaningful attempt to save the planet with an insane shrill message that green communitarianism is simply a Maoist scheme to abolish capitalism and replace it with eco-socialism.

With their lies about lead being safe in our gasoline and other catastrophic falsehoods, Big Car has continued making vast fortunes for those who are part of it. The immense amount of money they can spend on buying our legislators and those who are supposed to be administering our government agencies has made Big Car immune to having to tell the public the truth.

Until 1970, these issues were the sole domain of state and local officials. The results were devastating.

In 2010, the Supreme Court decision in Citizens United v. Federal Election Commission (FEC) wiped out any chance that environmentalists could effectively compete with Big Car's massive spending advantage. In 2018, Big Car contributed almost $100 million to candidates running for Congress, outspending environmentalist lobbyists by a wide margin. In the following years, this disparity has only gotten worse.[26]

From 1998 to 2005, every time you filled up your car with gas from Exxon, a portion of that money was contributed to organizations waging war on any concerns about climate change. Exxon spent well over $30 million to convince us that climate change is a hoax—even though the corporate hierarchy at Exxon knew full well how devastating the result of climate change was going to be to their customers.[27]

For the last 20 years, Big Car has taken out full-page ads in *The Washington Post*, *The Wall Street Journal*, and *The New York Times* saying that climate change science is fake. It continuously stressed that anything that hurt its business to curb global warming was ill-considered and premature.[28]

During the first decade of this century, the combined annual income of the top 100 climate change denial organizations, including think tanks, advocacy groups, and industry associations, was over $900 million. It has now far surpassed a billion dollars—paid by people who know better to undermine the public perception of the climate change catastrophe.[29]

A who's who of right-wing advocacy organizations quickly jumped onto the climate change denial bandwagon. These well-paid patriots worked tirelessly to stir up doubt about the science behind climate change. They spread baseless rumors that the issue was a hoax created by United Nations bureaucrats. They ignored the data and facts and pushed unfounded lies to undermine public confidence in scientific truth. And they did all of this in the name of profit.[30]

It has worked. The countermovement launched by these conservative think tanks and lobbyists created an attitude of "environmental skepticism" that persists today. Some real champs who would rather make money than admit the sky is falling include the brothers David and Charles Koch, the Heritage Foundation, the Cato Institute, the American Enterprise Institute, and many others. Working in concert with Big Car lobbyists, they give about three-quarters of all their funding to the Republican party, which *The New York Times*'s Paul Krugman calls "the world's only major climate-denialist party."[31]

We don't have room to highlight all the fanciful lies that Big Car stooges have tried to foist upon us. Some of the whoppers include the esteemed senator from Oklahoma, Jim Inhofe, attempting to debunk climate change by bringing a snowball into the Senate chamber and gleefully tossing it around as if somehow being in a snowball fight would discredit the work of thousands of environmental scientists.

Even better was Alabama representative Mo Brooks standing up in Congress and claiming that the current sea level rise is caused not by melting glaciers but by coastal erosion and silt that flows into our oceans. Isn't it strange that nobody had ever noticed that before?

There are countless other examples of climate foolery being voiced by our leaders—universally, they are Republicans. They seem to genuinely believe that thousands and thousands of scientists worldwide are part of a massive coordinated hoax. They never tell us who's secretly behind the coordination of these scientists to spread misinformation about the reality of climate change. Instead, they ask us to sit back, relax, and enjoy the bountiful gift our creator has given us in the form of the internal combustion engine.

THE BIG DOWNSHIFT

In the last few years, however, after having spent hundreds and hundreds of millions of dollars lobbying to delay or block any possible impact on their profits that climate change legislation would have caused, Big Car had no choice but to suddenly see the light.

Table 2.1 shows what the 2022 Fortune 500 feature in *Fortune* magazine reported that the supergiants of the oil industry made.

Basically, they were awash in record profits. They made this money by producing an ocean of oil. The International Energy Agency, which tracks this kind of stuff, estimated that in 2023,

TABLE 2.1 OIL INDUSTRY PROFITS

Big Oil companies			
Company	Revenue (USD)	Profit (USD)	Brands
ExxonMobil Corporation	$286 billion	$23 billion	Mobil Esso Imperial Oil
Shell plc	$273 billion	$20 billion	Jiffy Lube Pennzoil
TotalEnergies SE	$185 billion	$16 billion	Elf Aquitaine SunPower
BP p.l.c.	$164 billion	$7.6 billion	Amoco Aral AG
Chevron Corporation	$163 billion	$16 billion	Texaco Caltex Havoline
Marathon Petrolatum	$141 billion	$10 billion	ARCO
Phillips 66 Company	$115 billion	$1.3 billion	76 Conoco Jet
Valero Energy Corporation	$108 billion	$0.9 billion	—
Eni S.p.A.	$77 billion	$5.8 billion	—
ConocoPhillips Company	$48.3 billion	$8.1 billion	—

Note: Table reproduced from Wikipedia, "Big Oil," last modified November 23, 2024, https://en.wikipedia.org/wiki/Big_Oil. Data based on Fortune 500, 2022.

the production of over one hundred million barrels of oil daily would contribute to further profits.

What will these companies do with their hundreds of billions of dollars in profits? They'll do what they've always done:

avoid paying as much as they can in taxes, do gigantic buybacks of their outstanding shares of stock, and reward themselves with obscenely lavish lifestyles.

What they won't do is chip in to help pay for the damage their product is causing. In 2022, more than $300 billion in damages were caused by floods, heat waves, storms, and wildfires related to climate change.[32]

Big Car finally realized that this devastation could no longer be dismissed as "bad science." So instead, they've now jumped on the environmental bandwagon. They spent a couple of hundred million dollars in 2023 on significant media messaging to show how supportive they currently are in helping us fight climate change.

Perhaps we should change the classic phrase of "putting your money where your mouth is" to "putting your money where your media is." Last year, Big Car spent less than 3 percent of its profits on low-carbon projects. They spent the rest on expanding the destruction of our planet and making themselves even richer.[33]

One last note about the people in our government who are supposed to be protecting us from these people. According to the *Washington Post*, three out of every four lobbyists who work for Big Car previously worked for the federal government. That means that the people who are supposed to be protecting us from Big Car are in a very compromised position.

If you know that a couple of years down the line, you're going to be stepping into a cushy, high-six-figure job, odds are that you're not going to bite down too hard on the hand that's about to feed you.

Ronald Reagan summed it up best when he said, "Politics is supposed to be the world's second-oldest profession. However, I have now come to realize that it bears a very close resemblance to the first."

3

HOW BIG CAR TOOK OVER THE WORLD (PART ONE)

The word *automotive* comes from the Greek word for self (*autos*) and the Latin word for motion (*motivus*). A little over a century after this machine's introduction to us, it has become an addiction we cannot do without.

Right now, you're probably thinking I'm meshuga. (For those who have not had the pleasure of hanging with Yiddish-speaking friends, the word is slang for someone who's crazy.) But I'm being serious. We are carholics, unable to last a full day without returning to our addiction.

Our society is already riddled with many other everyday addictions. Alcohol, nicotine, caffeine—most of us think of these as part of life. However, a carholic's addiction goes even deeper.

An addiction is a persistent and intense urge to engage in certain behaviors despite the harm and negative consequences that may occur. The word *addiction* comes from the ancient word *addictus*, which meant that a person was enslaved. The *Oxford English Dictionary* states that an addiction is not only to a substance but also to how a person uses that substance. In this case, that substance is your car.

"Don't be silly," you're thinking. But consider this: When you confront an addict, their first response in denying their addiction is, "Hey, I can quit anytime I want." Right now, the sad fact is that most of us couldn't quit using our private cars even if we wanted to. The second most common response from a user is, "I only use it when I need to." Sound familiar?

We are exposed to automobiles before we can even walk. They are with us every day. They are, besides the computer, the only machine we have in our school day's curriculum via countless "driver's ed" classes. We think we can live without them, which is what being an addict means.

Sure, we're all addicted to food, breathing, and sleep, among other common activities, but none of these are things we can do without. Later in the book, we'll discuss some of the more successful attempts to break free from being carholics and enjoy life without our cars.

Why is this important? Because unless we do something to combat the further spread of Big Car in the coming decade, your children and grandchildren will live in a horrible place. This book is a story about how our addiction to the car can potentially wipe out humans. In this story, you'll see how our addiction to the car has made us so dependent on this ever-evolving complex machine that we are on a clear path to making humans, like the other 99 percent of lifeforms on our planet during its multi-billion-year history: extinct.

How the car became an almost universally desired consumer object is a complex, interesting story. First, I will give you a thumbnail sketch of how we got here. Then I'll show how it changed the way our cities were configured. The critical point is to understand how Big Car radically altered humanity's mobility dependence by having us put all our eggs in one car-driven basket.

"Man is a tool-making animal," said Benjamin Franklin (as quoted by James Boswell in *The Life of Samuel Johnson*). Tools have propelled us out of the forest and into cities. The tools we've created are supposed to be value-neutral. Some have helped prolong our species' lifespan to almost unimaginable lengths. The tool that has had the most profound influence on humans in the past century is the automobile.

IN THE BEGINNING . . .

In 1885, no human being had ever seen an automobile. The number of cars on the planet was zero. In 2024, the one billionth car will join our earth's traffic jams. The most amazing thing about that number is that nobody planned it. We all just let it happen. We quickly and happily adjusted to the world that Big Car created for us. They caused us to move into cities, then leave our cities and move to the suburbs. They became a world-accepted method of showing one's status. We began caring as much about our cars as we did our families. With very little resistance, we allowed Big Car to take over our economies and our lives. In the name of mobility, we changed how humans lived. We became addicted.

Here's how it happened.

It started around 3500 BCE when some genius invented the wheel. The fact that humans had existed for hundreds of thousands of years without the wheel is often forgotten. One of the most interesting things about humans is how long it took us to come up with the modern standards we now use to meet our transportation needs. For most of the time humans have spent on the planet, we were able to live without needing to roll.

The entire concept of time and distance we now live by would be incomprehensible for most humans who lived in that pre-wheel world. The distances between peoples, although not at all geographically great, were still vast. Spending generations within the confines of your own immediate space was how most humans lived. Travel was expensive, time-consuming, and most importantly, dangerous. People traveled sometimes because they were pulled by the lure of easier and more profitable ways of living. More often, they traveled because they were pushed and pulled by disease, natural disasters, or—most likely—other humans wanting to take their stuff.

Another distinctive trait of humans is that they like their own spaces. To find those spaces often necessitated going to new uninhabited territories. That meant having to travel. At first, all travel was done on foot. If you were lucky enough to own a horse, then you traveled on horseback. Later, another genius figured out that horses and wheels could work together. He invented the buggy, which evolved into the carriage.

The carriage became the must-have vehicle for the privileged few. By the sixteenth century, it was the status symbol of the ruling classes. Every European city was soon brimming with ornate, opulently decorated vehicles. The traffic jam had been invented, especially in bad weather.

These early carriages were on four wheels and were drawn by two to four horses. Short-distance travel became cheap and convenient for much of the nineteenth and early twentieth centuries.

You could buy your two-wheeled buggy for between $25 and $50 in today's dollars. Buggies could easily be hitched and driven by untrained men, women, and even children. Hundreds of different buggy companies competed for market share. The wide use of buggies led to the grading and graveling of main rural roads and the paving of streets in many cities.

All of this continued until the start of the twentieth century. More and more of the world's population was moving into metropolitan centers, except they now all faced the same daunting problem: transportation was dominated by horses, and horses relieve themselves whenever and wherever they feel the urge.

This had always been a problem for cities, but with population growth came an increase in the number of horses needed.

By the end of the nineteenth century, London had over 300,000 horses a day coming into town. New York City had 150,000, and these beasts produced more than two thousand tons of manure daily! Add to that a quart of urine from each nag, and you now had every street in your cities reeking of horse filth. Rain only made matters worse. Tens of thousands of city folk died each year from the effect of these horse droppings turning into fine dust and entering human lungs. The world's cities had become smelly, uncomfortable, and unpleasant to live in.

Unfortunately, cities were where the jobs were. It was where you could make money much faster than laboring in the fields. The result was a fourfold increase in the urban population in a very short time; it also meant a fourfold increase in the horse population. Soon there was one horse for every inhabitant of an American city.

Horse droppings became the climate change issue of the day. If cities wanted to continue to grow, they'd have to do something about the horse. The animal in the city was unsustainable.

THE SHIFT TO CARS

Enter the automobile.

By the early part of the century, enterprising men and women realized they could make a motorized vehicle by simply dropping an engine into a metal box on four wheels. Power it with steam, electricity, oil, or eventually gasoline, and away you go.

Big Car began to form. It soon became far more powerful than any army, invading our cities and taking control of all urban spaces. And it did this with such astonishing rapidity that nobody had a chance to oppose it or try and stop it.

Some tried to warn us. For example, in 1911, the British writer Aldous Huxley alerted the public about what he called "the drug of speed." He wrote, "The car is now a plaything for society. Soon it will come to dominate this society and become a tyrant that we will be forced to revolt against."[1]

But Huxley and any others who attempted rearguard actions against the exponential spread of Big Car soon became roadkill.

Within a quarter of a century, Americans were no longer planning how Big Car would fit into their cities; now they were planning how to fit their cities around the needs of Big Car.

If we had to pick one man responsible for the automotive age, it would have to be Henry Ford. His invention of the assembly line to make cars changed America forever. Ford almost single-handedly converted the automobile from a costly luxury toy for the rich into an accessible conveyance that profoundly changed the twentieth century.

How Ford, a fellow who possessed only an eighth-grade education, could do this is a book unto itself. He began his career as

FIGURE 3.1 Henry and Clara Ford sitting in his first car.

Source: *The Truth About Henry Ford* (1922) by Sarah T. Bushnell. https://en.wikipedia.org /wiki/File:Mr_and_Mrs_Henry_Ford_in_his_first_car.jpg

an engineer with Edison Illuminating Company in Detroit and quickly rose to become its chief engineer. It was while at Edison that he first became interested in gasoline-powered engines. By 1896, he had built his first self-propelled vehicle. He called it the Ford Quadricycle. He showed it to Thomas Edison, who liked the idea enough to encourage Ford to continue his experimentation. Two years later, in 1898, Ford came up with what would become the model for the automobile.[2]

His car went through countless iterations until he was ready to take it to market. Originally called the Model A, he proceeded through the alphabet until satisfied with his final product. He called it the Model T.

A DISRUPTIVE INNOVATION

Harvard Business School professor Clayton Christensen came up with the concept of disruptive innovation. *The Economist* called him "the most influential management thinker of his time."[3] His big idea was that sometimes something comes along that is so innovative that it creates a whole new market.

When the automobile first arrived, it was only a disruptive innovation if you were a horse sharing the same road with it. Even after the car's popularity grew, it still took another thirty years before the transportation sector was disrupted.

With the introduction of the Model T, Ford forever disrupted the way humans would travel.

Known colloquially as the Tin Lizzie, Ford's car made automotive travel available to middle-class Americans. It was the most influential car of the twentieth century and went on to become, at one point, the most-sold car in history, with over 15 million eventually purchased. (In 1972, the Volkswagen Beetle finally surpassed it.)

Ford had decided that his car should be large enough for a family to sit in, but small enough for an individual to operate and care for. He would construct it of the best materials and produce it with the best men. It would be as simple as modern-day engineering could come up with. And it would be sold at a price that any man earning a decent salary could afford. He said, "I'm going to build a car a man could enjoy with his family and enjoy the blessing of hours of pleasure in God's great open spaces."[4]

The men (and rare women) who drove Ford's first cars were dramatically different from humans today. They were 50 percent lighter and four inches shorter. In fact, in the last hundred years, our species has undergone the most significant change to the human body in 50 centuries.

The original Model T itself wasn't much. It had four cylinders, so it could travel at three speeds, one being reverse. It had no speedometer, windshield wipers, or even doors. The dashboard had an odometer and an oil gauge, allowing the driver to know how much gasoline was left.

To start the car, you first engaged the hand brake. You then got out of the car and walked to the front of it and grabbed an enormous crank and gave it a mighty pull. This was an unpleasant, labor-intensive chore—and it could also be dangerous in that sometimes cars backfired, which could cause the person doing the cranking to break their arm.

Here's the whole step-by-step process:

1) Make sure the gear-shifting lever is in the neutral position.
2) The clutch pedal should be unlatched, the clutch engaged, and the brake pedal pushed forward as far as possible, setting brakes on the rear wheel.
3) See that the spark control lever, which is the short lever located on top of the steering wheel on the right side, is back as far

as possible toward the driver and the long lever, on top of the steering column controlling the carburetor, is pushed forward about one inch from its retarded position (in which the ignition timing is deliberately delayed).

4) Turn the ignition switch to a point marked "B" or "M."

5) Set the carburetor control on the steering column to the point marked "START." Be sure there is gasoline in the carburetor. Test for this by pressing down on the small pin projecting from the front of the bowl until the carburetor floods. If it fails to flood, the fuel is not being delivered to the carburetor properly and the motor cannot be expected to start.

6) When it is certain the carburetor has a supply of fuel, grasp the handle of starting crank, push in endwise to engage the ratchet with the crank shaft pin, and turn over the motor by giving a quick upward pull. Never push down, because if for any reason the motor should kick back, it would endanger the operator.

Hurrying back into the Model T, you now used a foot pedal to choose which of the two gears you wished to drive in. There was no accelerator pedal. A driver simply pushed a lever connected to his steering wheel to go faster. The cars were not easy to navigate at first; they didn't steer very well. But the fantastic thing about the Model T was that it worked.

Well, it didn't exactly work. It tended to break down often, but the true genius of Henry Ford was that his Model T was amazingly easy for the average person to fix. The Ford instruction manual, *How to Run the Model T Ford*, was for many years a massive bestseller. The car became its generation's IKEA. Tinkering with and fixing up one's car became one of America's favorite pastimes. A whole generation of Americans became mechanics. The Model T was made to be customized. There were over 5,000 different items from Ford available to order in the Sears catalog.

FIGURE 3.2 A 1925 Model T.

Source: Photo by Mitchell Taylor. https://en.wikipedia.org/wiki/File:1925
_Ford_Model_T_touring.jpg

In 1908, a poor woman's car stalled on a bridge in Detroit. To restart it, she'd have had to do all the above. A good Samaritan saw the woman struggling to try and crank her car engine back to life. He graciously offered to help. He was finally able to give the crank one last great pull and the car started. Unfortunately, the crank immediately fired backwards and smashed into the man's face. A couple of days later he was dead.

This wasn't just any ordinary man who got conked out. He was Byron Carter, a big shot in the car manufacturing world. One of his best friends was the founder of Cadillac, Henry Leland. Leland was devastated by his friend's death and vowed to do something about it. He contacted Charles Kettering, the founder of Delco, and asked him to come up with an electric starter for his cars. Kettering was already working with Ford on the idea. Soon both Fords and Cadillacs had electric starters. The crank was gone forever.[5]

OTHER EARLY ENTRANTS IN THE HORSE RACE FOR AUTOMOBILES

For a while it looked like steam cars might prevail. The Stanley Motor Carriage Company in 1902 came out with what was called the Stanley Steamer. It was quickly nicknamed "The Flying Teapot." It had an external combustion engine, which used fuel from outside its engine. This made the car safer and more reliable. Plus, people were used to traveling by steam on railroads and riverboats. By the second year of the new century, over half the cars registered in America were steamers. There is not a single documented incident of a Stanley boiler ever having exploded.[6]

The problem with the steamers was that they needed to be carefully taken care of. Plus— and this was the killer—they often took thirty minutes to warm up before they would start. Finally, they were terribly expensive. The 1924 Stanley 740D sedan cost $3,950. Compared with the less than $500 that Ford was charging for the Model T, it was really no contest.

FIGURE 3.3 F. O. Stanley and his wife Flora drove to the top of Mount Washington to generate publicity for their firm.

Source: Mount Washington Auto Road Archives. https://en.wikipedia.org/wiki/File:Driving_to_top_of_Mt_Washington_1899.jpg

Our last entrant in the auto addiction derby is the electric car, which was giving the internal combustion engine a run for its money. The reason was that electric cars could go fast. They held every land speed record of their day. In 1899 one of them went over 65 miles per hour.

The obvious problem, just as it is today, is that there were not many places for electric car owners to recharge their cars. The electric car often ran out of juice, and nobody likes to lug around extra batteries. Finally, with the advent of the First World War, the prices for the metals to make the batteries became too high for electric car companies to stay competitive. Soon they were a memory.

Within a decade of its inception, the Model T had taken over the world market. Ford soon had more dealerships and car salesmen than almost all other car companies in the world combined.

FIGURE 3.4 "La Jamais Contente," an electric car that set the land speed record in 1899; it was the first automobile to reach 100 km/h.

Source: Wikimedia Commons. https://commons.wikimedia.org/wiki/File:Jamais _contente.jpg

The way Henry Ford was able to do this was his adaptation of the assembly line to produce cars.

Other companies had already been producing various household items by using assembly lines. Ford had gone to see the Chicago meatpacking plants and instantly saw how using low-wage, low-skilled workers could produce massive amounts of product. The secret was to have the workers remain stationary and bring the work to each man's workstation.

Ford built his first plant in Michigan. It soon had an assembly line in which over 7,500 separate tasks were being done. Ford's plant reduced the time it took to produce a car from days to hours. By 1921, the Ford Motor Company had gone from producing eleven thousand cars at the start of the century to making over two million cars a year.[7]

The Model T was a brilliant product. It sold itself. In fact, Ford did not spend a single dollar on advertising between 1917 and 1923. During that magical period Henry Ford held fast to a simple idea: Design the Model T correctly, then just keep making the same car. The idea worked. Most everyone who bought a Model T was sure that this would be the only car they'd ever need.

In 1909, the cost of a Model T Runabout was $825 (equivalent to about $28,000 today). By 1925 that price had been reduced to $260 ($9,000 in today's dollars). In 1918, an astounding 60 percent of all the cars sold in America were Model T's. And they were all black. As Ford wrote in his autobiography, "Any customer can have a car painted any color he wants so long as it's black."

HENRY FORD'S BRAVE NEW WORLD

The other massive industrial change that Ford brought about was to almost single-handedly wipe out skilled labor in the American automobile industry. He did this in the year 1914 by offering the unheard-of five-dollars-per-day paycheck ($140 today) to his workers, most of them men. For most of the workers on Ford's assembly line, this was double the rate they had previously been receiving each day. His move was compared to "a blinding rocket firing through the dark clouds of the present industrial depression." It meant that men and women could finally get a decent wage for a good day's work.[8]

It was a brilliant move. One of the problems all assembly-line employers faced was enormous worker turnover. Doing the same mechanical task, hour after hour, day after day, on an assembly line was soul-numbing.

Ford had seen that his chief economic weak spot was the constant employee turnover on the assembly line. Retraining new employees was time-consuming and expensive. So, Henry Ford amazed the world and announced his five-dollars-per-day program. Within another decade the skilled craftsman in the automobile industry would be a relic, limited to a few survivors who worked on European luxury models. Now, everyone wanted to get a job on the assembly line. When Ford launched his offer in 1914, he immediately got over 15,000 job applications.[9]

It was easy work, although boring as could be. It paid well, so what did it matter if you weren't allowed to sit, talk to your fellow workers, or take unscheduled bathroom breaks?

Men and women flocked to Detroit. Ford was one of the first Northerners not to discriminate against Blacks: they got five dollars a day, the same as their white counterparts. Thousands of former fieldhands migrated to Michigan. Soon, tens of thousands had come north. Housing and food became a problem because Black people were segregated into neighborhoods that became ghettos. With this massive population boom, five dollars a day suddenly didn't go very far. Whole families piled together into crowded, strikingly unglamorous living spaces. The price of eggs, milk, and other staples skyrocketed. It was still a good living, relatively speaking, but it was a hard living.

Some historians feel that Ford's invention of the assembly line and the five-dollar day had a greater influence on the twentieth-century workforce than the Russian Revolution.

There is another seldom-examined facet of the new economic benefit that Ford offered to his employees: Ford now demanded that his workers conduct their private lives in ways he thought proper. He formed a "Social Department" within the company. Using investigators and support staff to keep an eye on his employees, Ford made sure that his new wages were only offered to those who didn't engage in gambling or excessive drinking, and who were not "deadbeat dads." You either lived Ford's way or went back to the highway. (Which hadn't been built yet.)[10]

This was the dark side of Henry Ford. He really didn't mind being called the "Mussolini of Industry"; he viewed it as a compliment. Ford was a perfect example of an egomaniac being rewarded for his severe dogmatism. He truly believed that he had superior powers in every decision-making situation. He'd been proven correct so many times that he, and the select circle of sycophants who surrounded him, felt his word was law. And why not? He had built one of the most successful businesses in American history—and he'd achieved it by insisting everything be done his way.

He was a man who helped change America. In Aldous Huxley's *Brave New World*, the world follows a calendar system designated by BF and AF: Before Ford and After Ford.

Ford really thought he could fix anything, including the United States. He seriously considered running for president. He was consulting with potential backers when his wife put her foot down. At a keynote address to the Daughters of the American Revolution, when asked about her husband being the next commander in chief, she replied, "Mr. Ford has more than enough to do just taking care of his business. The day he runs for President of the United States, I will be on the next boat to England." Thus ended what would have been a disastrous experience for the Ford Motor Company.[11]

THE FORD-HITLER CONNECTION

Ford had a couple of weak spots. For one, he was a vicious anti-Semite. He truly hated all Jews. He firmly believed they had started the First World War just to make money for themselves and that they had a master plan to take over the world. He'd sent urgent memos to his production department that no Ford parts were ever to be made of brass because "brass was a 'Jew' metal."[12]

The people who made his cars simply painted the brass over with black and Ford had no idea that "Jew metal" was still being used to make his precious cars.

He bought his local newspaper, *The Dearborn Independent*, and began publishing signed articles detailing how corrupt Jews were. According to Ford, Jews were all part of an international conspiracy that was running America. They encouraged young girls to wear short skirts and listen to jazz. His tirades included all facets of American life. In 1920, he wrote, "If fans wish to know the trouble with American baseball they can have it in three words—too much Jew."[13]

In 1923 he wrote, "Jews are the scavengers of the world. Wherever there's anything wrong with a country, you'll find the Jews on the job there." He funded countless schools across the country so that they could have square dance classes because he hated jazz, claiming Jewish people had created it.[14]

Nobody is sure why Henry Ford so hated Jews. He hadn't really met very many of them. But hate them he did.

A young Adolf Hitler became enamored with Henry Ford's writing. In fact, Ford is the only American mentioned favorably in Hitler's *Mein Kampf.* As Hitler gained power in Germany, he stayed connected to Ford. He had a massive picture of Ford behind his Munich office desk. Ford sent him a $50,000 check for his birthday.

When Adolf Hitler awarded Ford the Grand Cross of the Supreme Order of the German Eagle, Henry was beside himself with pride. This was the highest honor the Nazis awarded to distinguished foreigners. The very first one had been awarded to Mussolini.

The effect Ford had on the Germans cannot be underestimated. Here was one of the leading industrialists in the world espousing the code of Aryan racial superiority over all others and telling his readers that Jews were subhuman.

The Hitler Youth program was organized during the rise of the Nazis so that they could indoctrinate German children in their ideology. Since you couldn't get into a good school or have any prospects for a high-paying job if you had not been in Hitler Youth, soon every German parent had enrolled their *kinder* in the program.

One of the leaders of the Hitler Youth was Baldur von Schirach, also known as "the butcher of Vienna."[15] When asked why he'd deported 65,000 Jews to be exterminated in death camps in Poland, he said, "The decisive anti-Semitic book that influenced me and my comrades was *The International Jew* by Henry Ford."[16]

Published in 1922 with an astonishing half-million copies going into print, *The International Jew* was a four-volume set of anti-Semitic booklets put together by Ford and his editors. The book quickly had an enthusiastic following, especially in Germany. Post-World War I Germany was a poverty-stricken, defeated country. Germans looked at Henry Ford as a representative of all that was great about America.

It was not surprising that men like Baldur von Schirach and Adolf Hitler were attracted to Ford's writings. Schirach said that reading the book taught him how to become anti-Semitic. "The book made a great influence on myself and my friends because we saw in Henry Ford the representative of success, also, he represented a progressive social policy that we believed in."[17]

Hitler and Ford were a natural match. Like Ford, Adolf Hitler was obsessed with cars. Perhaps this was because he was afraid to get behind the wheel. He never learned how to drive a car. Nonetheless, as head of the Third Reich, Hitler was driven more miles than any other leader in history. There wasn't a car show in Berlin that Hitler didn't host. Most important, he initiated the construction of the autobahn and the thousands of miles of multilane highways that crisscrossed Germany. Hitler truly believed that the twentieth century would be the era of the motor car. This project provided a massive stimulus to a battered German economy and was one of the major factors in restoring Germany as a world economic powerhouse.

Indeed, his road system might have given Germany an enormous advantage in being able to quickly move large numbers of troops for fast and often devastating deployment against his enemies. The problem was that most of the men whose labor was needed to finish the autobahn were either working in munitions factories or fighting at the front. In addition, Germany simply ran out of money and material. Very few of the miles that had been promised were ever built under the Third Reich.

Years earlier, in 1924, Hitler's dear friend Mussolini had opened Italy's *autostrada*, literally paving the way for Big Car to inaugurate motorways reserved exclusively for automobiles.

Supreme Allied Commander Dwight D. Eisenhower, as we shall later see, was so greatly impressed by these roadways that one of his first initiatives as president was to try and bring such a system to the United States.

HITLER'S VOLKSWAGEN

It was a proud moment for recruit number 5,643,287 in the Nazi Party. A Czechoslovak citizen, he filed a declaration at the Czechoslovak consulate stating that he was now a true German citizen. He would finally be able to work with his new boss on building his boss's dream car. His whole life he'd been drawn to automobiles. He'd worked with Mercedes-Benz and other companies but had big ideas of his own. His new boss was Adolf Hitler, and the dream car was the Volkswagen—the "people's car," a car for the workers, a car that would be worthy of the new autobahn and would showcase Germany's superior technology

FIGURE 3.5 A Volkswagen on display in the Technik Museum Speyer.

Source: Stahlkocher, courtesy of Wikimedia Commons. https://commons.wikimedia.org
/wiki/File:VW_Typ_83_vr.jpg

FIGURE 3.6 Adolf Hitler inaugurates work on a stretch of the Autobahn.

Source: German Federal Archives. https://commons.wikimedia.org/wiki
/File:Bundesarchiv_Bild_183-R27373,_Reichsautobahn,_Adolf_Hitler_beim_1
._Spatenstich,_bei_Frankfurt.jpg

for the benefit of all those lucky souls now living in Hitler's new paradise, not just rich fat cats.

He succeeded beyond his wildest imagination. In the last year of the twentieth century, he was named "Car Engineer of the Century." His name? Ferdinand Porsche.

Within Hitler's close circle, Porsche was involved in the production of Panzer tanks and a self-propelled gun named "the Ferdinand" in his honor. He worked on the V-1 flying bomb for Hitler and was the proud recipient of one of the Reich's highest honors, the War Merit Cross. (Not bad for a former Jewish Czech subhuman.)

The Volkswagen was basically a German iteration of the Model T developed by Hitler's hero, Henry Ford. To promote

Volkswagen, Hitler pulled off a Donald Trump–worthy scam on the German people. He started to sell the Volkswagen to the general public before it went into production. The entire Nazi propaganda machine went into high gear to convince Germans that they had to be part of this "great big beautiful German tomorrow" by buying the Volkswagen NOW![18]

The German public responded by spending hundreds of millions of marks in down payments on the future dream machine. Not a single car was built. Instead, the Nazis used these funds to build factories for their war effort. Anyone who had made a down payment was out of luck. Trying to bring a class action suit against the Third Reich would have been lethal.

As we all know, this story has a happy ending. After the war, the Volkswagen was put into production. The occupying forces made the new German government pay back any unhappy investors who had survived the war. Each investor was also given a discount off the retail price of the new VW.

(Somehow most of these facts were left out of the 1968 Disney movie, *The Love Bug*, which helped make the Beetle both a hippie poster child of an era and the top-grossing film of the year, easily beating out Stanley Kubrick's *2001: A Space Odyssey*.)

Hitler's own car was an armor-plated Mercedes. The car was gigantic, weighing in at over five tons. It could go 110 mph and sat Adolf and his entourage in great comfort. The best thing about it for Hitler was that it was free. Daimler-Benz gave the car to the German dictator at no cost. This turned out to be a smart piece of business because immediately all the other heads of state had to have one. Mercedes was able to sell their ludicrously expensive bulletproof luxury car to the emperor of Japan, the dictator Francisco Franco in Spain, and even King Zog of Albania, among many others.

One of the great ironies of the twentieth century is that Emil Jellinek, an engineer who worked with the newly merged companies of Benz and Daimler Motors in 1926, along with designer Wilhelm Maybach, had built a new car with an engine that revolutionized car mobility. They named the car after Jellinek's daughter Mercedes. The car was touted as a car not just for today or tomorrow but for the day after tomorrow. The car became so famous that Jellinek changed his own name to E. J. Mercedes. (Probably the first time in history that a father exchanged his own name for that of his little girl.) The irony is that Jellinek and his daughter Mercedes were Jewish, so Hitler and his Third Reich cronies proudly drove the streets of Germany all those years in a car named after a nice little Jewish girl.[19]

In one of the truly boneheaded moves in corporate history, Henry Ford II, now running his father's company, was offered control of Volkswagen for pennies on the dollar. He called the car "a little shit box" and walked away from the deal.[20]

The British were also taken to the VW factory and were offered all its machinery to make it as an English car. They politely declined—and didn't even bother to ship any of the equipment back to Britain. (Perhaps if the British had taken control of VW, we never would have had the Beetles?)

So, Germany kept control of VW.

As for Ferdinand Porsche, he was captured by the French after the war and jailed for several years because of his tremendous contribution to the German war effort. Upon his release, he was somehow able to redeem his good name and start one of the most successful automobile companies in the world.

And the rest is history.

4

HOW BIG CAR TOOK OVER
THE WORLD (PART TWO)

By midcentury, Henry Ford had become one of the richest and best-known people on the planet.

For many years his dominance of the automobile industry was overwhelming. His massive publicity machine, run out of Detroit, was able to tell the American public about Ford cars without having to spend a cent on advertising. His network of local dealers spread the auto's popularity into every corner of the United States. A Ford showroom was in every city in North America. This brilliant idea of establishing a large network of sales hubs made purchasing one of his cars incredibly convenient. In less than a decade, driving an automobile had become an American pastime. City folks bravely formed motor clubs and explored every part of the country. Farmers adopted the car as a commercial vehicle to help their business. For many years the Ford Motor Company achieved a year-over-year sales increase of 100 percent.

Almost at once the "horse problem" was gone. Within a decade, the number of horses on city streets fell by a staggering 60 percent. Soon after, less than 5 percent of all city traffic was horse-drawn.

Ford's miraculous domination of the global car market was ended by one Alfred P. Sloan.

FIGURE 4.1 Alfred P. Sloan in 1937.

Source: Library of Congress. https://en.wikipedia.org/wiki/File:Alfred_Sloan.jpg

Sloan was the president, CEO, and chairman of the General Motors Corporation. Trained in electrical engineering at the Massachusetts Institute of Technology at the end of the previous century, Sloan developed and implemented some of the most profound changes in the history of American commerce. His impact on consumer behavior still lives with us today.

Mr. Sloan's motto was "a product for every purse." He ran General Motors with just three goals: profit, profit, and profit. Above all else, the primary object of General Motors was not to make cars but to make money.

The result was that while the Ford Motor Company stagnated in the 1920s and early '30s, selling the same Model T to its customers each year, GM began making styling changes to its new line of cars. Every year a slightly different model would roll off the assembly line.

Then Sloan discovered Harley Earl, an automotive designer with an uncanny ability to give consumers what they wanted before they even knew they wanted it. He quickly became indispensable to Sloan and was elevated to the role of head of design for all GM cars. Nobody dared refuse Harley Earl; they all realized they'd have to explain to Alfred Sloan why they had denied GM's most prized asset what he wanted. In the end, most simply gave up and let Earl have his way.

Earl had begun his career as a coachbuilder—someone who manufactures bodies for passenger-carrying vehicles. His use of freeform sketching and modeling clay produced models of

FIGURE 4.2 Harley Earl in a Buick "Y Job," 1939.

Source: James Vaughan. https://en.wikipedia.org/wiki/File:1939
_..._Harley_Earl_and_%22The_Y_Job%22.jpg

future GM cars that Mr. Sloan and the other executives could easily visualize and understand. Thanks to this process, the GM team could begin planning how to build and market the new product. In less than half a decade, Earl had revolutionized automotive design and marketing.

Earl was also the first to come up with the idea of a "concept car." These were one-of-a-kind models put on display at motor shows to help gauge potential consumer interest. If the public seemed to respond favorably, GM would soon put them on their assembly lines and then in their showrooms.[1]

Motor shows were, and continue to be, central events: public exhibitions attended by anyone having to do with the sale and distribution of cars. Company representatives, dealers, car junkies, and journalists flocked to see what was on the transportation horizon.

At these motor shows, Earl would showcase new technology, styling, colors, and price points. It was the surest way for the industry to gauge customer reaction to "the new."

One of my favorite advertising creations of the Motorama was an industrial short film made by GM called "Design for Dreaming." Released in 1956, it tells the story of a woman who dreams that a masked man takes her to a Motorama. She's escorted past Buicks, Corvettes, and Cadillacs and finally taken to the "kitchen of the future." There, she bakes him a cake and then she and the masked man return to the Motorama; the two of them dance while looking at even more cars. The man suddenly unmasks himself and the couple jumps into one of the concept cars, a Firebird II, which featured a fiberglass body with seven short wings and tail fins, and they travel together on "the road to tomorrow." As they pull up to their new home, we get one final, wonderful product placement song from the man: "This dream house you and I will share. It was planned for us by Frigidaire."[2]

Before Sloan brought in Earl, nobody in the car manufacturing world cared much about how their cars looked. Cars were just large, black chunks of machinery used for getting from point A to point B, and the exteriors of automobile bodies were of no importance to either sellers or buyers. The Model T stayed constant. Henry Ford had been able to make a vast fortune by simply offering the same product to his consumers every year. Ford had told his engineers that the most important aspect of their job was to maintain the car's functionality and keep the cost down.

This all changed when Earl established a division within GM called the "Art and Color Section," later changed to the "Styling Section." It was a radical new approach. Now customers would be sold on how cars looked, not just how they functioned. Thanks to Earl's new approach, the wider automobile industry, which up to this point had never considered the tastes of buyers, had to contend with a whole new reality: People cared what their cars looked like. Earl and his "pretty picture boys" in the styling department turned GM into what we might call an automobile beauty parlor, Each year, Earl and his team would come up with dynamic changes—new forms, colors, and style trends—designed to awe and inspire the buying public.

Color played a central role in the GM marketing strategy, and Earl was also a color genius. Not only did his multi-toned cars change the landscape of American life, but his cars also gave buyers a chance to create their own color palette. GM was able to give consumers this choice thanks to its deep financial and corporate partnership with the American chemical company DuPont. Through this structural collaboration, DuPont came up with new, fast-drying paints in a wide range of colors. Now you could have a blue car, a red car, or even an orange one. The once-boring roadways of America became a rainbow of flashing hues. This was augmented by the advent of color TV; the United States soon became a cornucopia of different tints and shades. It shifted its consciousness from black and white to color.

By the 1960s, just as America was devoting massive resources to compete with the Soviet Union in space, Americans became obsessed with everything sci-fi and "spacey." The 1950s and early 1960s allowed Earl to make GM cars into earthbound space vehicles. His genius in harnessing the country's fascination with space into something they could drive on earth helped changed the consumer's relationship with cars.

In 1953, Earl took the name of a small U.S. Navy warship and introduced "America's sports car"—the Corvette. This car, helped by frequent appearances on the smash hit TV show *Route 66*, made one of Earl's concept cars emblematic of adventure and the American way of life. It became the most popular sports car in history.[3]

Sloan and Earl also came up with another innovation to induce people to buy cars: the implementation of planned obsolescence in the consumer car market. The idea was inspired, allowing GM to tap into the modern ethos of the midcentury American mind: "hipness." Jack Kerouac had coined the word for a new generation of Americans, whom he described as "hip." The term may have come from describing those who used opium as a recreational drug; to get the full effect of the drug, it was best to lie on one's side and smoke from a bowl of expertly served opium. One took the drug while "on the hip." No matter its origin, it became synonymous with things that were "cool," and cool was the ideal for the typical American consumer. If you wanted to display coolness, you did so through the ideas you discussed, the styles you wore, the way you spoke, and what you owned. Being hip was suddenly regarded as a very important personal asset.

FIGURE 4.3 Chevrolet Corvettes from (a) 1954 and (b) 1956.

Source: (a) by Greg Gjerdingen, (b) by Mr. choppers. https://en.wikipedia.org/wiki
/File:1954_Chevrolet_Corvette_(18863241390).jpg https://en.wikipedia.org/wiki
/File:1956_Corvette_Mt._Kisco.jpg

In an America whose citizens cared very much about what other people thought of them, it was vitally important to be regarded by others as hip. And what better way to define your hipness than by the kind of car you owned?

GM cashed in on this ethos by instituting an annual model change and linking each new model year with the very definition of "hipness." GM's plan was to make people want to trade in their perfectly fine cars for cooler new ones. The object was to convince buyers that their cars had become obsolete. They convinced drivers that keeping their old cars was a sign of economic failure. The strategy was particularly successful with parents who had to answer to their teenagers. Since what was hip was continuously changing, having the latest "cool" car was imperative. If you didn't, then you were a "square."

It all fit neatly into another one of America's favorite pastimes: seeking higher socioeconomic status through displays of consumer consumption. America had become a nation where consumer status reigned supreme. And GM also cashed in on this society-wide obsession. Through multimillion-dollar advertising campaigns, they made it abundantly clear to families that driving last year's car was definitely *not* cool. In a world where adults and children alike were terribly afraid of losing status within their peer groups, GM's message was well received, and sales continued to explode for the company. Soon it was the largest corporation in the world.

Yearly innovation is no longer a key marketing tool for car companies, but during this period it absolutely captured the nation's fancy. Car dealers also added theatrical flourishes of their own to pique consumer interest in new model years: In the weeks before new models were to be shown, dealerships would begin putting large swaths of wrapping paper over their showroom windows so that pedestrians couldn't see in, and buyers would not be allowed to enter the showroom until the day the car was presented to the public. These strategies worked. Crowds of curious potential buyers would patiently wait for the doors to open, and speculation about new models became a major topic of conversation at American dinner tables.

There is another reason why GM was the most profitable company on the planet: it saved a fortune on its machine parts.

Sloan and his team knew that, on average, GM had to buy new car-building tools every three years because the machines, under constant usage, simply burned out. By bringing in new machines to remodel their cars, GM could pass the cost of these new machines on to the consumer. It also meant that smaller companies couldn't compete with GM because they didn't have the resources to retool every three years. By getting their customers to upgrade to either a new model or, even better, a new higher luxury model, GM changed American consumerism and helped guarantee GM's continued market dominance.

What nobody seemed to care about was that the cars weren't really getting much better. Cosmetic changes provided very little value to the customer. The object was to get consumers to believe that their product had a limited shelf life—that it was becoming obsolete from the moment they drove it off the lot. In a society where being unfashionable was a consumerist cardinal sin, GM had come up with a brilliant idea. By introducing annual styling changes, they were effectively able to get the public to keep buying new cars, thus reducing the time between repeat purchases (what GM called the "replacement cycle"). Their strategy had worked.

Under the influence of midcentury consumerism, many Americans embraced two key beliefs: first, that their social standing in the community was even more important than their own competence or moral traits; and second, that because their superiority or inferiority to their neighbors could readily be determined by the kind of stuff they owned, they needed to purchase the newest car on the market in order to project higher social status.

Of course, in almost all societies that have ever existed, one's level of respectability has been predicated on one's possessions. After Gutenberg and the printing press, for example, one's status could be demonstrated by one's collection of books; the private library was a status symbol. In some cultures, especially in Asia, possession of jewels, pearls, and jade defined a person's position in the community.

By the time the automobile arrived, Thorstein Veblen had already introduced the phrase "conspicuous consumption" to define this aspect of human behavior. He pointed out that humans were quite willing to buy luxury goods and services to display their economic position in their community, and that these displays of economic power became synonymous with social status. To maintain a top position in the societal pecking order, one had to conspicuously consume.

H. L. Mencken summed it up beautifully: "Conspicuous consumption means I enjoy my bath because my neighbor can't afford one as nice as mine."[4]

The genius of Alfred Sloan was his realization that for consumers, signaling social status was not simply a matter of how much money one spent on a car; it also required a continual visual demonstration of how that car compared to others in the neighborhood. What better way to broadcast social signals about how well you were doing than by the car you parked in front of your house? Other luxury items—such as washing machines, vacuum cleaners, and television sets—were much less visible; they could not be taken for a stroll down the street. A new car, however, could be gleefully driven past the neighbors every morning.

And what of the homes in that neighborhood? Not surprisingly, the very structure and square footage of residential houses soon changed in response to the automobile. With cars now an indispensable symbol of social status, the garage quickly became an indispensable element of residential architecture. A garage was now integrated into the design of every new home, much like the bedroom or the kitchen. A complete house required a garage, a perfect extra room for showing off the owner's progression up the status-symbol food chain.

Sloan quickly established a pricing pyramid that allowed customers to define their place in the GM pecking order. From the lowest-priced Chevrolet, one moved on to a Pontiac, then an Oldsmobile, then a Buick, and finally—the top rung of the ladder of success—a Cadillac.

It was an idea whose time had come: "I own, therefore I am." Even more important, Sloan came up with a way for all his customers to afford these new status symbols. The General Motors Acceptance Corporation (GMAC) became the financing arm of the company. It allowed car buyers, for the first time, to be able to buy cars on credit.

Ford had always insisted that if you wanted one of his cars you had to pay the full purchase price in cash. There was no other way to acquire a Ford, so people saved and saved until they had enough money to buy and own their cars.

GM changed this model. The concept of paying in installments had been around for quite a while, but not for a product as expensive as the car. Banks have typically been conservative in their loaning practices; until a financial instrument has been proven to work they generally are afraid to try it. At first banks viewed car financing as a passing fad. They worried that if a car loan went bad, they would be stuck with repossessing, storing, and disposing of what basically was an expensive piece of metal.

Another big problem that GM overcame was America's relationship with debt. Borrowing money was considered sinful. This probably had a lot to do with the fact that only very wealthy

Americans loaned and borrowed money from each other. The average wage earner did not have this option. Going into debt was generally expensive and dangerous.

"Neither a borrower nor a lender be" was not just some catch-phrase from *Poor Richard's Almanac*. (Actually, it's from *Hamlet*.) It was also a weekly message delivered from American pulpits each Sunday. The very thought of living beyond one's means was sinful. It was allowing oneself to succumb to pride. The temptation of "easy credit" was used by the devil to lure honest men and women to become prideful and ultimately would lead to their demise. (Or so said the vast preponderance of the clergy, and those who had money.)

GM's management sensed that this idea was ripe for change. They were the first to make car loans and it became a veritable gold mine. Before Ford and the banks knew what had hit them, GM had established a cheap and easy way for the average American to own a car.

As with so many other messages put forth from the pulpit on how a good person needed to live, Americans ignored their religious leaders and hopped into their new cars. In one short generation, credit became so ingrained into the culture that "I borrow, therefore I am" soon became the underlying basis for American economic existence.

The widespread use of credit also allowed Sloan and GM one further benefit: They were the first car company to entice car owners to "trade up." They plugged into the reality that people wanted to show how their lifestyles were improving by the kind of model car they drove. Americans, in record numbers, began buying new cars over much shorter intervals. Soon more than 80 percent of all cars purchased in America were bought on credit. GM was now a monster company built on a mountain of car financing dollars.[5]

Ford, meanwhile, continued to offer the same meal over and over to its customers. Mr. Ford's black Model T started to look horribly old-fashioned. GM had given the consumer a whole new menu to choose from each year, with its kaleidoscopic world of color and body shapes. Soon, more and more customers began to upgrade to expensive newer models.

"You are what you drive" became America's national mantra. How cars were made and sold had been revolutionized. Americans were becoming more and more prosperous, and they wanted everyone to know it.

Big Car was changing our world.

5

THE ROAD

et's examine another essential facet of Big Car's dominance of the planet: the road.

Humans, once we came down from the trees, began following existing paths already created by other animals. We then began adding our own pathways. By 10000 BCE, these pathways were becoming roads. The oldest known paved road was built in Egypt. Additional stone-paved roads have been found in the Middle Eastern city of Ur dating back to 4000 BCE. By 3000 BCE, brick-paved streets had appeared in India. So, humans have been using roads for quite a while and they've been a vital part of our existence. They have also continued to improve over time.[1]

By 500 BCE, a Persian king, Darius the Great, finished construction on what was called the Royal Road. It was the superhighway of its time. A journey of 1,600 miles that ordinarily took ninety days on foot could now be accomplished on horseback in just nine days. Herodotus, an ancient Greek historian (known as "the father of history") who wrote a detailed account of the Greco-Persian Wars, was blown away by the sophistication of the Royal Road and its riders. He wrote, "Neither snow nor rain nor heat nor gloom of night stays these couriers from the swift completion of their appointed rounds." Sound familiar? Look at the inscription over your local post office.

However, nobody beats the ancient Romans as road builders. From 300 BCE they began to cover their empire with stone-paved roads. Many believe that the expansion and consolidation of the mighty Roman empire was a direct result of these roads. The roads were used to move vast armies quickly during military campaigns. Getting your troops to locations that will compromise the enemy gives your army a tremendous advantage.

The Romans were more than just great soldiers, though—they were also terrific businessmen. True, their armies vastly expanded their empire, but commercial trade is what kept Pax Romana the dominant force in the world for hundreds of years. With their sophisticated stone-paved roads they were able to connect their conquered territories and thus consolidate their rulership over them. Trade and the interchange of cultural ideas were then spread via the road system.

These roads were built through hills, across rivers, and over mountains. By the time the Romans were done, there were more than 250,000 miles of roads, many of which survived for over a thousand years and often are the same routes that many humans still use today.

Rome's new roads made travel faster, more convenient, and, most important, safer. They were well-used by both the populace and the military.

SURVEYING

Road construction, except for some of the materials now used, has not changed all that much since the Romans. The Romans knew that roads had to be engineered so that a roadbed could overcome any geographic obstacles in its way. This means the roadway must be graded by either removal of earth or blowing up anything in the way. It involves embankments, bridges, tunnels, and getting rid of any kind of living thing that might block the next mile of the road. Sadly, this often meant the end of miles and miles of trees.[2]

Over time, a whole new category of human enterprise was created: surveying. A surveyor was someone who went into the wilds to assemble and interpret geographical information so that additional roads and structures could be built. Surveyors have been around since before the pyramids. Their profession requires familiarity with the principles of geometry and trigonometry (and probably regression analysis, whatever that is). They are among those responsible for bringing the understanding of the laws of physics to our daily life.

Surveyors also hold considerable authority when it comes to construction. They tell us how and where our roads and other structures should be built. Besides addressing erosion, sediment control, storm drainage, and other environmental issues, surveyors also play a role in deciding who gets to stay on the land and who must be moved to make room for the new roads. We shall see later in the book what a profound effect these planned paths have had on our population and society.

One of the most important early surveyors was a nineteenth-century Scot, John Loudon McAdam (sometimes spelled Mac-Adam). He moved from his home in Scotland to New York City in 1770. There, he founded a counting house, which in those days meant he was the equivalent of a CPA. Although McAdam found keeping track of other people's business to be a boring and dreary job, he was good at it and made a fortune. After the Revolutionary War, he made the astounding decision to return to his native Scotland ("Go East, young man") where he was appointed surveyor for the Bristol Corporation.

McAdam's real passion was road construction. He was convinced that the quality of all roads would be improved if broken stones were carefully spread on roadways correctly. He was right.

So, it was no surprise when John sat down with a group of workmen at one of the sites he'd been put in charge of. Hundreds of workers sat in a circle, all holding small hammers. McAdam took out his own private hammer, picked up a stone, and gently started breaking it into six-gram pieces. He would then pop one of the stones into his mouth to see if it was the right size. If it was, he tossed it onto a growing pile of other two-centimeter stones in front of him.

When there were enough of these stones, other workmen carefully shoveled them onto the road. Within a short time, the existing road, which had previously been muddy soil, miraculously had a hard, smooth surface.

McAdam had invented a process that was to become known as macadamization, or macadam for short. It was the greatest advance in road construction since the Roman Empire. His new idea for road building meant that horse-drawn carriages could now easily travel on his roads. He made travel faster and more efficient, and these new roads were much easier to maintain. Soon, almost every major road in the world was using the macadam method.[3]

What were once simple horse paths became the main arteries that connected rural homes to market towns, fairs, and eventually large metropolitan cities. Although John McAdam's brilliant idea worked for over a hundred years, his roads eventually were worn down by constant usage. By the time the first automobiles came on the scene, roadways were a rough ride for both vehicle and driver.

CONCRETE

Over two hundred million years ago, during the Carboniferous geologic period, giant swamp forests dominated the Earth. These forests, over time, were buried in the earth. As they sank deeper, they came under extreme heat and pressure. The forests slowly began to change form and became what we today call bitumen, better known as asphalt cement.

Humans have been using bitumen both as an adhesive and to waterproof their homes since the fifth millennium BCE. The walls of Babylon contained bitumen. The Egyptians used it and called it "moom," from which we get the word "mummy."

A sticky, black, viscous liquid form of petroleum, bitumen forms asphalt concrete (commonly called asphalt) when mixed with crushed stone. It is the glue that binds together our streets, highways, airport tarmacs, and just about everything else we travel on. Most everything we drive on we can thank asphalt for.

In southwest Trinidad, there is a lake that has over ten million tons of bitumen in it. Canada has even larger deposits.

Over the last century and a half, it has become the most common material used to make our roads. In 1876, to celebrate America's one-hundredth anniversary, Pennsylvania Avenue was paved with asphalt.

The problem is that IT's getting expensive. At the beginning of this century, asphalt cost about $160 a ton. Five years later the price had jumped to over $320 a ton. Soon after it cost over $600 a ton.

This means that today for every mile of four-lane highway we build, it costs us about $300,000. The more roads we build, the more money Big Car rakes in.[4]

Cement is another binding agent that quickly sets, hardens, and causes material to cohere. It is mixed with crushed stone to make cement concrete (commonly called concrete). The concrete business is gigantic. Cement concrete is a common building material, and we also use it for almost everything we travel on. It has become the most widely used material on earth. The only other resource that humans use more than concrete is water. If the cement industry were a country, it would rank behind only

China and the United States as the largest carbon dioxide emitter in the world. This industry alone spews close to THREE BILLION TONS of carbon into our skies each year. That translates to almost one-tenth of all carbon dioxide (CO_2) emissions that go into our planet's atmosphere. It amounts to more than all aviation and shipping emissions combined.[5]

In addition to causing climate change, the concrete business is also a huge drain on municipal coffers. Most of the people in charge of our transportation needs seem determined to continue to spend and pollute because that's the way it's always been done. We're now into our fourth generation of city transportation planners and leaders who keep making the same misguided decision about how to deal with congestion and pollution: Just keep building more and more roads and eventually, everyone will be able to drive as fast as they wish. How's that working out? The people who govern us are trapped in a decision loop they can't—or, perhaps because of how well they are rewarded by Big Car, don't *want* to—break free of.

Later in the book we will provide some viable alternatives that they might want to consider instead of simply continuing to "throw good concrete after bad."

THE EXPANSION OF THE ROAD SYSTEM

Okay, back to our roads. Early motoring was quite an adventure. Any kind of inclement weather was an extreme hardship for the driver and the car. Most of the early cars were open-topped, and they did not yet have windshield wipers—indeed, they didn't yet have windshields. Roads were dangerously rutted with potholes and if one's auto broke down, there was virtually no help for the stranded motorist. Despite this, Big Car's popularity continued to grow.

At the time the Model T became America's car of choice, paved roads were still a rarity. Most roads were generally still made from dirt. The paved sidewalk was a great luxury, primarily used by big city stores to attract "foot traffic."

But the tidal wave of new automobiles soon resulted in a strident demand to improve roadways. People were now taking their new cars everywhere, and everywhere they went, the roads were terrible.

It was now time for the torch to be passed from the surveyors to the civil engineers. Civil engineering is a rather recent profession. (Except for Archimedes.) Before, we had people we called artisans. Brilliant stonemasons, master builders, and carpenters formed prestigious professional associations called guilds. These guilds carefully guarded the basic concepts of architectural design and construction.

There were also trained specialists called military engineers. They were responsible for making sure military tactics could be logistically carried out.

As humans moved from the country into cities, a professional engineering profession established itself. Having this professional training became a prerequisite for building such public works as roads, bridges, dams, sewage systems, canals, pipelines, and all the other structural necessities of big city living. This included public roadways.

Ex chao ordo—order from chaos—was their motto. It was, to them, simple math. They just needed to figure out how many lanes of roadway were needed to accommodate a reasonable flow of cars. When a street is laid out correctly, there should be no such thing as a traffic jam.

The first real transit routes through regularly trafficked areas in the United States were called thoroughfares. These roads were used by both pedestrians and cars. Many of the early roads went through city parks, hence the name "parkway." Soon parkways were being built all over the country. They generally had two lanes with a landscaped median and lots of open space on both sides of the road. These parkways evolved into roadways, replete with four-level interchanges, cloverleaves, and countless on- and off-ramps. They would travel above city streets; they would be safe and fast. The civil engineers named them "highways."

A highway is a major road that can carry any kind of automotive traffic. Also called freeways, tollways, or parkways, they are simply paved ribbons that we all use to get from point A to point B.

It makes sense that California, the poster state for automobile use, would have experimented with building one of the first highways. The Arroyo Seco Parkway (now called the Pasadena Freeway) was built in 1940 and quickly became a prime example of the transitional phase between early parkways and the freeways of today.

The opening of the Arroyo Seco was a gala occasion. The Rose Bowl queen was passed a peace pipe by Chief Tahachwee of the Kawie tribe signifying that his people were just fine with a multi-million-dollar parkway plowing through their land.

A tidal wave of construction followed. Within a decade, California was spending over $100 million a year on highway programs. A decade later the sum had increased to over $600 million annually.

The people initially responsible for these vast expenditures were called traffic engineers. They were almost all exclusively young or middle-aged white men. The California Division of Highways had twenty-five hundred engineers for most of the twentieth century and this included just one female. The number of female employees eventually "exploded" over the decades to seven.[6]

This in a profession that Thorstein Veblen predicted would be to the twentieth century what attorneys had been to the nineteenth.

FIGURE 5.1 Arroyo Seco Parkway. Photo by Steve Devorkin of Caltrans.
https://fhwaapps.fhwa.dot.gov/bywaysp/photos/36406

Perhaps the best example of what Big Car had in mind for us was exemplified at the 1939 New York World's Fair. There, millions of people were shown how the automobile would transform America. Called "Futurama" and set in a mythical projection of what Los Angeles would be like in the year 1960, General Motors showed us the magnificent lifestyle we would all soon enjoy because of the car. Traveling on wide, tree-lined freeways, in a fabulous infrastructure made exclusively for our cars, we saw how the car would lead us to a great, big, beautiful tomorrow. After watching it forty years later, I wanted to live there—and I'd grown up in Los Angeles in the 1960s.[7]

FIGURE 5.2 Detail of the Futurama diorama.

Source: Richard Garrison. https://en.wikipedia.org/wiki/File:Futurama
_diorama_detail.jpg

The man most responsible for our current road system was Dwight David Eisenhower. Nicknamed "Ike," he was the Supreme Commander of the Allied armed forces in Europe during World War II. After returning to America, he became a two-term president of the United States. While holding this august position, he provided America with the inspiration and funding for one of the largest public works programs in history.

During the war, Eisenhower had seen the autobahn in Germany and loved the idea of the American military having the ability to quickly move troops throughout our own country. Eisenhower also felt it was imperative for America to be able to quickly evacuate civilians from its cities. He knew that the Soviets had targeted these cities with nuclear weapons that would surely be used if there were to be another world war. Ike wanted to make sure that he could get Americans out in time to save them.

When Eisenhower was elected president, the United States had become a country with a solid middle class. People were making money, and spending a lot of it on cars. By the end of World War II, Americans, constituting about 6 percent of the world's population, owned over three-quarters of all the cars in the world. One in three people in the United States owned a car. If you laid all the cars available to Americans nose to tail, you'd have a line of cars that extended over two hundred thousand miles long. And gas was cheap. Americans wanted the freedom of the open road. If you built the roads, the cars would come.

The problem was that too many American roads were no longer so open. Instead, the tidal wave of new cars had also brought a tidal wave of congestion and spectacular traffic jams.

Everyone knew they were spending way too much time sitting in traffic. The *New York Times* reported that in Manhattan alone, people had lost over $1 billion worth of fuel in traffic jams in 1954.

But that didn't stop demand. People kept buying cars in record numbers. In the 1950s, General Motors made more money than any company had ever made in the history of the world. GM also ensured that Eisenhower's Republican party stayed friendly to their business interests by having all its dealers pay one dollar to the party for every car they sold.

The demand for a better road system was so insatiable that it spurred the federal government to do something it had been loath to try for most of our nation's history: intervene in the central planning policy of its constituent states.

Eisenhower sent the National Highway Act to Congress.

It was a federal takeover of an issue that had previously been the purview of local governments and their communities. It proposed to change the way we functioned as a democracy. Washington would now be in charge of how much money each state could spend on roads and, more important, where those roads would go. The federal government also would decide who would be displaced to make room for the new roads.

We would pay for the new roads by setting up the Highway Trust Fund—bankrolled by a tax that every citizen had to pay each time they put gas in their car. Most people had no idea that they'd agreed to pay this tax. It came to a few cents out of every dollar spent on gas at the pump.

The Highway Trust Fund would then take this money and use it to pay for road construction and other surface transportation.

At first, Eisenhower underestimated how difficult it would be to enact massive legislation to build roads in America. Interestingly, his most strident opposition to the bill came from the trucking industry.

Trucks had slowly but surely replaced the railroad as the most efficient way of getting goods distributed in our economy. The primary concern of the truckers was that the interstate highway system was going to be paid for out of their pockets. Eisenhower's plan called for a doubling of taxes on diesel fuel—the very gas that most trucks used. Truckers claimed it was an unfair burden, and that they were being asked to pay too much for the massive cost of building these new roads.

When the bill was first introduced in Congress, U.S. truckers sent over a hundred thousand telegrams to their representatives opposing its passage. They were quickly joined by the oil and rubber lobbies, who also faced sharp increases in taxes on their products if the bill was enacted. The result was that the original plan for a nationwide system of roads was soundly defeated in Congress.

However, like so many others, his opponents had underestimated Dwight Eisenhower. In a brilliant strategic marketing move, he wrapped the highway bill in the American flag. He first changed the name of the proposed legislation to "The National System of Interstate and Defense Highways Act." He then had his cabinet do a media blitz, explaining to the public that these forty thousand miles of new roads were vital for protecting America from the coming Russian attack. Finally, Ike spoke directly to the American people and convinced them that being able to travel from one end of the country to the other was their birthright. It was a necessary part of the American dream.

His strategy worked. A new version of the bill easily passed its next vote in Congress. The legislation called for the building of tens of thousands of miles of uniformly standard roads across America. These roads were intended to accommodate traffic in the United States for the next two decades. The specifications for how and where the roads would be built were solely up to the determination of the federal government. Since the feds were footing the bill, they'd have the final say over everything.

The Highway Act required that every bridge be the same uniform height. The exact specification was the height needed to accommodate a flatbed truck carrying an ICBM missile on it so the truck could safely travel under the bridge. Thus, a uniform minimum height of that exact amount became the standard elevation of every bridge on our highways—and remains so to this day.[8]

Within a generation, America went from being a country full of two-lane roads, often unpaved, to a place connected by new multi-lane paved freeways and highways—all provided for the public by Washington, D.C.

The law of unintended consequences reared its head for the truckers of America, but this time with wonderful consequences. Within a few short years, 80 percent of all freight transportation was being carried on highways by trucks. Because of the new roads, truckers were the direct beneficiaries of a new transportation system that would soon make them rich.

Like Henry Ford, the railroads didn't know what hit them. We had become a vastly different people than we had been just a generation earlier. Sixty million of us had left the cities to go live in the suburbs.

Shipping by rail, with most rail stations locked into downtown local neighborhoods, meant that goods had to have a second trip to be shipped to users in the suburbs. With the new roads providing convenient off-ramps for trucks, it was now much faster and cheaper to simply have trucks bring goods directly to the seller's warehouse or store.

A national system of highways, 90 percent paid for by the federal government (a.k.a. the American taxpayer), now shifted the economic game away from railroads and into the waiting arms of the trucking business. Fast shipping meant fast profits. The American trucking industry was soon able to build the most efficient supply chain in world history.

Within half a generation the interstate became the mode of travel for every kind of American. The widespread embrace of this new way to travel was remarkable.

We began paving everything that didn't move. The U.S. became a land designed for driving cars. We became the United

Parking Lots of America. We poured enough asphalt to build roads reaching to the moon and back. It was very expensive, and we would end up spending close to half a trillion dollars on roads for our cars.[9]

Big Car was very content.

In no time the highway system was carrying twenty-five times more traffic per mile than all the other road systems in the country combined.

As an additional benefit, the new road system was a massive windfall for America's economy. For every billion taxpayer dollars spent building the new roads, almost forty-eight thousand full-time jobs were created.[10]

In addition, almost inconceivable amounts of money were spent on the products necessary to build the roads. Over sixteen million barrels of cement were purchased, over a million tons of steel, eighteen million pounds of high explosives, and believe it or not, enough petroleum was used that if you poured it all out on the State of New Jersey it would bury the state's population knee-deep in oil.[11]

What did the United States have after spending the most money on any program in American history? At first, it had seemed as though these roads were going to make a semi-utopian paradise for us. The car now became a necessity for most Americans. The road map became an American staple. Local towns and then whole states competed to show that their roads were faster, safer, and newer than those of neighboring areas.

There was, of course, a cost. The new roadways did not really alleviate the traffic problem. Traffic remained part of a citizen's daily experience. We got used to sitting, often alone, in a piece of metal for hours at a time. In our new gridlocked nation, one-quarter of all the gasoline used by American cars was now being burned when the car wasn't even moving.[12]

For the most part, we, as Americans, accepted this lifestyle. The number of advertising dollars spent to keep the dream alive was staggering. A car with beautiful-looking people in it, most often on a road with no other cars present, still embodies what it means to be a free, happy American citizen. Some complained that it was now possible to drive from one end of America to the other without seeing a single thing of interest. Most people didn't care. Americans now had a second mistress: their cars.

Environmentalists raised concerns, arguing that these roads not only were devouring property that had once been occupied by people and their homes, but were also causing profound changes to ecosystems that had been there for tens of thousands of years. They pointed out that for large parts of our nation, the building of these roads was having the same effect on vegetation and wildlife that a violent tornado or even an atomic bomb would have had. Their concerns fell on deaf ears. People didn't care.

Rachel Carson, in her 1962 masterpiece *Silent Spring*, wrote, "The environment is fragile and the decisions we're making by building these roads will leave their marks upon them. By crisscrossing the great outdoors with giant, elevated ribbons of concrete and steel we will someday realize that these things are impossible to erase." She lamented that today cars slaughter significantly more game than hunting has ever done. Again, nobody cared.[13]

One issue that some people did notice was the pernicious consequences of our new highway system for people of color. The displacement of tens of thousands of poor Black and Hispanic citizens caused untold suffering to their populations. Often, without recourse, they were thrown out of their neighborhoods, schools, and churches in order to accommodate new roadways. Big Car framed it as a cure for "urban blight."

The bottom line is that at a cost of over $500 billion and still counting, the interstate highway system has been central to building the world we live in—a world in which driving and parking our cars is the end-all of urban planning. Roads and off-ramps are only built to accommodate automobiles. Whenever there is a battle for dollars in a city's budget, Big Car always wins.

One of the biggest casualties of the new roads was our public transportation systems. Big Car realized that wiping out public transportation systems simply made more room for their cars.

In Los Angeles County, around 40 percent of the land is devoted to the movement and storage of cars, with parking alone taking up the space equivalent to NINE Manhattans.[14]

We still operate on the premise that if we can just construct enough new roads, we'll solve traffic congestion. This idea has worked about as well as our war on drugs. Yet, as with our war on drugs, there seems to be an unwillingness to admit defeat or attempt change. We simply keep building more cars and more roads.

In this century there have been numerous attempts by members of Congress to change the math of the Highway Trust Fund. Some call for an outright suspension of the federal gas tax. Their opponents retort that this would halt all further expansion of the highway system. It would also eliminate all monies for road repair and maintenance. That makes the Trust Fund an economic third rail for both parties. Nobody wants the onus of being a member of the political party that got you stuck in traffic.

As a result, no politicians have ever wrapped themselves in the "asphalt flag" and made public transportation their issue. Instead, we just continue to pour additional money into our roads. California, one of the most environmentally progressive states in the union, recently enacted a gas tax, aimed mostly at widening and fixing the state's roads, that will pay out over $5 billion per year for the next ten years.

All attempts to limit further massive expenditures on expanding roads for cars have failed at both the state and national levels. Big Car's growth and dominance depends on concrete manufacturing and the laying of millions of miles of roadways.

As I write this book, no political party has offered a plan to try and combat what the Big Car juggernaut is doing to our nation.

According to author Ben Goldfarb, about forty million miles of roadway have been put onto the earth's surface. The United States has about six and a half million of these miles. Goldfarb describes them as "a totalizing ecosystem engineered for its dominant organism, the car." They disrupt animal migration, cause massive habitat loss, "taint" rivers, pollute soils, "besmog" skies, and "shatter biotic integrity wherever they intrude."[15]

6

CAR DREAMS

et's now look at how and why Big Car has been able to exert so much control over us so easily.

There wasn't one key moment when each of us had to have a car. Rather, it was a slow and gradual process that continues today.

I grew up in Los Angeles, a metropolis of seventeen freeway systems searching for a city. It was a "modern" city trapped in the twentieth century conundrum of car dependency.

During my course of my lifetime, California had been recreated—culturally, socially, and especially spatially—by its automobiles and freeways. We became a "car city." Most of our major streets were transformed into commercial arteries. Drive-in restaurants, movies, laundries, and banks could be accessed without leaving your car. Soon malls and supermarkets replaced many stores.

The State of California allowed you to legally obtain a driver's license at the ripe old age of 16. Being able to drive a car on one's own topped all religious rituals of the time. It was a secular declaration of adulthood and independence.

Young drivers formed a bond with their first car that was almost romantic. It gave them an amazing sense of freedom.

Of course, people already liked many of the mechanical objects that made their existence so much easier and more fun than that of their grandparents. The television and radio, for instance, were essential elements for keeping abreast of mainstream social life, but these items had become ubiquitous. Your car, however, was more than just a transmitter of culture: your car allowed you to think you were part of the American dream.

It was well known that Americans were willing to travel from home to work for about thirty minutes each way. The car dramatically increased the distance one could live from one's workplace. The idea of the semirural lifestyle exploded.

THE DREAM OF ENTERTAINMENT

One of the most important aspects of driving your own car was that you finally had total control of the radio. Remember, most kids still living with their parents didn't have the "right to the dial." The dial was often exclusively controlled by fathers and mothers, or any other adult in the room. This was incredibly frustrating for teenagers wanting to tune in to their favorite programs. Having to listen to or watch one's parents' favorite entertainment was boring. It was almost enough to make kids want to read a book. They didn't go to that extreme, though. Instead, they sat in the family room, willing to take in mind-numbing performances carefully produced for their parents' generation. It was still an easily accessed diversion, and it beat reading.

Young people driving cars on their own, however, could put on whatever they wanted to hear. Even better, they could do it at whatever volume they wanted. No adult was going to demand that they "turn that thing down!" Your car became your home-away-from-home entertainment center.

As kids started to experience sitting for long periods in stalled traffic, their music helped pass the interminable hours spent staring at the cars around them. Being your own DJ made the hours sitting alone in traffic equivalent to singing in the shower. You could "rock out" and nobody else really heard you. We got used to watching the people on all sides of our vehicles singing, often with great gusto, as we all waited for the interminable traffic to start moving again.

The car radio also became a navigational tool. Drivers could calculate the distances between their destinations by the number of tunes they could listen to on the way.

New cars made it incredibly easy for young drivers to find their favorite songs. They simply pushed a button, and a song was there for them. The car became a teenager's private jukebox.

Big Car, like the rest of America, recognized the seismic shift in the marketplace. Detroit didn't just become youth-oriented, it became youth-obsessed. Big Car finally understood that young people had purchasing power. They began to make cars for kids. Ford, knowing where the kids would hear about their new Mustang model, sent hundreds of free Mustangs to youth radio disc jockeys. It was a brilliant sales idea, and in 1964 they sold over a million cars.[1]

The car quickly became a testing ground for getting media to consumers. An arms race ensued among car manufacturers to determine which company could produce the most infotainment for their buyers. FM radios and cassette players became must-haves for all new cars.

One of the unintended consequences of all of us listening to countless hours of in-car entertainment was the increasing homogenization of American English pronunciation. National radio networks in the U.S. favored a specific dialect referred to variously as Network Standard, Broadcast English, or Network

English. As a result, the use of regional dialect declined, with many talking in the same melodic tones as their car radio DJs. The cultural phenomenon of artists finding a nationwide audience can be directly traced to all of us having heard it on the car radio.

The advent of "talk radio" made drivers feel less alone and abandoned while sitting behind other cars on congested roads. By the 1970s, you could tune in to interesting programming on NPR. Alternatively, you could listen to your favorite belief system's spokesperson and get hourly updates on how horribly the other side of the political spectrum was behaving.

In 1932, Richard M. Hollingshead, Jr. nailed a large white screen between two trees in his backyard in New Jersey. He then set his old Kodak projector on the hood of his car and put a radio behind the screen. He experimented with blocks to determine the proper height necessary for a car to clearly see the screen.

The following year he opened the world's first drive-in movie theater. His pitch to his neighbors was, "Come to my theater, everyone's welcome and we don't care how noisy your children are." A little more than a decade later, there were over four thousand drive-in theaters in America. People could now see movies in the privacy of their own car.[2]

Thanks to an RCA microbroadcasting system, each car in a drive-in could hear a film's soundtrack in stereo from a speaker that hung on the driver's side window. Parents, who were raising the largest generational cohort in American history, could bring their pajama-clad little ones to the movies with them. No more having to pay for a babysitter—and bottles and diapers were easily on hand in the car. It was an idea whose time had come.

The rise of color television played a significant role in the decline of drive-ins, as audiences were increasingly captivated by vibrant, at-home entertainment. America's major energy crisis of 1970 also played a major role: the entire country adopted daylight savings time, which meant drive-in movies had to start an hour later and often could only show one feature a night, which wasn't enough for the theaters to make money.[3]

Soon, though, we were able to provide the narcotic of online movies and TV shows to any child trapped in the backseat during a long car trip or a traffic jam. Making the automobile into an entertainment home for our kids seemed a reasonable price to pay for congested travel.

In perhaps the most ingenious use of public education by any industry, car companies were able to insert themselves into every kid's life through the schools. They made learning how to operate a car part of the American school system. Driver education became part of every school's assigned curriculum. In addition to math, English, and history, nearly every American teen was being introduced to Big Car.

An unintended consequence of this was the widespread exposure of teenagers to some of the most unimaginatively gory films ever screened in public classrooms. This was before Hollywood had begun to produce their highly profitable genre of "slasher films." Well before such classics as *The Texas Chain Saw Massacre*, teens were watching driver education safety films chockfull of extreme closeups of youngsters who had been killed in car crashes. Brutally mangled young drivers were shown in detail while a serious adult voiceover told kids not to let this happen to them. The only positive aspect of this horror show was that attendance was almost 100 percent on the days these films were shown in driver's ed classrooms.

Today, the average car's dashboard has far more instruments than astronauts Neil Armstrong and Buzz Aldrin had to cope with on Apollo 11's first moon mission. Companies like Google, Apple, and others have collaborated with most major automobile manufacturers to come up with systems that allow the driver to engage in a plethora of smartphone activities while driving. Web browsing, social media, and, of course, video chatting are now standard practices in every car's infotainment package.

Almost every automaker in the world has now moved virtually everything needed to operate one's car onto touch screens. To operate these hyperscreens, drivers have to take their eyes off the road. According to the National Highway Traffic Safety Administration, over 3,000 people a year are killed as a result.[4]

It's astonishing that nearly 90 percent of all human-created data that has ever existed was generated within the past two years.[5] And we are constantly immersed in this sea of data. Our cars now have so many instruments to retrieve and display information—on analog displays and digital screen images right in front of you—that massive cognitive overload is occurring. Even during the pandemic, there was a rise in traffic fatalities.[6]

True, our driving machines are often as big as tanks, which has helped raise the motor vehicle fatality rate. A pickup truck or giant SUV probably has a much better chance of wiping you out than the old family sedan did.

Still, using your smartphone while driving dramatically increases your chance of smashing into other things. Thousands and thousands of dead motorists are found with their phone still clutched tightly in their hand. Over a quarter of all traffic fatalities last year were phone-related. The insurance industry puts that figure closer to one-half.[7]

A distracted driver is a bad driver, and bad drivers kill people. Yet 75 percent of us use our phones while driving. We send text messages or watch an adorable little cat trying to eat ice cream. That's fine if you're sitting at the office or at home. It's not so good if you are sitting in a vehicle that weighs several tons and is traveling at seventy miles per hour. One possible reason why Europe has far fewer traffic fatalities is that so many more of their cars are stick shifts, thus requiring the use of both hands while driving.

The problem isn't even that people are driving one-handed (which is against the law). The problem is our minds. If you're making a deal, trying to get a date, or just catching up with an old friend, you're often not paying full attention to your driving.

Car companies have done us no favors by building video screens into their dashboards. Now, any idiot can text while they drive. Why not? Why would a video screen even be in the car if it wasn't okay to use it while driving at 70 mph? Our habits of scrolling and swiping don't stop when we close the door of our car and start the engine. The billions of dollars that advertisers now spend for in-car advertising on these screens can attest to that.

Proficient lobbying has made sure that there is no state or federal law to prevent this. Big Car, instead of trying to solve this problem, has instead generated a dashboard coolness competition where the goal is to build more and more complex screens into our dashboards. The result is deadly, but like so many other things about the car, it's a price we seem more than willing to pay.

Entertainment and Big Car were a natural fit. Magazines and newspapers made sure that, in return for the massive amounts of ad revenue they received, there was very little investigative reporting ever done about Big Car and its lethality. The fact is, we are currently losing as many people on the roads *each year* as we lost in the entire Vietnam War. But no one wants to publicize that.

Everyone knows someone who knows someone who has died or been hurt in a car accident. Those people, however, are other people.

In 1925, the director King Vidor made a silent film called *The Crowd*. It's about a guy who finally gets a job. He triumphantly returns home to tell the good news to his wife. As she steps out into the street to greet him, she's killed by a passing vehicle. It was the first time in a movie that Big Car was depicted as the Grim Reaper.[8]

When MGM (Vidor's studio) saw the film, Vidor was ordered to take the scene out. He argued that it was necessary for the film to make sense. But the powers that be had a lot of Big Car friends and wanted it gone. That same year King Vidor's earlier movie for the studio, *The Big Parade*, became a tremendous commercial success. It was said to be one of the finest movies of the silent film era. So, five-time Academy Award-nominated director Vidor told the studio to stuff it and put the scene in the movie despite their protestations.[9]

Of course, although people saw what Big Car's product was doing on the big screen, it still survived. Home entertainment on wheels was way too powerful to be stopped by one movie—or by anything else.

THE DREAM OF FOOD

I've been told that before cars, Americans actually dined. Now we just gulp. This is a direct result of fast food. Car-culture cuisine, a whole new form of food consumption, has been introduced to us and we can't get enough of it. The objective is to speed up the time necessary to get food into our systems so that we can immediately get back on the road. For many, eating fast is now considered the standard way to ingest calories.

Our cars have become our private dining halls. It began with the expansion of our highway system. In no time, drive-in restaurants grew like mushrooms along America's new roads. We deeply appreciated the convenience of not wasting precious travel time by having to stop for meals or chew our food slowly.

FIGURE 6.1 McDonald's sign.

Source: Sam Smith. https://en.wikipedia.org/wiki/File:Harlem_Micky_Dz.jpg

Soon Big Car had found perfect solutions for American motorists who wanted to eat and run. Fast service, fast food, and fast reentry to the freeway were offered by a wide variety of bright neon-colored signs beckoning hungry travelers to stop in. Instead of a gold rush, the whole country had a "food rush."

People have always eaten away from home. In ancient Rome, every major metropolis had street stands offering various food-stuffs. Usually, a large counter with a receptacle in the middle would feed numerous street folk. By the Middle Ages, every major urban area had street vendors that sold pies, waffles, pancakes, and various cooked meats. In a world where vast throngs of pilgrims traveled to holy sites, there were always plenty of willing customers.[10]

With our new car culture, mass-produced food specially designed for commercial resale made speedy service a top priority. Drive-through restaurants evolved into chain establishments, featuring standardized menus with items shipped from central locations to each individual restaurant. Reheated or precooked ingredients are served in takeout containers, turning fast food into a global pastime. There is almost no place one can escape fast food. McDonald's even has a restaurant and McCafé in the Louvre.[11]

The fast-food industry has grown into a nearly trillion-dollar global business in Big Car's lifetime. Pizza Hut is now located in almost one hundred countries and has over a hundred locations in China alone.[12] McDonald's spends nearly three times as much money on advertising than do all water, milk, and produce advertisers combined.[13]

Fast-food outlets have succeeded in "fattening the herd." The food served in most of these places is high in saturated fat, salt, and sugar and contains a staggering number of calories. This kind of food has been directly linked to vast increases in cancer, obesity, high cholesterol, and heart attacks—which means that Big Car is also "culling the herd."

In short, the car has changed how we eat. We've become a nation that struggles with obesity. We eat ten billion doughnuts a year, and obesity kills three times as many of us as malnutrition does.

There is, however, one bright note to all of this: no two countries with McDonald's restaurants have ever gone to war with each other.[14]

Just another contribution by Big Car.

THE WIENERMOBILE

Merrillville, Indiana, is an out-of-the-way small town of thirty thousand or so. Nobody there had ever seen anything like George Molchan's funeral. George was a big man in Merrillville, which was ironic because Mr. Molchan was a midget. That day, the cemetery was packed—and parked near George's gravesite was a car in the shape of a hotdog. It was the Wienermobile, one of the few beneficial contributions that Big Car may have made to Western civilization.

George had ridden in the Wienermobile, a unique car shaped like a hot dog on a bun, to countless promotions for over thirty-five years. The car was used by the Oscar Mayer company to promote their hot dogs, and George had served as Little Oscar.

Each day George would dutifully appear at schools, children's hospitals, and grocery stores to promote the Oscar Mayer brand.

FIGURE 6.2 Wienermobile.

Source: Scottfamily5. https://en.wikipedia.org/wiki/File
:Wienermobile-Bologna.jpg

(continued on next page)

(*continued from previous page*)

For decades, there wasn't a festival or parade that he hadn't been glad to participate in. George's job was to ride in the Wienermobile and toss little "wiener whistles" shaped like a hot dog with the company's distinctive logo on it, into the crowd. Kids lucky enough to score one would immediately start blowing into it and hear the distinctive Oscar Mayer theme song.

The Wienermobile was also featured in many of the company's television advertisements and Molchan was a certified "C-list" celebrity. After twenty or so years the Wienermobile was relocated, along with George, to Disney World, where he held court with his car for the next decade and a half.

As Molchan was gently lowered into his grave, those assembled began to sing his theme song: "Oh, I wish I were an Oscar Mayer wiener, that is what I'd truly like to be. 'Cause if I were an Oscar Mayer wiener, everyone would be in love with me." The assembled throng than all blew their wiener whistles as a final tribute to George.[15]

THE DREAM OF SEX

Come away with me, Lucille,
In my merry Oldsmobile.
Over the road of life we'll fly,
Automo-bubbling, you and I.

To the church we'll swiftly steal,
And our wedding bells will peal,
YOU CAN GO AS FAR AS YOU
LIKE WITH ME,
In my merry Oldsmobile.

1905 MARKETING JINGLE

Adults have always been involved in the sex lives of their children. At one time this was necessary because tribal and other communities needed to regulate the number of mouths they had to feed. By the Victorian age, restrictive societal norms for the young had entered their golden age. Girls simply weren't allowed to be alone with boys. A chaperone was a prerequisite for any couple spending time together on social occasions. The chaperone's sole responsibility was to make sure men did not have their way with young girls, ensuring "propriety of behavior."

For the most part, it worked. If a fellow wanted to see a gal, he'd have to come to her house to court her. There he'd be met by a full assembly of interested parties who kept a watchful eye on him while he was with the young woman.

This all began to change with the bicycle. The bicycle erased distance, shrinking the world and expanding the area in which one could search for a suitable mate.[16]

Elizabeth Cady Stanton, one of the driving forces of nineteenth-century American women's rights, wrote that the bicycle was not just a woman's ride to suffrage but also to a free future.

The bicycle changed the way women were chaperoned. It changed the way women dressed. Bloomers and pantaloons made it possible for women to ride a bike. Soon freewheeling women flying along the road with the wind in their hair became what the new womanhood was all about.

Cars then surpassed the bicycle as a means for couples to spend time together. This was because cars were a great place to be intimate. Early cars came with wide, car-length running boards. Young people figured out that covering these boards with pillows and blankets made for a pretty comfortable place to be able to lie down next to each other. (A chaperone's worst nightmare.)

FIGURE 6.3 A 1931 rumble seat in a Ford Model A.

Source: Stephen Foskett. https://en.wikipedia.org/wiki/File:1931_Ford_Model
_A_roadster_rumble_seat.JPG

Soon the rumble seat, an upholstered exterior seat that folded into the rear of the automobile, became another favorite "necking" area.

After World War I, America's moral compass on sexual freedom changed dramatically. The enormous spread of automobiles fit perfectly into the new zeitgeist. Drive-in movies became known as "passion pits."

American kids had, in a generation, gone from not being able to be alone with each other to being able to do whatever they wanted in the comfort of their own cars. This quickly spread throughout the world. (A recent survey stated that 88 percent of all Italian adults have had sex in an automobile.)[17]

For the young, even more than access to music, access to each other was a dream come true.

THE DREAM OF TRAVEL

J. Edgar Hoover, former director of the FBI, called motels "a home of disease, bribery, corruption, crookedness, rape, white slavery, thievery, and murder" in a 1940 issue of *The American Magazine*. He warned married couples that they most likely would be sleeping on mattresses previously sullied by people who had engaged in illicit relations.

This was becoming a big problem for a travel-happy nation. Roads were starting to improve, making longer trips easier—but unless you wanted to sleep in your car, finding a suitable place to spend the night was a challenge.[18] Travelers mostly had to rely on seedy, run-down motels to try and get a good night's sleep. The choice of lodging was limited and often unsafe.

Howard Deering Johnson barely made it out of sixth grade. A hard worker who loved ice cream, he ate at least one cone a day. After he hit it big, he kept an ample supply of flavors in the freezer of his massive Manhattan penthouse. He fervently believed that ice cream was not fattening. He would go on to develop the largest restaurant and motel chain in America, numbering over one thousand outlets throughout the country.

Howard Johnson, a food junkie and stated that his hobby was "to talk and eat food all day," created the first modern restaurant franchise on the planet. His new idea was brilliant: He would let independent operators use his name for their restaurants, and he would provide the food, supplies, and his easy-to-recognize logo in exchange for a fee. Johnson also realized that centralized buying for a specific menu would lower the cost of food items so the average family could afford them. His genius resulted in a brand-new way for Americans to dine out on a working man's wages. His restaurants—and later motels—were clean and family-friendly and provided a tidal wave of comfort foods for weary travelers. His company became the

FIGURE 6.4 Hotel and restaurant greats in 1979, from left to right: Patrick O'Malley (Canteen Corp.), Barron Hilton (Hilton Hotels), J. Willard Marriott (Marriott Corp.), Col. Harland Sanders (Kentucky Fried Chicken), Jim McLamore (Burger King), and Kemmons Wilson (Holiday Inns).

Source: Tucker.mccormack. https://commons.wikimedia.org/wiki/File :22_-_Hotel_and_Restaurant_Greats.jpg

largest commercial food supplier and lodging operator in the United States.[19]

Before the advent of the interstate highway system, most Americans slept only in their own beds. While children might occasionally have a sleepover, the norm was to sleep at home, in the same familiar bed. Once married, you and your spouse slept in your marital bed for the rest of your lives.

The car changed that forever.

Another man who helped change everything was Charles Kemmons Wilson. He had taken a road trip to the nation's capital with his family and was appalled by the conditions they encountered on the way, including bug-infested rooms with roadside food that you wouldn't feed your pet. Worst of all, they didn't feel safe. Mr. Wilson decided to do something about it.

Mr. Wilson founded a quality roadside hotel that he called the Holiday Inn. He had gotten the name from his architect, who suggested it as a joke based on a 1942 hit musical starring Bing Crosby and Fred Astaire, with music by Irving Berlin. The movie—a smash hit—was called *Holiday Inn*. It features the iconic song "White Christmas," a tune played so frequently during the holiday season that that it's nearly impossible to step into a bank or supermarket without hearing it. (It also earned Berlin the Academy Award for Best Original Song.)

Roadside hotels were the perfect idea for the newly forming American system of travel. Wilson made sure to build his hotels only on streets near the new highway offramps. He provided an inexpensive, clean, and above all, safe place for families to spend their nights. He put small swimming pools in the motel's courtyards and made the habit of staying at a Holiday Inn a family tradition. It was pure genius. The idea soon grew to become one of the largest hotel chains in the world, with over a thousand separate locations and over two hundred thousand rooms to rent.

THE DREAM OF THE OPEN ROAD

The car trip soon became part of the American experience. The spectacular growth in car sales and the expansion of the interstate highway system made America a nation on the move. Every family wanted to "see the USA."

Millions of American families loaded up their cars and ventured throughout the United States. The vacation-by-road trip

Bertha Ringer, born late in the nineteenth century in Germany, had everything a woman could possibly want: a substantial dowry, an insatiable curiosity about motors and how they worked, two wonderful sons (Richard and Eugen, now in their early teens), and a husband (Carl) who was also her business partner. He'd become her partner when she gave him the money to start a motorcar company.

The problem was that Carl was a bit of a coward. He and his engineers had built a model for a motorized car, but he was afraid to road test it. Roads at that time were made for wagons, not cars. Carl was terrified that his (and his wife's) investment would be lost if he took the car for too long a drive and it got damaged.

Finally, early on August 5, 1888, Bertha had had enough. She sneaked her two boys into the *Motorwagen* and proceeded to take the first road trip in world history. Bertha wanted to show her husband and the world that the machine worked, so she decided, without telling Carl, to take the car and drive sixty miles to visit her mother. It was the first time any human had ever driven a car that kind of distance.

She changed the world forever.

Before her Columbus-like voyage, trips by motor cars were typically very short and simple drives, often made with the assistance of a mechanic. Her trip resembled one of Homer's epic journeys. The car she set off on was a motorized tricycle with a rear-mounted engine. Before she'd gone very far, she had to use her own hairpin to clean out a blocked fuel line. Quickly thereafter the car began to overheat, so she used her garter as insulation. The wooden brakes on the car began to fail so she stopped at a country cobbler's and instructed him on how to install leather onto the brake pads, thus inventing the first pair of brake linings. It was one hell of a trip.

When she finally returned home to her relieved husband, the whole world wanted to hear about her trip. The accompanying publicity helped bring Bertha and Carl's company its first sales. The Carl she was married to, by the way, was Carl Benz. The rest, as they say, is history.[20]

became a national pastime. Holidays and road trips became synonymous. Roadside vacation stops, resorts, and camps appeared wherever roads were available. By the 1930s tens of millions of people were taking holiday motor trips. The time needed to cross our continent had been reduced from months to days, and there was almost no destination a willing driver couldn't now reach.

Motor tourism was literally a get-rich-quick scheme that worked. In fact, road trips became so popular in America that a National Road Trip Day was established and is still observed every Friday before Memorial Day.

Big Car didn't hesitate to serve these new motorists. For example, automobile laundries began to appear to help motorists keep their new cars spotless. "Everything back but the dirt" was how they advertised their service. They were fairly primitive, with virtually no automation; instead, they had brigades of bucket- and brush-wielding workers who scrubbed the car with simple soap and water. The car was then hand-dried, and the many brass components that had been added to modern cars were deftly polished. The whole car wash process took about half an hour per car, and it cost the equivalent of a typical office worker's hourly pay ($1.50) for the service.

The first automated car laundries, now called car washes, began in the 1930s. A car was loaded onto a conveyor belt and traveled through a cleaning tunnel in which overhead sprayers dispensed

FIGURE 6.5 The car wash as we know it, such as the one in this 1974 photograph, was developed from automation methods pioneered in the 1930s and improved on in the 1950s. Photo courtesy Orange County Archives. https://www.flickr.com/photos/ocarchives/12442962655

soap and water down onto the car. Soon automatic brushes were added, followed quickly by automatic air blowers to help dry the cars off. These new car wash facilities could clean almost two hundred cars per hour. Like so much else about the car, having it look brand spanking new added to its status and coolness.[21]

THE DREAM OF SHOPPING

It's 150,000 years ago, and a man (people didn't have names yet, so let's call him Myles in honor of my esteemed publisher) is very happy. The reason Myles is so pleased is that he's found an almost perfect piece of obsidian.[22]

Obsidian is what lava becomes after it erupts from a volcano. When it rapidly cools it becomes a crystalline solid with closely packed atoms. A piece of obsidian bulges on one side because the material, although very strong, is not quite strong enough. What's great about the bulge is that you can crack off these extra pieces of lateral material and shape the piece of glass into different forms.

Myles does this with his hammerstone, a tool common in almost every early-civilization human's tool kit. It's basically just a rock that, before the age of metalworking, allowed the user to forcefully strike an object. Since obsidian is hard, brittle, and amorphous, smashing down on it with a hammerstone fractures it. Do this enough and you get a distinctive oval-and-pear-shaped hand axe (often referred to as a thunderstone). The hand axe was the veritable Swiss Army knife of prehistoric times: they were used to butcher animals, dig for water and tubers, and even remove tree bark. We could even liken it to the modern cell phone: the ultimate status symbol for any *Homo erectus*.

Myles spent the rest of his day walking to a settlement that had become a favorite trading site for humans throughout the area. There, he carefully laid out his various tools for others to examine. Since he was one of the greatest magnetostratigraphic (how's that for a Scrabble word?) practitioners of his day, his hand axes quickly drew much interest.

Myles already had a more than suitable mate, so he swapped his goods for a scraper, a knife, two sickles, and a microlith. (These were primitive arrowheads that could be used as spear points.)

The point is that humans have been trading goods and services with each other for quite some time. Trading centers and marketplaces have long been part of the human experience. As the evolution of humans progressed, the exchange of goods and merchandise transformed as well. Fixed locations became standardized.

By the Middle Ages, trade fairs allowed the trading of goods from all over the world. Banking systems were developed so money could cross political and territorial borders. Hand-to-hand markets were closely regulated by local authorities and became the standard method of exchanging goods.

It was also during this time that Central Asia became the economic center of the world. In the west, various republics, mostly maritime locales such as Genoa, Pisa, and Venice, were dominant players in world trade. Mercantilism ruled the planet.

Now, let's fast-forward and see the impact that Big Car has had on shopping.

Victor Gruen was an Austrian-born architect who came to America in 1938. A rather short man, he arrived speaking no English and with only eight dollars in his pocket. In 1941 he moved to Los Angeles. Within the next twenty years, he would become perhaps the most influential architect on the planet.

It all happened because of a blinding snowstorm that took place in Detroit in 1948. Gruen and Oscar Webber, head of Hudson's, the second-largest department store in America (Macy's was number one), were stuck in an office together.

Hudson's had long been considered one of the grandes dames of retailing and now Oscar wanted Gruen to tell him how to make his stores better.

Gruen's story offers proof for why you should NEVER throw any idea away. Years earlier, Victor had, as a thought experiment, put together a prototype of how he thought Americans might shop after the Second World War. He'd come up with the idea of mixing the functions of retail shopping with everyday life. His vision was that shopping would take place in centers that were fun to be in. They would be places where people would want to hang out together: places that were not merely utilitarian (offering shoppers goods and services), but also epicenters of social amusement where cool, hip people would want to be.

One of the basic rules of economic profitability has always been that the more time a retailer is able to spend with a prospective buyer, the better the chance of making a sale.

As luck would have it, Mr. Webber was about to build a new Hudson's department store in the Twin Cities suburb of Edina, Minnesota. He fell in love with Victor's idea, and they decided to build it together. In 1956, the first enclosed, climate-controlled shopping mall in America opened. Called the Southdale Center, it had almost thirty acres (1,300,000 square feet) of retail space. The J. L. Hudson Company had already made shopping at their Detroit store a family occasion—even today, you can find an old Hudson's shopping bag or box in many older Midwestern homes. Hudson's was a place where families enjoyed being with each other. But now people were moving to the suburbs. How could Hudson's keep those customers? The answer was Victor Gruen's shopping center. It would continue Hudson's tradition of making shopping into a family outing.[23]

The shopping center idea worked, and soon there were shopping malls, usually anchored by department stores such as Hudson's, throughout the United States and the world.[24]

A supermarket or mall was now within easy driving distance for most suburban families. In the U.S., the federal government made sure that money flowed into these businesses by enacting new tax laws that allowed for massive depreciation. No longer did an investor have to wait half a century for an investment to pay off; now it took only a few years. So, people drove to shop, and America grew and prospered.

What the bazaar had been to eastern Asia, the mall became to twentieth century shoppers, and Big Car made sure that the only way you could get to these consumer havens was in one of their cars.

These are just some of the reasons that private car usage became irresistible to all of us. Let's see the price we've had to pay for these dreams.

7

LEAD HERRING (PART TWO)

As you may recall from chapter 1, regulators were trying to find out why the carnage at Ethyl Corporation's plant had occurred. Their concerns were finally addressed by Robert Kehoe, Ethyl's highly paid scientist. He enthusiastically assured the regulators that the claims against Ethyl's product were irresponsible alarmism, proudly citing a study in which 100 pigs, rabbits, guinea pigs, monkeys, and dogs had been exposed to leaded engine fumes every day for eight months and had shown absolutely no signs of lead poisoning. (He did add that one of the dogs had five puppies.)[1]

Kehoe's study wasn't just flawed, it was a flat-out lie. Nonetheless, the so-called doctor asserted that baseless claims had cost Ethyl Corporation an untold amount of stress and money. The so-called regulators completely agreed: The fact that a respected doctor, who had worked with the U.S. government during World War I in the field of poison gases, testified that ethyl was not at all toxic was good enough for them.

A very few in the medical profession were horrified. One of them, a Yale physiology professor, went on record at the *New York Times* saying that if he had the choice between tuberculosis and lead poisoning, he'd choose tuberculosis.

Kehoe's two big lies were that lead is natural to the human body, and that a poisoning threshold existed. For the next fifty years, this became the accepted scientific reasoning for government regulators, the media, and worst of all, the public. To millions of people, Kehoe's science was regarded as truth. He was held in such high regard that the *Archives of Environmental Health* devoted an entire issue to honoring him.

The folks at Ethyl Corporation had another scientist on their bench who was even worse; in fact, he might rightfully be considered the worst scientist of the twentieth century. His name was Thomas Midgley, Jr., and environmental historians have described him as having had the most adverse impact on the atmosphere of any one living organism in Earth's history.[2]

The direct damage inflicted by Midgley was not limited to the Earth's atmosphere. On October 30, 1924, he participated in a press conference to show how safe Ethyl Corporation's new product was. One of the key ingredients in the new product was tetraethyl lead. This was the "secret sauce" of the company's new fuel additive: when mixed with gasoline, it was a guaranteed cure for engine knocking. Midgley first poured the mixture all over his hands. He then held a bottle of tetraethyl lead under his nose for a full minute. The fact that just a few months earlier, this one-man environmental disaster had been seriously ill from exposure to lead poisoning made his willingness to take one for the Ethyl Corporation team all the more heroic.

For years, scientists had been working trying to find some kind of gasoline additive that would finally keep car engines from making so much noise. Midgley and another brilliant scientist, Charles Kettering, were at the forefront of this research. Henry Ford himself became involved in their project; he sent them a mixture he called "H. Ford's Knock-knocker." It didn't work.

FIGURE 7.2 Clair Patterson.

Source: Wikimedia Commons. https://commons.wikimedia.org/wiki/File
:Clair-patterson.jpg-e1660456364696.jpg

In 1921 they hit pay dirt with a product that author Joseph Roberts described in his book *Ethyl* as something that smelled like
Satan's gym locker. It was tetraethyl lead (commonly called ethyl),
the same product that Midgley had just spent a minute inhaling.

The first time tetraethyl lead was put into a gas tank was in
1923, in Dayton, Ohio. Later that year, in a brilliant publicity
stunt, Kettering and Midgley convinced several drivers in the
Indianapolis Memorial Day race to use tetraethyl lead in their
racecars. After 500 miles of racing, ethyl-based cars had claimed

the first three places in the race. The ensuing publicity swept ethyl into the public's consciousness.

Somehow the issue of toxicity was given to the United States Bureau of Mines to investigate. Midgley wrote a paper on the subject titled "Poison Hazards in the Manufacture and Use of Tetraethyl Lead" in which he stated that the only danger to humans from the product was if people were foolish enough to handle large concentrations of the material.[3]

The hearings were contentious. At one point, Dr. Alice Hamilton of Harvard Medical School approached Kettering and called him a murderer. He brushed her off by simply stating that if she could find something better to put into gasoline to reduce knocking, he'd hire her on the spot and double her salary. Hamilton sadly shook her head and said, "I'd never work for someone like you."[4]

Alfred Sloan at GM quickly weighed in. Sloan said that if it was impossible to make the product safely, they'd pull the plug on it. This, of course, would have cost his company millions and millions of dollars. The plug remained firmly in place.

Sales of ethyl were suspended for a short time, but it was finally determined that there were no grounds for prohibiting the use of the new additive. Newspapers everywhere proclaimed, "A bill of health for Looney Gas!" At once Ethyl Corporation was again putting lead into their product. Soon signs at gas stations all over America were proudly proclaiming ETHYL IS BACK![5]

For the next forty-five years, Robert Kehoe and Ethyl Corporation were able to keep all scientific research on the effects of lead on humans safely hidden in their labs. Nobody was ever given access to the studies that were done on how toxic lead was to the human body. It remained Kehoe and Ethyl Corporation's dirty little secret.

Dr. Kehoe issued a statement to the American public in which he claimed that the health and welfare of his workers and the people of our great nation were his greatest concern. In his authorized history of Ethyl Corporation, author Joseph Roberts describes Kehoe as follows: "Quite as remarkable as the scientific achievements of this man was his reputation for professional honesty."[6]

The result was that lead pollution has increased by over 625 times compared with the levels of a hundred years ago. And to this day, Ethyl Corporation denies that its product poses any greater public health risk than that of gasoline itself. Tell that to the over 170 million Americans alive today who lost a collective 824 million IQ points from childhood exposure to exhaust from leaded gas, or to the five thousand Americans who died annually from lead-related heart disease over this almost half-century.[7]

Let's take a quick look at why lead is such a pernicious substance. Lead poisoning, also called plumbism, is a form of metal poisoning that occurs when lead enters the human body. It can have severe effects on the brain, as lead mimics calcium and disrupts critical processes necessary for brain function. Over time, as lead accumulates in the body, it triggers irritability and memory problems; if exposure continues, it can lead to anemia, seizures, comas, and even death.[8]

Lead is a cumulative toxicant that poses significant risks, particularly for young children. Lead doesn't just target the brain—it also accumulates in teeth and bones. No safe threshold of lead exposure has been identified; any level can have harmful effects on human health. According to Jerome Nriagu, the world's leading authority on the history of lead poisoning, it may have been the key factor leading to the fall of Rome. Lead was in the pipes of their wonderful aqueducts and in their jewelry and other everyday objects, often at extremely high levels. Before we pass judgment on these antiquated Romans, however, you should know that you have over ten times the amount of lead in your system than those Romans had.[9]

Lead pollution in the atmosphere is entirely due to human activity. The worst thing about lead poisoning is that its adverse effects on kids are likely to persist throughout their entire lives.

But humans are resilient. If a single individual—a Robert Kehoe, for instance—can do incalculable harm, it is also the case that sometimes one or two individuals can change everything for the better. That's what happened with lead. For almost half a century, Big Car collected and hid the data on what lead was doing to human brains and bodies. Our old friend Robert Kehoe guarded this information with intense secrecy and kept it hidden deep in the files of Ethyl Corporation. He refused to share what he knew with other scientists, calling the information proprietary. Nobody seemed to care.

But a couple of people *did* care. One was Professor Derek Bryce-Smith, a young academic at King's College London. In 1954, Bryce-Smith innocently asked for a sample of the lead additive being put in people's gasoline, only to be told it was too toxic to be shared. This piqued his interest. After repeated queries, they relented. The sample came with stern instructions: if he spilled any on the floor, he'd have to rip up the entire floor. And if he got any on his fingers? It would be absorbed through his skin, and he'd go mad and die.[10]

This really got the young professor's attention. If the stuff was so highly toxic, why were we letting countless tons of it escape from our cars into the atmosphere? He committed the cardinal sin of continuing to ask embarrassing questions about lead.

Big Car pounced. Bryce-Smith was bitterly attacked by virtually the entire scientific establishment. Alone and marginalized, no other chemists would join his scientific quest. He later

FIGURE 7.1 Kettering on the cover of TIME magazine in 1933.

Source: TIME Magazine. https://en.wikipedia.org/wiki/File:Time-magazine
-cover-charles-kettering.jpg

understood why: these same scientists were deeply indebted to
Big Car for providing them with almost all their research funding.

A few years later, across the Atlantic, one of the true scientific superheroes of the twentieth century was also starting to ask

questions about lead. His name was Clair Patterson. An accomplished professor at Cal Tech, Patterson was a leading light in the field of geology; he was one of the scientists responsible for discovering how to accurately determine the exact age of our planet by radiocarbon dating of organic material.

Patterson intuited that the earth and meteorites all contained radioactive isotopes of carbon. His experiments also introduced him to lead. He realized that all his samples had way too much lead in them. Where was it coming from? Everywhere he looked, including his own lab, everything was teeming with lead. How could this be?

In 1956 he published an article called "Age of Meteorites and the Earth." It was the first time that the true age of our solar system was established. The accompanying publicity made him a bit of a media star. All he would give reporters, however, was the simple statement, "We did it." Always a modest fellow, he generously shared the credit for the discovery with other scientists.[11]

Patterson remained perplexed about why there was so much lead in everything. In 1965 he went to Antarctica and began taking ice core samples. Amazingly, ice samples from 100 BCE were fully contaminated by lead.

Something was up, but nobody would listen to him. He was finally able to publish a paper called "Contaminated and Natural Lead Environments of Man." Despite being published in an international journal, it got virtually no attention except from the notorious Robert Kehoe. Kehoe unleashed the power of Ethyl Corporation against him. He also demanded that Patterson get out of Kehoe's field and stick to geology. But Patterson refused to back down.

Next, in a truly nefarious move, four executives from Ethyl Corporation came to Pasadena to visit with Patterson. They couldn't have been friendlier. They showed him a full resume of ongoing projects that the corporation was working on. They then offered Dr. Patterson a job that would pay many times his current salary. He could have his own lab and whatever staff he wished, with one small caveat: he was not to study lead.

Instead of accepting this generous offer, Dr. Patterson showed the men the door.

In no time things got very dicey for him. His contracts with almost every research organization in his field were abruptly ended. The United States Public Health Service severed its relationship with him. He was even tossed out of the National Research Council, a supposedly neutral organization whose stated goal was to seek authoritative, objective, and scientifically balanced answers to scientific questions of national importance. Dr. Patterson had been working on a National Research Council panel investigating atmospheric lead contamination and was far and away the leading expert in America on the matter. Yet his services were no longer wanted.[12]

Patterson didn't back down. He continued his work independently. Ethyl Corporation upped the ante.

Patterson's boss at Cal Tech called him in for an emergency meeting. There was a lot of pressure being put on him by a member of Cal Tech's board. Unfortunately for Patterson, one of the big shots at Cal Tech was also a board member of Ethyl Corporation. He had reminded Patterson's boss that Ethyl Corporation had been extremely generous to the University, and he'd hate to see the relationship end.

Patterson was a tenured professor, so his boss couldn't really fire him. But without any means to fund his research and with the University not offering him assistance, he was, in academic parlance, screwed.

Left with very few options, Patterson packed up his equipment and went into exile up in Lake Tahoe. This was one of the most fortunate occurrences of the last century.

To be continued . . .

8

THE CORVAIR

et's take a look at a car that profoundly influenced the automobile industry, and not in a good way.

Penny (not her real name) had come to Washington, D.C. to escape the crushing boredom of her rural hometown. Once she reached the big city, she tried various dead-end jobs and quickly realized that her most precious asset was not her mind, but her body. Amply endowed, Penny eventually was recruited into the world of prostitution.

One night, she was hired by a guy who called himself a "cut-out." She imagined he worked for powerful individuals, and she knew her job would be to compromise a john by having him filmed having sex with her. This, unfortunately, had become a common practice in high-stakes corporate shenanigans, but it paid Penny very well and she didn't mind.

This tradition of entrapping men through sex has been around forever and is still prevalent. Many think the Watergate break-in was an attempt to find evidence about top Democrats and call girls. In fact, one of the initial schemes Gordon Liddy presented to then-Attorney General John Mitchell in his "Operation Gemstone" plan was to lease a boat at the 1972 Democratic

FIGURE 8.1 New '61 Corvair.

Source: Wikimedia Commons. https://en.wikipedia.org/wiki/File
:%22NEW_%2761_CORVAIR%22_car_art_detail,_1961_-_Ed
_Newman_Chevrolet_-_Matchcover_-_Allentown_PA_(cropped).jpg

convention in Miami and load it up with hookers whom Liddy would then film having sex with high-ranking Democrats.

Penny wasn't having much luck with her target. She'd been surprised at how rumpled and unseemly his clothing was, and his shoes looked like something a twelve-year-old would wear.

She'd tried every trick of her trade and the young man, while always courteous, had soundly rebuffed her offers of "a good time upstairs." Finally, she just gave up and left the poor guy alone.

She reported back to her people that there was no need to continue to book the room in which the cameras had been placed. He wasn't going to have sex with her.

These men were working through other safe "cutouts" (intermediaries) for the General Motors (GM) Corporation and had been trying to get the goods on this guy for some time. His name was Ralph Nader.

GM's goal was to try and run a smear campaign against Nader that would get him to back off from his investigation of what they hoped would be a hot-selling car for them. They had hired a group of private investigators to search for any kind of embarrassing incidents that he might have had in his past. They had tapped his phones and pored over his financial records but had found nothing. They urgently needed to find something to shut him up. He was about to blow the whistle on a car that would soon gain the reputation as the least safe car of the twentieth century.

In fact, Penny had been wasting her time and GM's money. This man's sense of propriety was legendary. Once, as a guest on the children's program *Sesame Street*, he had refused to join the cast members in singing a line from the show's signature sign-off. The line was about being kind to a "person that you meet each day." He protested, arguing that the proper way to sing this song that millions of kids heard daily was "a person WHOM you meet each day." PBS and the *Sesame Street* producers finally gave in, and the man Penny had been trying to lure up her room was allowed to sing it his way.[1]

Nader had, over the last couple of years, launched a campaign that Big Car considered both dangerous and likely to cut into its profits. He had dared to bring up the issue of car safety.

Nader had a perfect platform to air his concerns. His former boss in the U.S. Senate was going to hold hearings about Nader's recently published book, *Unsafe at Any Speed*.

The book hadn't caused much of a stir when first published. Then, Nader let the world know that GM had tried to bully him into shutting up. He sued them and they paid him a settlement of several hundred thousand dollars. Even worse for Big Car was that the news of GM's ham-handed attempts to shut him up had aroused a great deal of sympathy for Mr. Nader. The American public was upset by the idea of a powerful corporation wiring his phone, trying to entrap him with call girls, and hiring a team of unsavory men to follow him—so upset, in fact, that his book became a best seller.

Nader's book showed how GM had resisted the introduction of safety features such as seat belts for the car because it would lower the car's profit margins. Now, suddenly, Americans were discovering that this corporate strategy was not limited to General Motors—in fact, the entire automotive industry was building cars that were just plain unsafe to operate. For one of the first times in its existence, Big Car had to play defense.

Nader's book served as a wake-up call for anyone—i.e., most of the world—who held the view that the automobile was necessary and good. Nader had shown that the car could be a deadly companion. He pointed out that if you added up all the Americans who had died in all the wars our country had ever fought, those numbers would be significantly smaller than the number of Americans who had died on our streets because of cars. When you factor in the billions of dollars lost each year in property damage caused by cars, it paints a damning picture of what cars were doing to us. It was no wonder that GM was willing to spare no cost to silence this man.

What really scared Big Car was that for the first time someone was showing the public the true cost of doing business with them. Nader showed that our economy had lost over $300 billion in less than a century due to property damage, injuries, and traffic deaths. That's close to one thousand dollars for every person living in the United States. It's 1.3 percent of our annual gross national product. And, as if all the above wasn't enough, half of all litigation now occurring in American courtrooms is directly related to automobiles.[2]

This should have been a wake-up call. Nadar had convincingly demonstrated that Big Car was an expensive killer of human beings, but people didn't care. Car culture maintained its hold on America and around the world.

Nader's book was principally a critique of one of GM's new cars, the Chevrolet Corvair. Its name was a portmanteau. (I promised my wife I would use that word at least twice in this book.) The name Corvair was a combination of two GM models, the Corvette and the Bel Air. The Corvair was the first mass-produced American car with a rear-mounted, air-cooled engine. GM made several million of them and priced them reasonably—under two thousand dollars—to compete with the inexpensive new imports entering the U.S. market. It became the *Motor Trend* magazine Car of the Year in 1960. *Car and Driver* magazine described it as the most beautiful car to appear in America since World War II.[3]

One of the biggest problems with the Corvair was the powerful rear-mounted engine. American drivers were used to front-engine cars, and the new Corvair handled differently than they were used to, especially when driven at high speeds and a turns. The result was predictable: it's what happens when an out-of-control car collides forcefully with a highway barrier, tree, or any other solid object. Soon GM was facing hundreds of lawsuits involving car crashes of their beautiful new Corvair.

The death knell for the car came when Ralph Nader uncovered internal documents that showed that people within GM knew there was a problem with their new car. In a crystal-clear moment of industrial greed, they decided that instead of spending money to fix the problem, they would just hope that the problem went away. They decided to roll the dice with people's lives. GM could have simply added a roll bar, but that would have meant a costly recall and the negative publicity that came with it. Instead, GM's bean counters determined that it was simply cheaper to pay off a few mangled victims of Corvair rollovers. Their math was probably sound, but they didn't count on one intrepid crusader who would make them wish they had simply fixed the car in the first place.

It was one of the few times that the world got to stop the steady incursion of Big Car.

The media feasted on Ralph Nader. His congressional hearings about the injuries and deaths caused by GM made national headlines, and media outlets presented GM as a profile in corporate irresponsibility. Suddenly the Car of the Year had earned the title of "un-safest car of the year." Sales of the Corvair tanked, and soon it was a relic of the past.

For the rest of the twentieth century American car makers competed fiercely with their foreign counterparts. First the Germans, then the Japanese, and then many other automobile producers discovered that Americans would gladly switch car brands if the price was right, the car was safer, and the car looked good. The result was a seismic shift in car ownership. Buying American became a low priority for the public. Millions and millions of foreign vehicles joined the already crowded byways of America.

9

CAR NIGHTMARES

For many years I wrote screenplays. If I had come to a studio with a script about aliens or some other power that killed tens of millions of humans in a short time while the humans simply refused to fight back, I would have been laughed out of the room. But that is exactly what has happened with our species and Big Car.

In the United States, motor vehicle crashes are far and away the leading cause of death in the workplace: one out of every three workplace deaths is due to Big Car.[1]

Driving is very, very dangerous for humans. Every year tens of millions of people around the world are seriously injured in traffic collisions. Well over a million of them die each year. Close to a hundred thousand of those people are children under the age of five.[2]

What this means is that for every three thousand cars you see each day, one of them is going to kill someone.[3]

Car crashes cost our planet over a hundred billion dollars each year.[4]

FIGURE 9.1 A crashed car.

Source: Thue. https://commons.wikimedia.org/wiki/File:Car_crash_1.jpg

THE NIGHTMARE OF INJURY AND DEATH

The duchess was bored. It simply wouldn't do for the wife of a grand duke to just sit around the house. (Or, in this case, the palace.) So, she rang for her chauffeur and told him she wanted to go out for a ride in her new toy.

The toy was an Alliance automobile that her husband had recently brought back from Paris. It had cost almost one thousand dollars (about $35,000 in today's dollars). She carefully ensconced herself in the backseat and told the driver to take her to the nearby village.

A quick note about the term chauffeur. It's obviously French and originally meant stoker. The earliest cars were steam-powered, which meant that someone had to heat up the steam by

Mary Ward was a remarkable woman. Born in Ireland in 1827, she began collecting insects and conducting experiments with them that far surpassed the typical abilities of children her age. Throughout her life she struggled to stay connected to scientific inquiry: learned societies and universities wouldn't dream of accepting women into their august halls. But this didn't stop her from becoming highly skilled as a naturalist. She was an early microscopist and a published author—and her contributions to science were sufficient to have her included in the *Oxford Dictionary of National Biography*.

Sadly, Mary Ward is remembered today as the first person to be killed by a motor vehicle. In 1869, her cousin built an experimental steam car. The steam car's engine was powered by an external combustion engine, as opposed to the internal combustion engine used in all almost all cars today.

While trying out her cousin's new car, Mary was thrown from the vehicle while it was taking a nasty bend in the road. She tragically fell under the car's wheel and died almost instantly from a broken neck. Her grieving cousin immediately destroyed the car.[5]

lighting a fire under the engine and then stoking it. However, the original use of the word came from a late eighteenth-century gang of vicious thieves. These thieves would break into homes and beat the owners until they revealed where the family's treasures were hidden. If they refused to talk then the gang members would light a fire in the living room and burn the soles of the victim's feet. "Jack the Scorcher" was the name of the gang's notorious leader. Years later, when early cars demanded a similar treatment, the name chauffeur was a natural fit.

The feeling of the wind blowing against the duchess's hair was intoxicating. She indicated to the chauffeur that she wanted him to go faster. As the car sped up, a small boy darted into the road. The Alliance met the boy head-on and sent him sprawling to the side of the road. The chauffeur stopped the car and started to get out, but the Duchess grabbed his arm and told him to drive on. She had things to do in the city.

Neither the chauffeur nor the duchess was prosecuted. Why would they be? The prevailing ethos of the time was that roadways were now for cars, and this was just another bitter pill the "little people" had to swallow.

At the start of the century, in the British Isles, there was a suggestion that all pedestrians should be legally empowered to discharge shotguns at any car that was speeding. Although this suggestion appealed strongly to the sporting instincts of the Brits, it never caught on.

Across the pond in America at the start of the twentieth century, Mr. Henry Hale Bliss often visited Central Park. For much of his sixty-nine years, the New York real estate dealer would take the Eighth Avenue trolley to the park and walk over to the sailboat pond to view the larger-than-life bronze statue of Alice in Wonderland. He loved that she was playing with her kitten, while the White Rabbit and the Mad Hatter attended in the background. ("Mad as a hatter" was a phrase used to describe the folks who, while making hats, were exposed to excessive amounts of mercury fumes, which tended to make them act irrationally.)

One day, Bliss had no sooner jumped off the moving trolley when a taxicab plowed into him. It crushed his head and chest, and he died soon after.

The driver of the taxicab explained to the authorities that a large truck had been occupying the right side of Eighth

Avenue and he had simply been trying to get around it by edging closer to the trolley. He was arrested and charged with manslaughter. A jury subsequently acquitted him on the grounds that he had not been negligent and had shown no malice toward poor Mr. Bliss.

This was the state of pedestrian rights at the beginning of the car age.

Let's examine how the battle for supremacy over the world's roadways was easily won by Big Car over the next fifty years.

By 1920 or so, horses were, at long last, gone from most urban streets. Public transport services such as trams, trolleys, and buses were being cut dramatically. The streets now belonged to Big Car.

The problem was that streets had long been the passage-ways for people as well—so the streets also still belonged to pedestrians.

These streets became death traps for pedestrians. The num-ber of traffic fatalities rose into the tens of thousands. With the growing number of cars, it became the responsibility of pedestri-ans to avoid being run over.

Sadly, many of the early deaths caused by cars involved chil-dren. The Grim Reaper was now behind the wheel and for a generation of young ones trying to cross streets, the price was very high. Some cities tried to introduce safety regulations, but they did little to protect children. When the thousandth child was killed in early 1921 in New York, the city raised a memorial wall. It made no difference.

At the start of the car era there were very few restrictions on who was allowed to drive cars or how the automobile was to be driven. For a decade or so there was no such thing as a driver's license. Finally, in 1910, New York made chauffeurs get them. A few years later the state of New Jersey made all drivers pass

FIGURE 9.2 "Sacrifices to the Modern Moloch" cartoon.

Source: James, *St. Louis Star*, November 6, 1923. https://en.wikipedia.org
/wiki/File:Sacrifices_to_the_Modern_Moloch.jpg

a driving test before they could get a license. Eventually the rest of the United States followed.

Cities also turned to law enforcement to try and bring some order to our motorways. The traffic cop was invented.

These poor souls had to stand in the middle of traffic and give hand signals to impatient drivers to let them know when their cars could speed across intersections. It didn't do much good.

In 1899, a New York City cab driver named Jacob German was arrested for speeding down Lexington Avenue. Mr. German had been driving at the breakneck speed of 12 miles per hour. Thus, the traffic ticket was invented.

Traffic tickets now come in two forms: a moving violation, which includes any time one is caught exceeding the posted speed limit, or a parking violation. Parking tickets tell you the amount of money you now must pay for parking your car either in the wrong place or at the wrong time.

Tickets are supposed to be used as tools to keep people from driving too fast or too recklessly. We've all seen how well that's worked.

Next, traffic lights were installed at some intersections and drivers began using hand signals to alert others where they were headed. The traffic signal also helped separate cars from pedestrians. Children learned from an early age, "Green light go, red

The fastest speeding ticket ever issued was in England to one Daniel Nicks, who was convicted of driving his Honda Fireblade motorcycle at 175 miles per hour. He had to do six weeks in jail but got his driver's license back. The most expensive ticket ever given was to Jussi Salonoja of Helsinki, Finland. Salonoja's family was very wealthy, and in Finland fines for speeding are based on the offender's last known income. He was fined a whopping 170,000 Euros for driving 80 km/h in a 40 km/h zone. Finland has now given quite a few tickets in the six-figure category, and it seems to work. Its traffic accident mortality rate per 100,000 inhabitants is 3.8, one of the lowest in the world.[6]

light no!" The UK came up with what are called pelican crossing signals. Activated by pedestrian call buttons, they display "walk" signs for crossers to follow. They also keep pedestrians together so they can be seen by motorists.

It still did no good. Civilian deaths continued to increase.

Big Car then came up with the brilliant idea of shifting the responsibility of road safety onto the pedestrian. They invented the crime of jaywalking. (A "jay" was a nickname for a country bumpkin.) It was no longer the car's fault if a jaywalking pedestrian was struck by a car.

Specific parts of the road were now designated for herding troublesome civilians across traffic. Crosswalks or pedestrian intersections were marked with distinctive white lines to indicate where pedestrians might cross without being jaywalkers. Early crosswalks were first constructed in shopping areas, and then at schools, to help protect vulnerable pedestrians. Rules were established so that cars no longer were allowed to simply plow into anyone on the road. If a pedestrian was within the crosswalk lines, drivers had to stop—at least until the pedestrian had crossed, after which the driver could take off.

Everyplace else on the road belonged to the car, and if you happened to stray into their space and got splattered, it was your fault.

Enter one of the least known but most interesting Americans of the twentieth century, Augustus Thomas Post, Jr. Among Mr. Post's many other distinctions, he had multiple wives and spent the last quarter of his life with a man. He was also an original member of one of the preeminent young boys' organizations in America, the Sons of Daniel Boone, which was later folded into the Boy Scouts of America.[7]

Post was one of the first civilians to descend in a submarine. He was the thirteenth man to ever fly solo in an airplane.

FIGURE 9.3 A pelican crossing.

Source: Jaggery. https://commons.wikimedia.org/wiki/File:Towards_a_Leominster
_Bypass_pelican_crossing_-_geograph.org.uk_-_6302390.jpg

He predicted in 1919 that "a man is now living who will be the first human being to cross the Atlantic Ocean through the air," and convinced a rich hotel owner to put up the $25,000 in prize money won by Charles Lindbergh for doing just that in 1927.[8]

If nothing else, Mr. Post should be remembered as the first person ever to use a checkered flag to indicate the end of a race. He did this while participating in one of the first road rallies in the U.S. For these early rallies, which were instrumental in getting Americans acquainted with new car models, automobile manufacturers would send their new models to compete against each other. The bragging rights for the winning car helped spike sales.

To help sponsor these rallies, Post formed the Auto Club of America, now known as the American Automobile Association (AAA). Today, "Triple A" is a national association and service organization with over 60 million members.[9]

When Mr. Post founded AAA in Chicago in 1902, he and Big Car were a perfect fit. They both foresaw a future in which the car would dominate the world. They both knew there was a fortune to be made from that domination, and they both worked hard to make it happen.

Post was also an early recipient of a New York City traffic citation. He was driving his car down Riverside Drive at ten miles per hour when a policeman on a bicycle pulled him over. Shortly after that, he was again given a traffic ticket for driving his car in Central Park. The Parks Commission had banned cars in the park because it "spooked" the horses. Post and a small group of rebels kept coming into the park; eventually the city relented and began to let them drive their cars in the park.

AAA grew amazingly fast, and every city wanted to be included in their maps and travel guides. (These maps and guides were only available to white people. Discrimination against African Americans by AAA continued long into the twentieth century.)

What AAA did best for Big Car was to act as its media spokesperson. At first, AAA simply spread horrific stories about jaywalkers who had caused heart-wrenching harm to innocent drivers. Very quickly they were able to swing public perception toward believing that most traffic deaths were the result of careless pedestrians. Their campaign to convince America that roads were for cars, not people, was an unqualified success.

Post later brought a horde of assistants into the mix to help spread the message: the Boy Scouts of America. Throughout America, tens of thousands of young scouts suddenly began patrolling streets and issuing citations to anyone foolish enough to try and cross at the wrong spot. If you were daring enough to do so, you would likely face being accosted by a boy scout loudly blowing his whistle and pointing at you. The young man would then rush up to you and issue a "scout citation" informing you of the correct way to cross a street. In no time, most people simply walked to the corner and used the new crosswalks.[10]

It was a perfect smokescreen to take the onus of car deaths away from Big Car—and it worked. Huge fines were issued to jaywalkers. In Saint Louis, one sad boy was caught jaywalking, and a special school assembly was held. There, the unfortunate lad was tried before a jury of almost one thousand of his peers. He was found guilty and sentenced to clean blackboards for the rest of the term. (Yet sometimes change does happen: on January 1, 2023, the State of California decriminalized jaywalking.)

The idea of using children to participate in Big Car's domination of the road reached its logical next step with the establishment of the Junior Safety Patrol. The patrol's job was to have older kids walk younger kids across the streets. Before the end of the century, there were Junior Safety Patrol members in almost every community in America. In 2024 AAA sponsored over half a million kids in fifty thousand schools.[11]

In every school, becoming a crossing guard is an honor. You get to wear a cool Sam Browne belt, and AAA gives ample badges and other shiny objects to make every kid want to participate. Former safety patrol members include over twenty astronauts and Presidents Carter and Clinton. Donald Trump does not seem to have ever joined a single safety patrol.

AAA is also a highly influential lobbying force in Washington. They opposed the Clean Air Act because it would take money away from building new highways. They were at the forefront of the fight against vehicle emissions standards, and they've opposed almost every EPA restriction on smog and tailpipe emissions that was ever entered into legislation. Even today they continue to lobby actively against many public transportation projects.

In the last seventy-five years no major highway or traffic safety legislation in America has been passed without AAA's approval. They are adamant that the 18 cents per gallon in federal taxes at the pump should be used exclusively to fund highways. They were among the most strident opponents of the Kyoto Protocol and worked tirelessly to oppose the American Clean Energy and Security Act.

Big Car did sometimes have setbacks. One was in 1935 when freelance writer Joseph Chamberlain Furnas published a story in *Reader's Digest* called "—And Sudden Death!" The editors of the *Digest* printed the article with a kindly warning that their readers might need to throw up after reading Mr. Furnas's story. The piece was a slow-motion, detailed description of the horrors of a deadly car crash. It became the most-reprinted article in the *Digest's* history.[12]

For a brief time thereafter, automotive safety was discussed responsibly. The article was debated everywhere in America. Most people in the U.S., by that time, had seen some kind of automobile accident. But it was mostly strangers in those cars. Suddenly, the focus shifted to the possibility of the people in the article being oneself or one's own family.

With the article becoming a national sensation, Big Car swung into action. General Motors CEO Alfred P. Sloan took out full-page ads in newspapers around the country. He let readers know that he was all too aware of what was wrong with driving in America: The roads were just way too slow for today's cars. If we just had better roads, everything would soon be fine. The Automotive Safety Foundation was now founded by General Motors.[13]

AAA continued to work the public education angle, and soon other organizations also began to fight for Big Car. The American Highway Users Alliance was founded by General Motors in 1932. It merged with the Automotive Safety Foundation and the Auto Industries Highway Safety Committee; and together they became powerful lobbyists for Big Car. One of the things Big Car does best is to shower money on congresspeople and senators in the form of campaign contributions. The amount given by Big Car to our elected officials has made these legislators beholden to them. If dollars are the "mother's milk" of politics, then Big Car is a massive teat.

What have we gotten by having Big Car oversee our transportation system? The answer is clear: an obscene amount of spending on our highway systems, lack of progress in road traffic safety, and no elected officials brave enough to advocate for reducing traffic congestion.

Finally, with the looming threat of greenhouse gas emissions that would put Florida under water and burn down California, some politicians are beginning to stir and take a hard look at the impact Big Car is having on us. However, if candidates continue to have to beg for money to keep their elected positions, Big Car seems immune to any immediate action.

Meanwhile, too many people were still being run down by cars.

When traffic fatalities began rising, various agencies set out to determine why so many deaths were occurring. Wayne State

University is a public research university in Detroit, Michigan. It is also the home to some of the most advanced research in the crash test dummy field.

Researchers' first test subjects were human cadavers, which were placed in cars for collision tests. The goal was to recreate what a high-speed accident does to a human body. They also conducted experiments by dropping heavy ball bearings onto cadavers' heads to simulate the force of a skull being crushed. In other tests, they would drop cadavers down elevator shafts onto steel plates. They even strapped something called an accelerometer to the cadaver's head to measure the effects of acceleration in a head-on collision.

Unfortunately, these early experiments didn't produce much useful data, in part because the cadavers used in these experiments did not accurately reflect the typical demographics of automobile drivers and passengers. Most of the cadavers used in these experiments were elderly individuals, as they were among the few available that hadn't experienced violent injury. Also, public outrage erupted when it was revealed that the cadavers of children were being used. Suitable cadavers simply weren't that easy to find.

Enter Lawrence Patrick.[14] Professor Patrick inspired the creation of the crash dummy. While teaching at Wayne State, he made himself into a human crash test dummy. With his institution's approval, this brave man strapped himself into a rocket sled and was then repeatedly smashed into things. (A rocket sled, used by the Germans used at the end of World War II to launch their rockets, is a testing platform capable of reaching very high speeds.)

After each crash, the good people of Wayne State would rush to the sled and check to see how the crushing blows to his head and body had affected poor Professor Patrick.

One afternoon Patrick allowed a fifty-pound pendulum to slam into his chest. This was supposed to show the effects of a steering column banging into a human. He survived, but one of his students had had enough and decided to make what he called a "crash dummy." This eventually became a 172-pound, 5'9" man who could take the professor's place in the driver's seat for future crash tests. The tests revealed how and why humans were being butchered in car crashes, and allowed engineers to come up with some basic design changes in how cars were made.

Amazingly, the public still didn't seem to care much about safety. What really mattered to the buying public was how the car looked. Crashes happened to other people.

Before Robert McNamara foolishly led America into the Vietnam conflict, he was the head of Ford and worked hard to try and get basic safety features put into his company's automobiles. He came up with a program for Ford called the Lifeguard package. It was a total flop, according to the company; his boss, Henry Ford II, is reported to have said, "McNamara is selling safety, but Chevrolet is selling cars."[15]

Test dummies, traffic lights, pedestrian zones, the Boy Scouts, and jaywalking laws still weren't making a dent in the fatality rate of the number of humans being killed by cars. See the nearby table for a breakdown of the number of Americans killed in car-related incidents in recent years.

In 2023, 337 people were killed by cars on Los Angeles streets, an increase of almost 10 percent from the year before. According to the Los Angeles Police Department, deaths on LA roads have doubled in the last decade. As the *Los Angeles Times* wrote, "If a serial killer were on the loose killing more than 300 Angelenos every year, we would launch a citywide hunt to end it."[16]

So long as our streets continue to be built solely for cars to get quickly from one place to another, people will continue dying. During the time it's taken you to read this far in the chapter, another half-dozen Americans have been killed in traffic accidents.

TABLE 9.1 AMERICANS KILLED BY CARS (2013–2021)

2013	*32,893*
2014	*32,744*
2015	*35,485*
2016	*37,806*
2017	*37,473*
2018	*36,835*
2019	*36,355*
2020	*38,824*
2021	*42,915*

Source: David Shepardson, "U.S. traffic deaths jump 10.5 percent in 2021 to highest number since 2005," Reuters, May 17, 2022, https://www.reuters.com/world/us/us-traffic-deaths-jump-105-2021-highest-number-since-2005-2022-05-17/.

FIGURE 9.4 Traffic congestion.

Source: Blair Pittman, Environmental Protection Agency. https://commons.wikimedia.org/wiki/File:TRAFFIC_CONGESTION_AT_SOUTHWEST_FREEWAY_AND_LOOP_610_INTERSECTION_-_NARA_-_545884.tif

THE NIGHTMARE OF CONGESTION

When a human being is congested, it means they have excess fluid in their system. Doctors advise us to reduce that congestion so that we can be in good health. When a city is congested, it means they have excess traffic in their system. Cities are advised to *add* to the congestion by building more and wider roads. If humans don't recover from congestion, they become sick and sometimes even die. The same is true for our cities. How did we arrive at our current predicament?

One of the main reasons is that Big Car was the most important mover of American prosperity in the last century. If you combine the payrolls of assembly line workers, steelworkers, and rubber workers over the past century, along with the profits of the oil companies over that same time, the resulting figure represents a staggering portion of our gross national product. Add to that motels, suburban housing, and vacation resorts and it seems as if the purpose of our nation was simply to produce, consume, and drive our cars.[17]

Humans in the twenty-first century have become hypermobile travelers. We take frequent trips, often over great distances. From walking to riding horses, then advancing to bicycles, cars, and eventually planes, humans have dramatically increased the speed at which they travel over the last century. Now, however, our hypermobility is being threatened by worldwide congestion.

As automobile use rose dramatically, the people in charge of administering our roadways came up with what they were sure was a perfect solution to traffic congestion: simply build more roads to accommodate the new traffic. They could have tried to dissuade people from wanting to use cars all the time by promoting the use of public transit, but instead they did the opposite: They began to destroy trolley, tram, bus, and other public mass transport systems to make more room for automobiles. By the Second World War, all major U.S. cities were building their infrastructures exclusively around cars.[18]

The Interstate Highway System spread the idea to the suburbs and made car dependence essential. Urban sprawl was the result of large numbers of people moving out of urban cores into surrounding areas (suburbs); the sociological impetus for this urban exodus is sometimes referred to as "flight from blight." This rapid influx into previously undeveloped land near cities has led to uncoordinated growth, communities without consequences, and severe traffic congestion.

It has also meant leaving behind cities' low-income and minority populations. With limited or nonexistent access to transportation, these communities face continued overcrowding of downtown urban areas. Given that many of these residents rely completely on public transportation, they have largely been excluded from the benefits of the Highway Trust Fund, which prioritizes car infrastructure. The result has been a steady decline in available transportation resources and services. Urban residents are left with overcrowded, inadequate, and often dangerous travel options.

Not to keep singing the same note, but much of this stems from old-fashioned greed. Americans have historically shown resistance to paying taxes. In the 1920s the United States formalized a specific type of tax loophole known as like-kind exchanges. This strategy allows people to buy agricultural land just outside the city and swap or trade it for an urban property they have just sold, all while avoiding any form of capital gains tax. The result? Enormous profits. This made it both affordable and highly lucrative to leave the city for the suburbs.

The result of this tax treatment was the exponential growth of suburban communities. Suburban sprawl has resulted in a massive increase in the number of miles driven annually by Americans—which means that pollution-causing vehicle emissions have also vastly increased. Add to this all the other health risk factors that sprawl has brought about, such as a sharp decline in physical activity because of increased driving, and it is little surprise that rates of hypertension and obesity are skyrocketing in the U.S. At the same time, the residents of these sprawling, costly communities struggle with exorbitant expenses for basic services like power, sewage, water infrastructure, and general maintenance.

The biggest problem is that all these people consume road capacity at the same time. This has led to one of the grand misnomers in our language: "rush hour." First, nobody is rushing. Instead, they are stuck behind the person in front of them in massive traffic jams. And this kind of peak congestion can last much longer than an hour.

Once again, Big Car was confronted with what seemed an insurmountable problem. There were simply way too many cars on our streets. They no longer could blame pedestrians for traffic problems, so they came up with a new culprit: the street.

Our streets were no longer big enough or wide enough to service their product. They thus introduced a whole new epoch in American transportation, called "highway safety."

Those who controlled the purse strings and shaping of our environment all agreed to play along. Big Car decreed that we owed it to the car to have more space for it to function. Even after the completion of the Interstate Highway System, the largest and most expensive public works project ever attempted by humans, drivers demanded more roads.

We began to pave everything that didn't move. Not since the pharaohs had such a vast public works program been attempted. And it wasn't cheap. At millions of dollars per mile, we've already spent half a trillion dollars to accommodate Big Car's need for more roadways, and we're far from finished.

Big Car has ordered us to "pave, baby, pave." They have, until very recently, made sure that all battles for transportation dollars in local, state, and national budgets are won exclusively by Big Car.

The seventy-five largest metropolitan areas of our country experienced almost four billion vehicle hours of delay last year. That's over six billion gallons of wasted fuel. It cost us about seventy billion dollars in lost productivity. The annual estimated cost of congestion for every driver in America comes out to over one thousand dollars per person in our major cities.[19] Thirty percent of this congestion is, believe it or not, cars looking for parking.[20]

A small percentage of drivers on America's roads are known as "super drivers." The average American driver travels a little over 13,000 miles per year. By contrast, superdrivers (about 10 percent of the driving public) drive over 40,000 miles per year and are responsible for almost one-third of all the gasoline used on the road. If we could get these people to switch to electric cars, there would be a staggering reduction in car emissions and global warming.

About twenty million Americans account for over 35 percent of gasoline consumption on our roads. They use more gasoline than is burned each year in Brazil, Canada, and Russia combined.

Sadly, a majority of superdrivers are from low-income families and won't be able to afford electric cars for years. By focusing on the number of electric cars sold rather than on who is using them, we plunge further and further into climate catastrophe.[21]

THE NIGHTMARE OF PARKING

Let's look at parking. As we all know, you can't just drive to where you want to go and simply get out of your car and leave it. I mean, you can, but there's a good chance your car will have been towed when you return. Instead, you must find someplace to park it. Car parking uses up a tremendous percentage of space in our cities. It's estimated that as much as half of North American city centers are for parking multi-ton machines that we use less than 5 percent of the time.[22]

As with so much else in human existence, where and how to park our cars has been left to government bureaucrats. This has resulted in modern parking codes that are designed to provide the maximum amount of parking using the minimum amount of urban space. The result is that American cities now have eight parking spaces for every car in their municipalities.[23] Our cities are jam-packed with parked cars. If you could magically see a city devoid of anything else except parked cars, you would think that the purpose of the city was simply to store automobiles.

The most prevalent form of car parking is the parking lot. This is simply a large, paved area devoted exclusively to stockpiling automobiles. These lots vary from immense acres of asphalt for shopping malls and sports stadiums to smaller spaces crammed into urban streets and alleyways.

Every city in America has a municipal zoning ordinance that tells its citizens where they can and cannot leave their cars. The ideal is to somehow meet the demand for parking during peak times during the day. Residential and business districts obviously have different rules when trying to figure out how many parking places will be needed.

It's all very scientific. No city planner would be caught dead without a copy of the *Parking Generation Rates* guidebook.

FIGURE 9.5 A vertical parking lot structure in New York City.

Source: Tomwsulcer. https://commons.wikimedia.org/wiki/File:New_York
_City_parking_lot_structure_for_cars.JPG

This guidebook instructs our city officials on the perfect way to park their constituents' cars with head-spinning, complex formulas. Lucky for them—and consequently, for us—the guidebook has made parking into an exact science. The guidebook enables these traffic engineers to extrapolate from their data to find the perfect way for us to park our cars. These scientific geniuses can determine exact parking ratios that help them determine the number of parking spots everyone will need each day.

I mean, it's all based on science. What could possibly go wrong? Anyone who's ever had the pure exhilaration of being late for a meeting and unable to find a place to park can thank these engineers—and their puppet master, Big Car—for making life so convenient for us.

From an environmental standpoint, parking lots are a major source of water pollution. Their impermeable surfaces seal off the lots, preventing rainwater from permeating the soil. Instead, the water flows into sewers and eventually into oceans, lakes, rivers, and estuaries. Along the way, this runoff picks up all kinds of wonderful things: oil, chemicals, dead animals, bacteria, grime, and most everything else that isn't nailed down or under asphalt. Over one-third of the pollution in our water systems is a result of this brilliant scientific planning.[24]

Carlton Cole "Carl" Magee was a lawyer from Iowa with a big idea. He was also a newspaper publisher who had moved to Oklahoma City to become the editor of the *Oklahoma News*. Magee claimed to have come up with the Scripps newspaper chain's motto that is still used today: "Give Light and the People Will Find Their Own Way." (It was stolen from Dante.) In his capacity as newspaper editor, he had been asked by the Oklahoma City Chamber of Commerce to help abate the city's terrible traffic congestion.

Magee quickly realized that the congestion was being caused by the scarcity of downtown parking places. There were enough parking places overall, but everyone preferred the same downtown parking places and many wanted to leave their cars there all day long.

People were used to pulling up to their local store, walking in, buying their merchandise, and carrying it back out to the car. That no longer worked because now there was no place to pull up and park in front of your favorite store. The result was a severe drain on these downtown shops' profits.

Carl came up with the brilliant idea of putting a coin-operated timer in front of every downtown parking place. He called them meters. The first five-cent piece was put into a meter in July 1935. Soon Oklahoma City's coffers were awash in coins from Magee's great idea.[25]

Other communities immediately noted this surprising new cash flow. They already controlled the curbs in front of the stores. All they had to do was put up meters. In fairly short order, Americans learned and accepted that you had to pay to park your car.

But of course, not everyone embraced the idea. For generations, people had considered streets to be public property, and curbside parking—be it for a horse, a wagon, or a car—to be a fundamental right. Not being able to simply leave their cars on public streets just seemed wrong, and there were even legal challenges to the new system.

There were also operational challenges. If your meter ran out of time, you got a parking citation and had to pay a hefty fine to the city. This required a workforce to record parking infractions and then collect the related fines. A whole new low-paying job was created: the parking enforcement officer. These traffic wardens were almost exclusively women. America, and in patriarchal fashion, they were soon dubbed "meter maids."

Another idea that traffic engineers began experimenting with was the one-way street. The invention of the one-way street took place on the evening of September 7, 1934, when Robert Willmott, captain of the SS *Morro Castle*, died in his sleep. The ship, on its way from Havana to New York, was perhaps cursed because almost immediately after he died, a fire broke out in one of the ship's storage lockers. The fire spread and burned through the ship's electrical cables and the *Morro Castle* went completely dark. A strong northeast wind developed and suddenly the entire ship was on fire. The Coast Guard and crew members were helpless, and the ship's lifeboats had nowhere near enough capacity to save all of its passengers or crew. By the afternoon, the ship was abandoned, and survivors and the recently deceased captain were brought by local crafts to the New Jersey shore.

Soon there was an enormous flock of sightseeing traffic to watch the poor SS *Morro Castle*'s terrible demise. The streets leading to the dock were gridlocked. The local police chief, desperate to get help to the surviving passengers, decided to designate the only northbound street to the shore as one-way going north, and the street one block over one-way going south. This is the first recorded history of one-way streets being used to try and solve the problem of traffic congestion in America.[26]

Like so many other ideas attempting to solve the problem of too many cars and not enough streets, this desperate solution didn't really work. By the end of the day, 137 passengers and crew of the SS *Morro Castle* had been lost.

There are very few humans on the planet today who are immune to the problem of traffic jams. Simple supply and demand create a worldwide daily interaction between too many cars and not enough road or parking space. The result is congestion.

In the United States, with over one hundred and thirty million people commuting between their houses and places of work each day, traffic has become an annoying circumstance that we've learned to live with. Big Car's solution has simply been to try and reduce congestion by building more roads. This has turned out to be about as smart as fighting obesity by loosening your belt.[27]

Over a hundred and forty million Americans drive each day, and that's just to get to work.[28]

Those drivers don't realize it, but they are each participating in what economists and social scientists call "the tragedy of the commons": individuals acting independently and following their own self-interest, and thereby depleting a shared resource. This does not always align with what benefits the common good.

The result of each person trying to get where they want to go at the same time each day is extreme traffic congestion. And even after all this time, we still cannot fully predict the specific conditions under which these traffic jams will occur. They can be caused by individual incidents such as a crash or a car breaking down. The ripple effects of these individual events, in turn, often result in "the cascading failure" (one of my favorite phrases). This is a failure in a system of interconnected parts in which the failure of just one or a few parts leads to the failure of all the other parts. One part fails and the probability that the entire system will fail increases almost exponentially. In the case of cars, the result is massive traffic congestion. This same congestion leads to pollution, ozone depletion and, of course, global warming.

Different cities have tried various solutions to try and reduce traffic. Many of the world's largest cities, including Singapore, Stockholm, and London, have levied congestion zone pricing on drivers. If you want to enter London's city center, the standard charge is 15 pounds a day, or about $19. (No charge between Christmas Day and New Year's Day.) And yet, London is still full of traffic.

Everything from managed lanes to high-occupancy vehicle lanes, to bus lanes, to letting drivers use highway shoulders during peak traffic times has been tried. Nothing has worked.

We have paid an enormous cost for this congestion. Here's a short list of the hours wasted and the per-driver costs of congestion.

Congestion continues to be a nightmare. We widen the roads, and the result is that more people show up to drive on them. That means cars' impact on the environment becomes increasingly worse. It means money that could have been spent on alternatives to automobiles, such as mass transit, is never available. It means more greenhouse gas emissions, which must be

TABLE 9.2 COSTS OF CONGESTION PER DRIVER

	City	Hours wasted per vehicle	Cost of congestion per driver
1	Boston, Massachusetts	149 hours	$2,205
2	Chicago, Illinois	145 hours	$2,146
3	Philadelphia, Pennsylvania	142 hours	$2,102
4	New York City, New York	140 hours	$2,072
5	Washington, D.C.	124 hours	$1,835
6	Los Angeles, California	103 hours	$1,524
7	San Francisco, California	97 hours	$1,436
8	Portland, Oregon	89 hours	$1,317
9	Baltimore, Maryland	84 hours	$1,243
10	Atlanta, Georgia	82 hours	$1,214
11	Houston, Texas	81 hours	$1,199
12	Miami, Florida	81 hours	$1,199
13	New Orleans, Louisiana	79 hours	$1,169
14	Seattle, Washington	74 hours	$1,095
15	Stamford, Connecticut	74 hours	$1,095
16	Providence, Rhode Island	70 hours	$1,036
17	San Diego, California	70 hours	$1,036
18	Austin, Texas	69 hours	$1,021
19	Sacramento, California	64 hours	$947
20	Dallas, Texas	63 hours	$932
21	Denver, Colorado	63 hours	$932
22	Hartford, Connecticut	61 hours	$903
23	Minneapolis, Minnesota	52 hours	$770
24	Charlotte, North Carolina	49 hours	$725
25	San Juan, Puerto Rico	46 hours	$681
26	Cleveland, Ohio	44 hours	$651
27	Columbus, Ohio	43 hours	$636
28	Milwaukee, Wisconsin	41 hours	$607
29	Detroit, Michigan	39 hours	$577
30	San Antonio, Texas	39 hours	$577
31	Boulder, Colorado	37 hours	$548

Source: Katie Pysyk, "Gridlock woes: Traffic congestion by the numbers," Smart Cities Dive, March 27, 2018, https://www.smartcitiesdive.com/news/gridlock-woes-traffic-congestion-by-the-numbers/519959/.

reduced if we are to survive on this planet. And yet the Los Angeles County Metropolitan Transportation Authority, known as Metro—i.e., the entity responsible for how ten million citizens of Los Angeles travel—plans to add an additional 300-plus miles of new highways and extensions in the next few years. This will result in cars driving an extra thirty billion miles! It will also produce an additional 10 million metric tons of CO_2 into the climate. Are these people living on the same planet as we are? And this is from just one county in one state.[29]

Until the people in charge of controlling congestion realize that expanding highways to reduce congestion is doing the exact opposite and only bringing more cars onto the newly completed roads, we will be trapped in an unending cycle of folly. Rather than building a sustainable lifestyle for our citizens by helping to reduce greenhouse gas emissions, Big Car is instead killing us softly with asphalt.

THE NIGHTMARE OF POLLUTION

At the beginning of the twentieth century, there was still great hope that humans could solve any problem the planet faced. And so it came to be that Dr. Henry Antoine Des Voeux went to London for a meeting of the Public Health Congress. He was shocked and depressed by the quality of air in England's capital. In his speech, he said, "It requires no science to see that something is being produced in great cities which is not found in the countryside. This something is a smoky fog."[30]

The good doctor had always loved a good portmanteau, a blend of words combined to form a new word. He decided to name this new, smoky fog that hung over most of London "smog." The word caught on and has been with us ever since.

FIGURE 9.6 Highland Park Optimist Club wearing smog-gas masks at a banquet, Los Angeles, 1954.

Source: Los Angeles Daily News Photographic Collection. https://digital.library .ucla.edu/catalog/ark:/21198/zz0002q06p

On July 26, 1943, in the midst of World War II, there was widespread panic in Los Angeles. Thousands of residents were trapped in the city by a thick fog that made their eyes sting and their noses run. You couldn't even see a few blocks ahead. The Japanese had obviously launched a chemical warfare initiative against Los Angeles.

But it wasn't a nefarious Japanese attempt to kill Angelenos that day, it was the exhaust plumes coming out of Angelenos' cars. Photochemical smog produced by internal combustion engines was being released into the Los Angeles atmosphere that day by the massive influx of cars and factories now in the city. Los Angeles had been built in a large basin, and its geography now trapped these fumes like a giant bowl. Big Car had declared war on LA.

The irony was that so many of the recent transplants had come to LA for its clean air. Tens of thousands had moved there hoping to cure their tuberculosis and other respiratory diseases. Now their lungs were burning.

Los Angeles has always been a perfect host for smog. The first inhabitants of the area called Los Angeles "the valley of smoke." Its geography, weather, and other factors make it a wonderful place for smog to hang out. Most of LA lies inside a long, flat basin surrounded by the ocean on one side and mountains on the other. Cold ocean currents bring down air temperatures and result in a massive inversion layer, which simply means that air, instead of decreasing in temperature, increases. The result is that a thin layer of air remains hanging above the city and can't escape from the basin. This air quickly accumulates pollution from our cars and has nowhere to go. The mixture of this trapped air and pollutants becomes smog. Breathing that smog is not healthy.

Los Angeles Mayor Fletcher Bowron announced that the villain was a factory in downtown LA called the Aliso Street Manufactured Gas Plant, and he immediately shut it down. He promised that Los Angeles would completely eliminate the problem of bad air in the next few months.

Dr. Arie Haagen-Smit, a chemist at the California Institute of Technology, was not as optimistic. He had been the first to recognize that perhaps ozone was the primary source of the smog that was choking the basin in which he lived, and also deduced that perhaps this ozone was being created by the partially unburned exhaust from cars when that exhaust was hit by direct sunlight. He went public and said that it wasn't a factory

Southeast of Pittsburgh there is a small mill town called Donora. One day in 1948, people in Donora knew something was wrong. They couldn't inhale without having to cough. By the end of the day, over twenty had died and almost half the town was suffering from severe respiratory problems, all caused by smog. The event is commemorated at the Donora Smog Museum, which serves as a reminder of this now-overlooked chapter in American environmental history. Stan Musial, the all-star St. Louis Cardinals slugger, was on the Donora High baseball team.[31]

or a slipup at an oil plant that was causing the massive increase in irritation of the eyes and respiratory problems. It was, he said, a direct result of all the new cars streaming into the Los Angeles basin and polluting it.

Nobody paid him the slightest bit of attention.

What exactly is pollution? It's simply the introduction of contaminants into the environment. These contaminants are mostly caused by human activities. When chemically mixed into certain constituent parts, they have a devastating effect on our species.

Worldwide, pollution kills almost ten million people a year.[32] That's one out of every eight hundred humans on our planet. Air pollution accounts for three-quarters of these pollution deaths.

Air pollution is the presence of substances in our atmosphere that are dangerous for living beings to inhale. It contributes to a wide range of serious health problems, including respiratory infections, lung cancer, strokes, and heart disease. This "bad air" also seems to lower our IQs.[33] It's also now been shown to cause dramatic increases in depression. It's just not good for us to expose our bodies to these compounds.

The fact that 90 percent of the people on our planet breathe dirty air each day is certainly not beneficial for our species. Along with the millions of lives it claims, air pollution also causes massive losses in productivity for the world economy—to the tune of over five trillion dollars a year.[34]

How does Big Car contribute to pollution? It manufactures the internal combustion engine that until a few years ago went into every automobile made, and then sells the gasoline fuel that these engines turn into pollution.

Even if you excused the immense amount of noise pollution cars cause each day, you can't overlook the direct pipeline between car exhaust and human bodies. Add to this the severe ozone depletion due to the particulate matter coming out of cars, and you have a direct assault on human health and well-being.

The culprit is carbon dioxide. It was the first gas to be discovered and called a discrete substance in 1640. (The word gas

It is a colossal misnomer to call gasoline "natural gas." It has now been shown that natural gas has a similar carbon footprint to other fossil fuels, and yet (or perhaps because of this) energy companies have used this name in the last two decades to distinguish their product from coal gas. Like the industries that promote "natural" foods and other "natural" consumer products, Big Car hopes to convince consumers that natural gas is environmentally friendly. In a recent poll, 77 percent of voters held a favorable view of natural gas over methane-based products. Interestingly, Republican voters tend to view natural gas much more favorably when it is instead called "fossil gas."[35]

is derived from the Greek word for chaos.) Carbon dioxide is a natural component of our atmosphere. Given off by both plants and humans, it is an essential component for life on our planet. But because of the current levels it has now reached, it may well be the essential component in the extinction of our species.

The Earth's atmosphere, which is simply the layer of gases (air) retained by our planet, is held in place by Earth's gravity. This is how life was able to come about. It protects our existence on the planet, allows liquid water to form, and gives us the luxury of greenhouse gas which, until very recently, helped us reduce temperature extremes.

The problem is that we now have twice as much carbon dioxide in our atmosphere as we did in preindustrial times.[36] This is because of the billions of metric tons of CO_2 that are belched out of our cars when they burn fossil fuels. It is the leading pollutant in our environment.

Humans make CO_2 in record amounts. Each time you drive your car you increase the level of it in our atmosphere. We now are measuring levels of the gas that have not been seen in hundreds of thousands of years. The planet's vegetation and oceans are no match for it, and we can't stop ourselves from continuing to poison our species. It's no longer merely a carbon footprint; it's now a carbon highway to human extinction.

Temperatures rise because of carbon dioxide. It exerts a greater warming influence on our planet than all other known gases combined. We emit over thirty billion tons of it per year. (Volcanoes contribute less than 1 percent of that.)[37]

The number of humans dying each year because we use cars in the United States is over 25,000.[38] We remain one of the dirtiest countries in the world, and it's only getting worse. Just another proud contribution to our species from Big Car.

THE NIGHTMARE OF TRAFFIC "PROFESSIONALS"

Until very recently I'd never met an engineer. In fact, I didn't know anyone who knew anyone who had ever met an engineer. Since I was executive producer of the film *Revenge of the Nerds*, you'd think I'd have had some exposure to the profession. But not a one.

The word engineer is derived from the Latin words for "to contrive" and "cleverness." Traffic engineering in this century doesn't seem to be living up to its name.

John Smeaton was an eighteenth-century British engineer and is widely regarded as the father of civil engineering. Others argue that the distinction could also rest with Thomas Telford, a Scot, who was called "the Colossus of Roads."[39]

In the United States before 1907, there was no formal require-ments for being recognized as an engineer. This resulted in countless poorly constructed roads and bridges. Finally, the great state of Wyoming created an engineering board of examiners.

To become a traffic engineer is not a swift or easy process. You first must get your bachelor's degree at a four-year college in some sort of engineering discipline. This means taking a great many math and science courses. After that, you get to spend five to seven years of grueling study in the specific branch of engineering you've chosen. Then you take a battery of tests, and when all of this is successfully completed you can call yourself an engineer.

Here's how the organization dedicated to making sure that engineers know their stuff, the Engineers' Council for Profes-sional Development (which became the Accreditation Board for Engineering and Technology in 1980) defined engineering: "The creative application of scientific principles to design or develop structure, machines, apparatus, or manufacturing processes, or works utilizing them singly or in combination; or to construct or operate the same with full cognizance of their design; or to forecast their behavior under specific operating conditions; all as respects an intended function, economics of operation and safety to life and property."[40]

Even better, the National Society of Professional Engineers has a code of ethics that states that engineering is an important and learned profession. "As members of this profession, engineers are expected to exhibit the highest standards of honesty and integrity. Engineering has a direct and vital impact on the quality of life for all people. Accordingly, the services provided by engineers require honesty, impartiality, fairness, and equity, and must be dedicated to the protection of the public health, safety, and welfare."[41]

One can imagine young engineers throughout America raising their right hand and swearing adherence to the highest principles of ethical conduct on whatever engineers might use as a secular bible. In Canada, when one becomes an engineer, they get to have a private ceremony known as the "Ritual of the Calling of an Engineer" during which they are presented with the coveted "Iron Ring."

Pretty cool for a profession that throughout history was sometimes consigned to building siege engines and catapults.

Miller McClintock, described by *Fortune* magazine as "the top man in his industry," had a number of "traffic tricks" up his sleeve.[42] The self-styled expert on traffic control developed what he called the "friction theory" of traffic. His big idea was that streets in cities should no longer be viewed as public utilities for everyone; instead, they should only be used for cars. The result was that all over America, in the name of road efficiency, cars were segregated from the rest of human transportation.

Miller McClintock was director of Harvard University's Albert Russel Erskine Bureau for Street Traffic Research. The institute was named after the former president of Studebaker. Mr. Erskine was not a lucky man. He was an avid Notre Dame football fan and had the brilliant idea of starting a production line for a car he would name the Rockne, in honor of Notre Dame's famed football coach, Knute Rockne. Less than two weeks after poor Mr. Rockne joined the company, he was killed in an airplane crash. Studebaker still went full steam ahead with launching the car. Unfortunately, it was in 1932, the bottom of America's Great Depression—not an auspicious time to try and get folks to buy new cars.

Studebaker lost its shirt, pants, and everything else it had on. Mr. Erskine, a broken man, put a gun to his heart and ended his torment shortly thereafter. What better fellow for Harvard to name a traffic school after?

McClintock's influence on future traffic engineering was immense. Being an engineer, he deeply believed that the only criterion for any utility is efficiency, and since engineers were the only ones who really knew how to measure efficiency, we should turn the streets over to them. After all, we'd already done that with gas lines, water pipes, and sewers. Why shouldn't streets be the same? McClintock's viewpoint won, and engineers were designated as the pros who would handle the problem of traffic on our streets.[43]

Publicly elected officials in cities were now being replaced by professional engineers. The mayors and police departments had obviously failed in solving traffic problems. It was time for the pros to take over.

To serve the public interest, engineers were given the right to work on fixing the problem. The first thing they did was clear the sidewalks of clutter so that pedestrians wouldn't trespass on their precious roadways. Goodbye newspaper boys, kiosks, and sidewalk vendors. Get lost—we're making these streets into efficient speed corridors.

Next, they went after curbside parking. Come on, that's two extra lanes for cars to use!

They put up more traffic lights to ensure a steady flow of traffic through downtown streets.

As described earlier, they used the schools, Boy Scouts, and other organizations to teach the public that there was a new "king of the road": the car. If you were on foot, there were now clearly marked areas for you to cross the street. Traffic etiquette was transformed by these engineers. Our streets now firmly belonged to Big Car.

What these men (women were a rarity in the profession) really did well was to gain access to public transport money. The public was willing to turn over their transportation budgets to these "experts." Finally, there would now be people who could bring regulation and tidiness to our streets.

Mr. McClintock and his engineers were social scientists, a term commonly in use since the nineteenth century. Their discipline was one of many addressing human society, behavior, and social structures. According to these early traffic engineers, fixing our roadways was just a matter of understanding science. They promised that in no time traffic would be halved, and that if given the proper resources they could wipe out congestion completely.

Everyone jumped on their bandwagon. Chambers of commerce all over the country began to champion them. And, of course, who loved these engineers and their new ideas the most? Big Car.

Big Car put their full resources and media know-how into convincing Americans that these engineering efficiency experts would take care of everything.

Most cities, as mentioned above, had already placed significant trust in the engineering profession by this time. They had already granted engineers substantial authority over managing public utilities, so it seemed logical to extend that control to the design and management of streets. One of the primary engineering solutions for irresponsible and reckless driving was to build bigger and wider roads that would (in theory) remove the danger. Wide, multi-laned highways, free of pedestrians and especially children, would make streets safe again; indeed, cities would only need to give a competent highway engineer enough concrete and steel, and traffic congestion and accidents would be a thing of the past. Well-engineered roads would lead directly to well-engineered driving. It was all very scientific.

Thus began the most dramatic change to American urban space in the history of our country. Vast tracts of land, often already densely populated, were bulldozed into flat ribbons of pavement. Fences blocked access to these highways. Pets, children, pedestrians, and anything else that would slow the productive movement of a speeding car were pushed out of the way. Everything possible was done to make these roads exclusively for cars.

Big Car began slashing their way through our cities. They didn't care if people already lived where the roads were planned. Also, in one of the most profound changes in urban history, cities ceded their property rights to the federal government, which had already become a willing partner to the interests of Big Car.

All of this was done in the name of fighting traffic and making roads safe again. Pleas for motorists to slow down, such as the slogan "Better belated than mutilated," were lost within the intoxicating promise of wide, fast-moving thoroughfares connecting one's town to the rest of America.

Big Car couldn't have been more pleased. It's easy to forget that in 1886, before the start of the twentieth century, the U.S. Supreme Court had already ruled that the equal protection clause of the Constitution protects corporations as well as private persons. And hadn't it been the folks with money who had greatly improved our standards of living? Give them our streets. What could go wrong?

McClintock and his traffic engineers held the misplaced belief that cars didn't need to sacrifice speed for safety, and that with the right scientific thinking you should be able to have both. A great big beautiful—and fast—tomorrow was right around the next corner.

To begin solving the problem, these traffic engineers first did what bureaucrats with access to large public funds often do: They began to hire each other to do "feasibility surveys." Every facet of traffic would be looked at. "I survey, therefore I am" could well have been their motto. Since these were scientific studies, and numbers never lie, these surveys would give the engineers the necessary tools to build the perfect automotive city. Again, what could go wrong?

The first thing their numbers showed them was that fast traffic was smart traffic. Increasing travel speed on any street would obviously result in increased capacity for more cars. They began to experiment with putting traffic signals in downtown areas to speed up the flow of traffic. They issued glowing reports about how well their ideas were working. One engineer's report actually said that driving our streets now can't help but make you smile as if you're in a fairy tale.

What could go wrong? Many things, in fact. The first problem was that a driver couldn't just bring his or her car downtown and walk away from it. No, they had to find places to park. This was now causing the thing engineers hated the most—inefficiency. Their new surveys revealed that car drivers needed ten times as much street space as public transportation riders. They kept this discovery to themselves.

Engineers became increasingly frustrated as downtown streets didn't neatly fit into their scientifically crafted models.

The actual problem was that traffic engineers had collected data that in no way accurately told the story of how the public was using their streets. Since cars in the city were already taking up about a third of the surface area of most towns' streets, something had to be done.

Things really began to turn ugly between the people and the engineers when it was "scientifically" decided that curbs could no longer to be used to park a car indefinitely. They prevailed upon those who ruled the cities to pass laws severely limiting the amount of time one's car could remain parked at the curb.

It was too late. American cities had given themselves over to Big Car. Urban streets no longer belonged to the people; cities now belonged to the automobile.

Today, traffic engineers work with other professionals to create what's called an intelligent transportation system (ITS). This is the plan for how a metropolitan traffic system should be designed. Besides trying to decide how to prevent congestion, one of the main interests of our government in ITS planning is now about homeland security. Because all new ITS systems involve extensive surveillance of our highways, this has meant bushels of federal dollars being spent on planning for mass evacuation of people from urban centers. (President Eisenhower would be proud.) Because of the effect of Big Car on our environment, homeland security is now a central component of all ITS planning.

One can only wonder if the billions spent on this might have been better used to find a way to make traffic move when we're not on fire or being flooded, rather than spending our resources protecting us from being attacked by the Russians.

Remember all the studying and hard work that it takes for traffic engineers to get their certification? In theory, this should protect against the dangers expressed in one the most famous engineering maxims: "garbage in, garbage out." But the methods used to teach these folks are still deeply rooted in the past. Textbooks often are from twenty or thirty years ago. The foundational principles for streets and highways are based on the facts and figures of yesteryear's urban planning failures.

Year after year, the people who are supposed to be advising our cities bring with them antiquated concepts—and worse, ideas that have been proven not to work. The teaching of traffic engineering in America fits perfectly into Einstein's definition of insanity. They continue to simply expand roads and then are disappointed when these new roadways immediately become just as congested as they were before billions of dollars were spent widening them.

The salient fact is that even with enormous new computer processing power, engineers have not been able to come up with any kind of general plan to control traffic. Instead, they have come up with complex models of traffic patterns. Using both empirical data and theoretical systems of analysis, they have come up with models that allow them to make traffic forecasts for the rest of us. Using what they call a demand model, they follow a formula developed in the 1950s by our early computer systems. What could go wrong?

There is probably not a single person reading this book who has not sat in a bottleneck on these scientifically laid out highways and seen road construction taking place on either side of their car. As they said about Watergate, "Follow the money."

Another "hero" of our traffic woes is the Metropolitan Planning Organization (MPO). This is a federally funded policymaking organization composed of representatives from Washington and various local governments. The idea of forming the MPO was to try and have some semblance of regional cooperation with the federal government in laying out our new roads. Since the engineers alone couldn't solve traffic problems, bureaucrats joined the planning process.

When a tidal wave of federal funds swept across America in the 1950s, all the rules for planning and paying for transportation changed. Before then, Washington had studiously avoided getting directly involved in local transportation decisions. Now, with Uncle Sam signing all the checks to pay for these new roads, Washington could dictate how and where this money would be allotted. That meant that they could now tell states where they had to lay their roads. It was the U.S.A. way, or no highway.

Suddenly, a slew of MPO policy committee members, none of whom had been elected by the local citizenry, had legal authority over where the roads would go.

In 1991, with the enactment of the Intermodal Surface Transportation Efficiency Act (an oxymoron just waiting to happen), MPOs expanded their authority even further. Now, all state transportation officials were required to report to MPOs on any decision-making plans involving traffic congestion. Like so much else, addressing traffic at the federal committee level only made things worse.

George H. W. Bush promised that by having his people in charge, we'd have cleaner air, better energy conservation, and (for some reason) total social equity in our road systems. His plan to integrate our transportation system into a "seamless" movement of goods and people worked out about as well as his war on drugs.

Federal MPO budgets doubled. The MPO became the go-to body for requesting the funding for dealing with traffic and congestion. Adding another layer of bureaucracy to try and solve how to deal with Big Car did exactly what one would expect: It simply made the problem more intractable. Having to deal with bureaucratic bottlenecks did little or nothing to make our roads less congested.

Since almost half of all congestion is a result of improperly planned, designed, constructed, and maintained highways, a grateful nation can only offer a sincere "thanks a lot" to the engineers and MPOs of the United States.

THE NIGHTMARE OF RACISM

Most of what we've looked at so far has been how Big Car has affected White people. What it's done to Hispanics, African Americans, and other communities of color is even worse.

In the early years of Big Car, traffic fatalities were significantly lower for people of color than for White people, especially for children. This was because cars were often too expensive to buy for people in non-white communities, who generally earned far more meager salaries. As more and more cars began to speed through their communities, however, more traffic deaths quickly followed.

More alarming was the impact of so-called "urban blight," a euphemism referring to the wholesale disruption of entire communities to make more room for cars. Traffic engineers and others soon came to use the term as shorthand for describing the social and structural deterioration in areas of large cities that had (according to them) once been a well-functioning part of the city but now had fallen into decay following an influx of people of color.

These areas were defined by their low quality of life and living standards, high instances of crime, lack of political clout, and high levels of pollution.

The result was "white flight," a massive migration of white people away from these same areas. Big Car, having brought about the advent of the national highway system, provided a perfect means of escape. The 1950s and 1960s saw a mass migration of white people out of our downtown communities.

Add to this the restrictive covenants, redlining, and overt mortgage discrimination practiced by cities, banks, and individual homeowners outside of overcrowded minority cities, and vast numbers of people of color were forced to live lives that were much different from those who migrated to the suburbs.

One problem quickly led to another. Lack of adequate banking and insurance meant that these communities of color were trapped by what author Laura Pulido has described as environmental racism.[44]

What this meant was that making it to the suburbs was something only middle-class and working-class whites were entitled to do. Mortgages by the United States Department of Veterans Affairs (VA) and the Federal Housing Administration were only available to Whites for purchasing new houses:

> "Recommended restrictions should include provisions for: prohibition of the occupancy of properties except by the race for which they are intended. . . . Schools should be appropriate to the needs of the new community, and they should not be attended in large numbers by inharmonious racial groups."[45]

With the new highway system transporting suburbanites to downtown jobs, it now meant that most of the monied population was outside the city. Shifting the tax base away to the suburbs meant that urban decay worsened in the cash-starved cities.

Urban planning decisions were now being made not by the local populace but by people whose socioeconomic decisions were often overtly racist, particularly in the American South. There, local governments used highway road construction to carve up Black neighborhoods. They had the federal government construct interstate highways through majority-Black communities. These communities, within a generation, became home to populations of the poorest proportion of people in our country—people who did not have the money to leave their shattered communities.[46]

Finally, being in a car when you are a person of color is dangerous—not only because of the countless traffic fatalities that occur, but also because of the law.

When a non-White teenager becomes old enough drive a car, they are often given "the talk." A parent sits down with them and explains the dangers of being on the road.

In America today there are more than 50,000 traffic stops a day made by our nation's police.[47] A disproportionate number of these involve Black and Brown motorists. These stops frequently lead to tragedy.

The danger of incarceration always looms. A broken tail-light, a turn signal that wasn't activated, or a full stop that didn't occur—the litany of causes and pretexts for these occasions is seemingly endless.

Once pulled over, drivers of color face the imminent threat of financial hardship, going to prison, and sometimes death.

One of the reasons that people of color fear being pulled over is that often their communities use the traffic ticket as a revenue generator. Being stopped and given a citation can lead to a cascade of financial hardship for the driver.

For example, if the driver cannot get off work to go to court to make a plea, they are smacked with staggeringly high penalties. If they don't pay these fines at once, they run the risk of being jailed. Cities throughout the land of the free have disregarded the ability of the driver to be able to pay. "No payment, no pavement" is their motto.

Judges almost always side with the police and the city and turn the matter over to collection agencies, which charge exorbitant fees. Add to that the court costs, and the ticket cost, and the result is that countless people of color just give up and drive without a license. If they are then pulled over again, they go to jail and must pay even heftier fines.

Sadly, far too many municipalities, starved for financial resources, have been using this method to be able to fund themselves.

For those who are jailed, the problems have only just begun. Because they are unable to work, their credit rating is ruined. Upon release, they are now subject to predatory lending schemes. The most egregious of these is that, believe it or not, car financing lenders will only give them money to rent or buy top-of-the-line luxury cars.

They cannot, even with a financially solvent friend or relative willing to cosign for them, get into a new Toyota or another mid-cost automobile. Instead, they are pushed into getting a Mercedes or other high-end car. For far too many of these people, it's only a matter of time until the car is repossessed.

As NYU professors Julie Livingston and Andrew Ross recently reported in a *New York Times* op-ed piece, "Fiscally squeezed by austerity policies, officials extract the funds from those least able to pay." That is a form of regressive taxation. They also note Malcolm X's observation that "racism is like a Cadillac; they bring out a new model every year."[48]

THE NIGHTMARE OF SEXISM

"To attract men, I wear a perfume called "New Car Interior."
—Rita Rudner

When Big Car first appeared, everything about it was masculine. You also needed a fair amount of strength just to operate it. It was a high-maintenance item, and the user had to be willing to muddy themselves and get covered in grease. And it was manifestly not built for women: not only did early cars require the turning of a very difficult-to-operate crank to get the machine started, but most of them were built so that most women's feet couldn't even reach the pedals. Women were also not generally allowed easy access to money. As a result, virtually all first-generation cars were owned and operated by men.

Today, although 85 percent of all car-buying decisions are made by women, the car manufacturing business is still dominated by males. Less than a quarter of the people who build cars are women. An even smaller percentage of females exist in "Big Car" managerial roles.

Believe it or not, it was the fight for women's suffrage that finally opened the world of cars to women. The auto symbolized freedom in the fight for women's rights. It was used to connect like-minded females across the country, and it provided the transportation to bring these women to Congress to state their case.

Early women activists taught each other how cars worked. They used their cars to travel to neighboring towns and enlist other women to join their movement. Driving automobiles draped in suffragette banners, they would pull into towns and gather signatures. The press loved them, and the cars themselves were attention-grabbers since the suffragettes would

adorn them with flags, flowers, and even suffragette hood ornaments. For many small-town residents, seeing a woman driving
was shocking enough. The freedom to travel displayed by these
women drivers must also have helped the suffragettes' cause
gain traction. Upon hearing their message, tens of thousands of
small-town women joined their cause. On one suffragette cara-
van, they were able to show up in Washington with over fifty
thousand signatures. Their petition was over 18,000 feet long.

The automobile and the suffragette movement became intertwined. One trip in 1916, sponsored by the National American
Woman Suffrage Association, traveled over 10,000 miles. At
that time very few women drove, roads were mostly unpaved,
and the women had to repair their own machines, which often
broke down.[49]

For men and women alike, travel was a mud-splattering,
dusty mess. No self-respecting woman would ever dare appear
in public wearing her driving outfit. Instead, women would pull
over before they reached their intended target and shed their
hats, shoes, scarves, and outerwear.

So, these early hand-cranked cars were not intended for
women to drive. Since they also didn't have power brakes or
power steering, most women had to practically stand up in the
driver's seat to reach the pedals.

By 1910, however, car design began to be more accommodat-
ing to women. When Charles Kettering developed an electric
starter (as discussed in previous chapters), women could start
their vehicles from the car's interior.

The first car to have a significant impact on women's access
to driving was the electric car, designed rather like today's golf
carts. Used exclusively by the well-off, they were easy to steer and
didn't leave their drivers a muddy mess. Henry Ford's wife Clara
would, much to her husband's chagrin, only drive in electric cars.

The Woman and the Car, written by Dorothy Levitt in 1909 advises women to wear the following:

- **Suit:** A two-piece skirt and jacket set. An extra sweater for warmth.
- **Blouse:** A button-down shirtwaist, very simple.
- **Dress:** A simple dress to match your destination (party, tea, vacation, etc.)
- **Underwear:** Petticoat and slip.
- **Smock:** Optional driving smock.
- **Coat or duster:** A long roomy fur coat in winter, tweed lined in mild seasons, or a light cotton or linen coat in summer.
- **Shoes:** Flexible leather sole pumps, slippers, or boots if not too restrictive. Gaiters to the knee.
- **Hat:** A flat-top beret, turban, sailor cap, or fur cap, with a motoring scarf wrapped around the hat and head.
- **Goggles:** A pair of driving goggles.
- **Scarf:** A neck scarf for warmth.
- **Gloves:** Soft leather gauntlet gloves year-round. Fur mittens for winter.

(1) *"Traveling for Suffrage Part 1: Two women, a cat, a car, and a mission".* *National Museum of American History. Retrieved August 24, 2020.*

But a key reason why women were encouraged to drive in electric vehicles had to do with ideas of sexual propriety: men were concerned that the vibrations of the internal combustion engine would provoke sexual stimulation in women. Men reasoned that because the early car was essentially a giant vibrator, they should keep decent women out of cars.

FIGURE 9.7 A 1916 ad for the Baker Electric. From the Collections of The Henry Ford.

After the Second World War, the relationship between women and cars changed dramatically. During the war, with so many men gone, women had stepped up to keep America's economy working. They also had made enough money to buy their own cars. Ford began a very successful ad campaign that said a woman's place was no longer in the home but instead in a Ford.

Suddenly it was important for families to own two cars. It was now every American's right to drive a car. Car salesmen called on women at home; they showed them all the colors now available for their cars and the various fabrics they could choose for their interior; they even gave them a choice of what kind of floor mats they wanted. Men may still have been selecting the engines, but women picked what the car would look like.

How a woman was to act when she was in a car was also clearly defined. The famous matriarch of manners, Emily Post, before skillfully making a fortune telling folks which fork to use and how to behave like a "perfect gentleman," was originally an early female car journalist. Her 1916 book *By Motor to the Golden Gate* follows her cross-country automobile trip from New York City to San Francisco. By the time her iconic book on etiquette was published a few years later, she had set new standards for what was proper for women in the auto age. No longer did a woman need to be chaperoned in a car; in fact, she could drive a male passenger. Twenty years later, at the height of her popularity, Emily Post published "Motor Manners: The Blue Booklet of Traffic Etiquette. She made it okay for women to be in the literal driver's seat.

Thanks to the post-World War II baby boom, America was now awash with children. "Big Car" never one to miss an economic opportunity, took an already-established, low-selling product and turned it into an economic bonanza: the minivan.

What once was regarded as a "hippie car" now became a housewife's car. Big Car understood that a new generation of

In 1994 Big Car discovered a demographic that had long been ignored: lesbians. One company in particular decided to make a car that lesbians would be drawn to. Subaru thus began to launch a series of brilliantly coded national advertisements under the slogan "Get Out and Stay Out." It worked; the car allowed an entire subset of Americans to drive out of the closet. Their most successful ad read: "It loves camping, dogs, and long-term commitments. Too bad it's only a car."

women needed a car that would help them meet their new world of professional responsibilities while, at the same time, ensuring a smooth transition from home to work. They could drop the kids at school, go to work, pick the kids up and drop them at Little League practice, race back to work, pick the kids up, and finally stop by the grocery store to pick up dinner. Most children were now being raised on the road, between thirty and fifty miles per hour.

A quick note about women and automotive safety: There was a pervasive and highly prejudicial belief that women were inferior drivers, and this prejudice was often encoded in popular culture: "My wife is a careful driver—she always slows down when going through a red light," was a frequent joke on television shows.

Car safety features were designed explicitly to protect the male body; all safety measures designed to safeguard drivers were made for men. One primary reason for this was that for years crash tests were done exclusively using male test dummies that were six feet tall. The federal government set its standards on car safety based on statistics that only used this model. It took generations before automobile manufacturers and the government finally conceded that their car safety features were only helping men (and men of a certain stature, at that).

Let's examine a few of the women who contributed to Big Car's success:

MARY ANDERSON

At the start of the twentieth century, the horse was quickly being replaced by other means of mobility. Almost none of these modes of transport had the accoutrements that we've grown to take for granted.

Mary Anderson was an already successful entrepreneur when she came to New York City in 1902. One particularly blustery winter day, while sitting in an electric trolley car, she became increasingly frustrated when the trolley driver stopped repeatedly, either to open his window and lean outside to clear the shield, or to leave the car and clean it by hand. Mary immediately came up with a brilliant idea. What if a device could be attached to the front window and activated from inside the trolley car? Her idea was to have a lever inside the vehicle that controlled a rubber blade on the outside of the windshield. The lever could be operated to cause the spring-loaded arm to move back and forth across the windshield. She had invented the windshield wiper. Anderson was granted a patent in 1906, but nobody wanted it. Remember, this is still many years before Henry Ford's assembly line. The most common response she received was: "We do not consider it to be of such commercial value as would warrant our undertaking its sale." Furthermore, many could not see the value of her invention and stressed the risk that the driver would be distracted by the operating the device and the moving wipers.[50]

Her patent expired and Mary Anderson never made a penny for her brilliant idea.

FLORENCE LAWRENCE

Lawrence was a major silent movie star during her lifetime. Appearing in over three hundred films, she was one of the most interesting women in early Hollywood. She is often referred to as the "first movie star" and was LONG thought to be the first film actor to be named publicly by her studio in order to sell theater tickets.

Besides her film career, Lawrence is credited with designing the first "auto signaling arm," a predecessor of the modern turn signal, along with the first mechanical brake signal. She did not patent her invention and also didn't make a single cent off of it.[51]

MARGARET WILCOX

Margaret Wilcox was tired of freezing from the cold in her husband's new car. At a time when women had very little control over the family automobile, she decided that, at the very least, she could stay warm. Early cars were open to the air, and taking a drive meant bundling up in a prodigious amount of clothing. Margaret realized that the car's engine was producing a great amount of heat. If she could just funnel some of that heat into the car, then every outing wouldn't be so uncomfortable.

So Wilcox invented the car heater. At the time she did this, women weren't allowed to hold patents, so she had to register her invention in her husband's name.

A few years later, when Henry Ford began to enclose his cars, he took Wilcox's invention and built it into his machines. Suddenly, it didn't matter how cold it was outside; the car's interior was nice and cozy.

Very few people have ever heard of Margaret Wilcox—despite the fact that her patent was finally registered in her name, and her car heater was named one of the top ten inventions of the century by *Inventors Digest*.

The National Inventors Hall of Fame was founded in 1973 to recognize individuals who had significantly advanced technology. With hundreds and hundreds of inventors and scientists as members, it took them twenty years to finally select their first female inductee. Only three are listed for their inventions for cars.

MARGARET "PEGGY" SAUER

Known as the "Damsel of Design," Peggy Sauer was instrumental in building GM car interiors that would appeal to women. Her interiors made sure that women could easily take care of their primary duty: being a housewife. She even came up with a minivan that included a small washer and dryer. Mom could now do a load of laundry while at soccer practice.

MARY TERESA BARRA

Mary Teresa Barra is the chair and chief executive officer of General Motors. Holding the title since 2014, she is the first female CEO in Big Car history.

She first came to GM as a teenager in 1980. Her first job was checking fender panels. Her paycheck from GM enabled her to pay her college tuition.

Forbes now ranks her among the ten most powerful women in the world. Her annual pay is the highest of all automakers: $22,000,000 a year.

Last year she was inducted into the Automotive Hall of Fame, joining such luminaries as Henry Ford, Charles W. Nash, Barney Oldfield, Ransom E. Olds, Alfred P. Sloan, Jr., and Jay Leno. She is one of only a handful of women among the hundreds of men in that hall of fame.

There are, of course, many other females who have contributed to the success of Big Car. Most have vanished into obscurity, overshadowed by the men they worked for.

Our discussion of gender and transportation would not be complete without addressing the sexual segregation of women in mass transit. This practice has a long and complex history. Today, in many countries, sexual assault and harassment of women on public transportation is so endemic that transportation spaces (often, railway and subway cars and taxis) are reserved exclusively for women. These measures have been introduced as a response to widespread groping and assaults, and are intended to provide a safer and more secure environment for women travelers.

A cursory survey finds this being implemented in the following places:

In the Egyptian cities of Cairo and Alexandria, the middle two cars are reserved for women, and some are even painted pink to denote them as being exclusively for women.

Mexico City implemented women-only buses in 2008, and the Mexico City Metro offers a number of women-only cars. They even have a women-only taxi and bus service called the "Pink Line."

Almost all long-distance travel systems in India have special compartments reserved for women only.

Indonesia's rapid transit buses have women-only areas in the front of each bus.

Tehran has women-only carriages exclusively for females.

The Manila Metro Rail Transit System designates the first car of its transit lines for women only.

Every train in Dubai's Metro System has one designated carriage for women only.

As suburbia grew, women needed cars. They needed them to buy groceries, take the kids to the doctor or to Little League and soccer games, drop their husbands at work or the train station, and do countless other activities. By midcentury, the car was a vital necessity for almost all women to satisfy their domestic responsibilities. Yet when families traveled together, the man was still overwhelmingly in the driver's seat.

THE NIGHTMARE OF DRUNK DRIVING

Now let's look at one last horrible consequence of Big Car: drunk driving. In the time it will take you to read this section of the book, somewhere in America a person will be killed in a car crash involving an alcohol-impaired driver. Every day in the United States, close to forty people are killed in drunk driving accidents. That's equivalent to losing a small town each year to alcohol-impaired traffic deaths.[52]

These car crashes kill about the equivalent of a small town each year and the estimated annual cost of these deaths is nearly three hundred billion dollars, accounting for "lost quality-of-life" costs.[53] This is not just a public health crisis; it's also a life-endangering threat to everyone on the road.

Humans have been getting intoxicated for most of our short history on this planet. Various solutions have done absolutely nothing to address the problem. In England, as far back as the Middle Ages, Poor Laws stigmatized drunkenness. A drunk person was set in the stocks for three days and nights, given nothing but bread and water, and finally banished from the town. Throughout the early modern era, England would pass much more stringent laws punishing the "undeserving," including drunkards. And with the advent of indentured servitude, drunkards were sometimes packed off to English colonies across the Atlantic or at the far corners of the world.

As early as 1874, Francis Anstie, an English scientist, realized that alcohol was excreted by breathing. But it would be almost 50 years before anything resembling a breathalyzer (another portmanteau!), a device to measure breath alcohol content, came into being. In early versions, drunk suspects were required to inflate a football bladder with their breath, which would then be tested for traces of alcohol.[54]

In 1931, the Drunkometer—a practical roadside breath-testing device—was developed at the Indiana University School of Medicine. The Drunkometer collected a motorist's breath sample directly in a balloon inside the machine. The breath sample was then pumped through an acidified solution and if there was alcohol in the breath sample, the solution changed color. The greater the color change, the more alcohol was present in the breath.

This would have been a great way to instantly get drunk drivers off the road, but for one small problem: It didn't work. Countless falsely high breath analyzer readings made the courts wary of allowing their findings to be used to convict drunk drivers.

One of the most common causes of falsely high breathalyzer readings is the presence of mouth alcohol. In analyzing a subject's breath sample, the breathalyzer assumes that the alcohol in the breath sample came from the lungs. However, alcohol may have come from the mouth, throat, or stomach; something as simple as burping or gastroesophageal reflux can greatly skew the breathalyzer results. A very tiny amount of alcohol from the mouth, throat, or stomach can have a significant impact on the breath-alcohol reading, in which case the findings are invalid.

Various companies entered a breathalyzer "arms race." The National Highway Traffic Safety Administration was the final arbiter and instructed the states to put implied consent laws into their driver's license agreements, which meant that any driver suspected of being intoxicated would be subject to evidentiary procedures such as breathalyzer tests. The results of these tests often lead to arrests for driving under the influence (DUI).

On May 14, 1980, Candace Lightner's thirteen-year-old daughter, Cari, got on a school bus being used by her local church youth group in Carroll County, Kentucky. Candace would never see her little girl again because a pickup truck driven by a drunk driver smashed into the bus in a head-on collision. It was the deadliest bus crash in U.S. history. Twenty-seven people on the bus were killed.[55]

Candace was devastated but decided to try and do something about the tragedy. She founded Mothers Against Drunk Driving (MADD). The Irving, Texas–based organization was an idea whose time had come. Within no time there was at least one MADD office in every state in America. These offices offered victim services and promoted alcohol safety. In 1985, Stevie Wonder wrote a song called "Don't Drive Drunk" that mentioned MADD.

Candace is no longer with MADD. She left saying that the organization "had become far more neo-prohibitionist than I had ever wanted or envisioned." She said she'd started MADD not to deal with alcohol, but to deal with the issue of drunk driving.[56]

MADD's telemarketers now raise over $40 million a year. CharityWatch (formerly the American Institute of Philanthropy) says that MADD keeps nearly 60 percent of the money it raises for Internet fundraising costs and management.

Like so much else, MADD may have become a victim of Big Car. In the same way that Big Car deflected the blame for pedestrian deaths onto pedestrians themselves, the blame for alcohol-related road deaths has been deflected onto alcohol rather than drunk drivers.

10

THE EDSEL

This was one of the best jobs that Teddy had ever had. For a few years he'd bummed around the country, doing various odd jobs, but he had finally ended up in his hometown of Dearborn, Michigan. He now sat on the roof overlooking one of Ford's giant manufacturing plants. He peered through his telescope from six in the morning until six o'clock at night. He was a Ford watchman, hired to look out for anyone foolish enough to try and sneak up to the plant's windows and take a picture of what was going on inside. If such an intruder appeared, Teddy was to instantly ignite a string of rather large firecrackers. This would be an intruder alert for the plant's heavily armed security guards. During his short tenure, nobody had tried to sneak a look into the intensely guarded structure.

Inside the mammoth factory, teams of production crews were hurriedly assembling one of the Ford Corporation's most precious commodities: the 1957 Edsel.

The reason I've picked this particular car to highlight is that it really is a lasting tribute to Big Car's total disregard for common sense. The car was about to become the most expensive launch of any product in world history. It had taken more than eight hundred executives, fifteen thousand workers, and the employees of

FIGURE 10.1 A 1959 Edsel Ranger.

Source: Redsimon. https://commons.wikimedia.org/wiki/File:Edsel_Ranger_2door
_Hardtop_front.jpg

Ford's twelve hundred dealerships to make sure this car would become a mainstay in American automobile commerce.[1]

Nobody except a select few of Ford's most trusted employees, had been allowed to see the finished product. Ford had spent millions teasing the public with hints about the astonishing new vehicle that they were about to allow every American to park proudly in front of their homes.

Newsweek magazine, one of the most widely read periodicals in the country, had just published a cover story on the car. But they hadn't really shown the car. The cover photo of the Edsel showed only the right front wheel and a couple of very revealing inches of the car's bumper.

E-Day, the date that Ford would finally let the American public view its masterpiece, was much anticipated. One of the major networks did a special about it. Photographs of pieces of the car were shown to tantalize the audience. All Ford dealerships showrooms had had their windows either boarded over or covered with newspapers so that nobody could sneak a look. This was big.

In September 1957, Ford finally unwrapped its present to America. They opened their showrooms and three million Americans poured in to see the Edsel.

Henry Ford II, called "Hank the Deuce" by his near and dear, was the oldest grandson of Henry Ford senior. He was also the oldest son of the man the car was named after—his father, Edsel Ford I. He was also the president of the Ford Motor Company.

He hadn't been happy about naming the car the Edsel. He felt there might be something demeaning about seeing his father's name spinning wildly on countless cars' hubcaps. He also remembered his father telling him about how often he'd been teased because of his name: "Did you say your name was pretzel?"

Henry's instincts had been well founded. The Edsel was a catastrophe for his company. The problem wasn't just that the car was ugly and often didn't work. It was that, so far, nobody seemed to want to buy it. Ford could shake that off. After all, he'd been able to sell the public all his other products. This just might take a bit more time.

He hired the biggest names in show business—Frank Sinatra, Bob Hope, Bing Crosby—to collaborate on singing the Edsel theme song:

> We want our friends to understand,
> When they observe our car,
> That we're as smart and successful and grand,
> As we like to think we are.

Huh?

Ford still wasn't ready to admit that he had been responsible for what is still regarded as one of the worst ideas in corporate history.

Edsel's problem was that the car was a total lemon. The trunk didn't open, the brakes often failed, hubcaps went flying off, and the push button gears specially built into the steering wheel didn't work. The surest sign that the Edsel was a total flop was that nobody was even stealing them.

A breathtaking 99 percent of the cars manufactured went unsold. Ford's corporate earnings that year looked like a ski slope.

In one last desperate, heroic fit of foolishness, the Ford corporation bought 1,000 ponies and shipped them to each of their Edsel dealerships. The idea was that any mother who brought her kid in could enter a raffle to win the pony. Dealers had no idea what to do with the poor beasts. Even worse was the stampede of mothers, whining in perfect Homer Simpson tones, "I want to see the pony, I want to see the pony, I want to see the pony!" The winners of the raffle, understandably, rather than taking the pony, instead accepted the alternative prize of a couple hundred dollars in cash. Countless Ford dealers were now stuck with a lot of ponies. (An even cursory study of animal husbandry would have revealed to the great minds of the Ford Motor Company that car showrooms are not a natural habitat for ponies.)

This was but one of the countless mistakes the company made in what's been described as the most colossal, stupendous, and legendary blunders in the history of American marketing. Ford lost the equivalent of almost two and a half billion dollars ($250 million in 1960 dollars). A couple of years later, with very little fanfare, the Edsel brand was quietly put to rest.[2]

As part of the brilliant rollout for their magnificent car, Ford had bought a sponsorship of one of the most popular programs then on network television, *Wagon Train.* To help promote the automobile, television viewers were gleefully invited to participate in an exclusive promotional contest to win a brand-new Edsel. On the last show of the year, it was announced that instead of a new Edsel, winners would instead be given a pony.

11

OUR CONTINUED LOVE AFFAIR WITH BIG CAR

By the mid-1900s, America's love affair with cars had reached its zenith. It was more than just sex appeal, although that helped. Rather, it was almost like a religious experience for people. The cars themselves had become amazing objects of adoration.

With luxurious tailfins and chrome galore, a mighty V8 engine, and every kind of accessory auto engineers could think up, the car became the dominant factor in how Americans defined themselves. No other technology or machine had ever had such a major influence on the culture.

There were songs about cars, movies about cars, books, and, of course, billboards everywhere that reflected our fanatical devotion to the automobile. Rarely, if ever, had humans displayed such passion toward an inanimate object. Since so often one's status was defined by one's "wheels," you became what you drove. When you were young, your family car told the whole block exactly how the family was doing. Everyone was an expert in the different models put out each year. Kids could identify cars with amazing accuracy. The "rocket jet" chrome and hood ornaments let everyone know exactly where one belonged in the car pecking order.

Big Car played into these beliefs by spending hundreds of millions of dollars in advertising to show you exactly how a car could redefine your existence. Driving a new Cadillac up to your favorite restaurant would tell the planet that you had arrived, that you had done so well that you were allowed to sit behind the wheel of America's premier symbol of success.

Sitting behind that wheel was not something for the fainthearted. While Big Car continued to make gargantuan profits each year, they didn't really put much of that money back into making cars safer for their customers. In part, this was because people who bought new cars cared way more about how they looked than about how safe they were. More important, safety costs money. Why rock the economic boat when demand remained at peak levels?

Midcentury cars were not safe. Dashboards were hard and unforgiving. There was no such things as seat belts. The dangers of lousy brakes and steering columns that slammed into (or even impaled) drivers were compounded by windshields that rained glass down onto the hapless driver and any passengers—unless you were thrown out of the car, whose doors often flew open on impact.[1]

Big Car, like the cigarette business, was brilliant in deflecting blame away from its own product. In the 1960s and 1970s, cars were killing more than 50,000 people each year—but the car companies shrugged this off as the fault of irresponsible pedestrians, bad driving habits, and poorly constructed roadways. Evidence of the harsh effect of emissions on people in cities was dismissed as simple alarmism and "quack" science.

The result was that for decades, Big Car was able to sell poorly designed cars with virtually no safety features to a willing public. The industry was allowed to keep polluting the air without any serious repercussions, and they were able to reap enormous profits while doing so.

Each year in America it was a big deal when Big Car's new models came out. Brilliantly using television, radio, magazines, and newspapers, Big Car would tease the public into impatiently wanting to see what was new.

When a car dealership's windows were finally uncovered so the public could see the new models, the whole community flocked to ogle the shiny new toys. Longer, heavier, higher-polluting models, many of them reflecting America's newfound fascination with space exploration, made the public yearn for these cars. The result was whopping sales and profits for Big Car.

For much of the twentieth century, the only sure thing in American commerce was that everyone wanted to buy, own, and drive their new cars. There was no appreciable anti-car movement. A true American was a true car enthusiast, and the prevailing mindset was, "You'll get me out of my car when you pry my cold dead foot off of my accelerator."

Big Car had become too big to fail.

After World War II the story of Big Car in America was one of unbridled success. Car ownership surged, tripling in the twenty-five years following the war. By then, there was virtually nowhere you could go in the United States without seeing a car. At one point, there were likely more cars than people with driver's licenses.

Most of Europe's car manufacturing plants had been bombed into extinction. They had been a prime target for both the Royal Air Force and the United States Air Force, and the newly developed aerial photography abilities of the two forces had eventually found almost every operating plant being used by the enemy. Massive bombing raids ensued, and the result was one of the key factors in the Allied victory. Hitler and his armies simply ran out of ways to transport things. We'd smashed them all to bits.

Our old friend Alfred Sloan, as part of GM's worldwide conquest, had by 1935 taken over full ownership of the German automobile manufacturer Opel. For many years, Sloan was known as "Hitler's carmaker." In 1935, Opel became the first German manufacturer to produce over a hundred thousand cars a year.

After the war broke out, GM surrendered their Opel operations to the Nazis. The plants quickly switched to wartime production of tanks and other weapons.

When the war was over the Russians got to Sloan's Opel plant in Brandenburg before General Patton did. They quickly dismantled what was left of it and took it to the Soviet Union.

Now, the fun part. GM went to the United States government after the war and asked for tens of millions of dollars in reparations for the damage their plants had suffered by Allied bombings. Mr. Sloan got every cent he demanded and rebuilt the Opel plants. He also decided to use one of the plants to make Frigidaire refrigerators, since he had owned the Frigidaire company since 1919. Your tax dollars at work.[2]

With all the major European automotive plants reduced to rubble by the war, America had an incredible advantage over the rest of the world's car manufacturers. No U.S.A, no highway. For a couple of amazing years, the only cars you could buy on the planet were, for the most part, made in the U.S.

Detroit was awash in money. They needed to keep production at peak performance before other autos all over the world started rolling off assembly lines. The result was cost of living pay raises for their labor force. This reduced the constant haggling with the auto unions, but more important, it kept their workers on the job.

The result was higher wages, a full labor force, and even more cars being made. More cars, more profits for everyone.

The amount of productivity in the automotive sector was epic in scale. Within five years of the war's end, the U.S. was making over 75 percent of all the cars in the world. They soon were selling over seven million cars a year, just in the United States.

These cars were lavishly engineered and available in almost any color the buyer could imagine, with a whole array of new looks and conveniences. Tubeless tires supported a giant piece of metal, replete with automatic transmissions and power windows. Americans were willing to buy anything that Big Car put on the market. Safety be damned!

The vast amount of money Big Car made for America helped establish the U.S. as the richest, most technologically advanced nation in the world. Big Car and America were intimately intertwined in a business relationship that benefited them both. While testifying before the U.S. Senate in the 1950s, Charles Wilson, the president of GM, proudly boasted, "What is good for the country is good for General Motors, and vice versa." Very few questioned his reasoning. Indeed, General Motors was synonymous with American prosperity. GM was the most powerful corporation in history. It was the first corporation to ever gross a billion dollars in annual sales. It was making and selling more cars than all its competitors combined.[3]

Ford, meanwhile, was hovering near bankruptcy. Alfred Sloan was so afraid that the Justice Department would come after GM as a monopoly if Ford went out of business that he actually sent Ford some of his top management people to try and save the ailing motor company.

America had become one of the greatest seller's markets in the history of our species. After years of not being able to buy anything because of the Great Depression and then war rationing, there was an overwhelming demand by Americans for products.

In the first few years after the war, trying to get a car was not easy. Often a buyer had to slip a small "consultant fee" under the table to the salesman simply to get on a waiting list to buy one of the much-coveted new postwar cars.

The bigger the car, the bigger the profit for the company, so GM decided to make bigger and bigger cars. Inside the company there had been discussions of providing a smaller, lower-priced model to the public, but the idea went nowhere. Any executive who might have had the nerve to suggest building smaller cars would have probably seen his career quickly end and he'd have to go work for Ford.

GM had started putting a new high-compression engine into all their new cars. Smaller cars were a poor fit for this new engine, which made big cars a necessity. The fact that these cars had to use high-octane gas didn't seem to matter to consumers. Again: bigger cars, bigger profits.

Alfred Sloan became the gold standard for all American managerial positions. By understanding that Americans would want to "trade up" to show their peers how well they were doing, Sloan was able to make GM the model of Western capitalism. Big Car had turned us into a nation of status seekers.

Sloan's new cars gave consumers what they wanted: new styling each year, automatic transmissions, and of course, bigger, higher-compression engines so that GM cars could blow by everything else on the road. The car became the symbol of affluence and abundance.

Sloan's alter ego, Harley Earl (see chapter 4), was swept away after the war by the new technology of the jet airplane. His new car models didn't just chug along—they were like rocket ships and gave drivers a sense that they were heading into the future.

GM cars became the personification of the "ugly American"— big, ostentatious, and painfully gaudy with excess chrome and

FIGURE 11.1 Spirit of Ecstasy, the bonnet mascot sculpture on Rolls-Royce cars.

Source: Damian B. Oh. https://en.wikipedia.org/wiki/File:Rolls-Royce _Spectre_Anthracite_(20-crop).jpg

The car mascot has been with us since the first car owner decided to put something on their car to show how cool they were. Big Car took the hint and almost immediately, specially crafted ornaments were put onto cars to symbolize the company. Garishly placed on the front center of each hood, they soon became objets d'art. Rolls Royce's subtly named "Spirit of Ecstasy" was the acknowledged adornment leader. She was popularly known as "Nelly in Her Nightie."

fins. American consumers not only accepted them but wanted even more "extras" on their cars to show off to their neighbors.[4]

American exceptionalism is the idea that the United States is different and better than all other nations. One of the most extreme examples of American exceptionalism was the 1959 Cadillac Eldorado, and its Chrysler sister the Imperial Crown sedan. Each car, with twin bullet-shaped taillights, looked like jet airplanes. Not only could these cars mow people down, but they could also impale young kids who were unlucky enough to run into them from behind. Production couldn't keep up with demand.

Public opinion, and more importantly the courts, continued to side with Big Car. It wasn't a Cadillac's responsibility to anticipate all the possible ways a person could harm themselves by crashing their car. Tailfins looked cool and if kids were being maimed by barreling into them while playing in the street, then kids were simply going to have to find another place to play.

It was another machine—the television—that really helped make American cars so dominant. Americans now spent an

FIGURE 11.2 A Cadillac Eldorado.

Source: Veesixteen. https://commons.wikimedia.org/wiki/File:59svl.JPG

extraordinary amount of their leisure time glued to their TV sets. While there, they were bombarded with ads for new cars.

It's hard to understand in today's media world, but in those days, viewers watched commercials. Yes, water usage in big cities often spiked as people rushed to the bathroom during commercial breaks, but for the most part everyone simply sat and mindlessly watched them.

One would have to have been a hermit in a cave not to be exposed to all this messaging about why one needed a new American car. Advertisers were able, in one short minute, to tell Americans stories that promised them prosperity, happiness, and a great, big, beautiful tomorrow. Madison Avenue and Big Car were perfectly suited for each other. The ad men were able to portray to millions of watchers how great-looking men and women bettered their lives by simply driving a Chevrolet or a Buick, or, if you really had made it, a Caddy.

Then Madison Avenue discovered teenagers. Within no time, cars became a "must-have" necessity for every young person in the land. Watching ads depicting their peers having fun driving rubbed off on a new generation of customers. "I'll die if I don't get a car, Dad!" became the mantra of every teen in the land.

Like most things that seem too good to be true, Detroit's plan for total domination of the automobile industry was no exception.

Sloan and GM, following Henry Ford's nearly disastrous earlier decision, decided it was best to stick with a winning strategy. All they would have to do was make each year's model a bit different and customers would flock into showrooms to buy them.

This time, they were wrong.

In Europe and Asia, auto manufacturers had realized that "dynamic obsolescence" was no longer a viable way of moving merchandise. They reasoned that superior technology, better design, and even automobile safety were the new selling points. It didn't take them long to catch up and quickly surpass GM and the rest of America's automobile manufacturing dominance.

Companies such as Renault, Fiat, and Rambler began to address the existing need in the American market for affordable, compact cars that would fit in a garage. Often these cars became a family's second car.

GM's response was to finally provide a smaller, cheaper car for the public—the Corvair.

We know how that ended.

12

ROAD SAFETY

For the next century, Big Car was able to keep international safety standards at bay. Basically, Big Car was assumed to be innocent unless overwhelming evidence was presented to show otherwise.

By 1966, however, the evidence of Big Car's lethal potential was overwhelming. The rising number of fatalities on American roadways had become too severe to ignore: road deaths had more than doubled since 1925. Daniel Patrick Moynihan's pivotal 1959 article "Epidemic on the Highways" had also helped to raise awareness.

America had reached its breaking point. The public demanded that Big Government finally take action to protect them. Things had to change. It became a popular enough issue that a few members of Congress became brave enough to forgo their yearly lobbying payoff from Big Car and take a stand. The Highway Safety Act was passed. Big Car was suddenly in trouble. There were too many bodies piling up because of cars. Something had to change.

On September 9, 1966, President Lyndon B. Johnson signed the act into law. Not being one to miss jumping on a political bandwagon, he had suddenly become a road safety advocate.

People have been trying to impose road safety laws since the inception of the internal combustion engine. In England, The British Locomotive Act of 1865 required any car with an engine to be led by a pedestrian waving a red flag. This was to warn others of the fact that a very loud machine—a "horseless carriage"—was heading towards them. These individuals were also legally obligated to help calm horses or other transportation animals that became agitated. If an animal showed distress, drivers were required to immediately pull over and stop the vehicle's engine. This may have been the last time that Big Car was tamed.[1]

That day, he told reporters that over the recent Labor Day weekend 29 American soldiers had died in Vietnam, and that over that same weekend 614 Americans had died in automobile accidents.

Johnson inaugurated the United States Department of Transportation whose mission would be "to develop and coordinate policies that will provide an efficient and economical national transportation system."

Suddenly there was hope that Big Car would finally be held to account. Maybe Big Car had finally run out of excuses. Congress had finally passed a bill that explicitly named Big Car as an agent of injury.

But Big Car was not so easily pushed aside. They immediately jumped onto the safety bandwagon themselves. Soon new models were being widely advertised as the latest in safe motoring. Big Car bragged of equipping this year's models with energy-absorbing steering wheels and headrests. They proudly announced that their cars now came with shatterproof windshields, even though the know-how of putting this kind of glass in cars had been around for many years. What they didn't care about was the fact that they had to include these basic safety features in their new cars because they had been mandated by Congress to do so. A grateful nation thanked them, and new car sales did just fine. Big Car had survived again.

Roadways also began to improve. Data showed that many traffic fatalities occurred on highway curves. Soon, centerline stripes and reflectors were added to roads. At last, the experts who oversaw our roads realized that signs and utility poles, which had caused countless fatalities, should now be breakaway so that ramming into them wasn't an automatic death sentence. They also realized that roads needed better illumination, and that barriers should be added to separate oncoming traffic lanes. As a result, head-on freeway collisions were sharply curtailed.

Guardrails also began to be placed on freeways. At first, they were made of hard steel and drivers crashing into them were still being killed at an alarming rate. Enter the American National Standards Institute. They were asked to provide testing standards for guardrails.

Big Car let the institute know they'd be happy to help out. Working together, they came up with a nifty test to ascertain the impact of a 10,000-pound load on the newly installed guardrails. The rails passed with flying colors. Only later did we find out that these tests had been conducted with vehicles traveling at a breathtaking *four miles an hour* when they crashed into the guardrails.

According to the Insurance Institute for Highway Safety, a van or a sport utility vehicle (SUV) with a hood height over 40 inches (basically all of them) are 45 percent more likely to kill pedestrians than smaller cars.[2]

Since the tests clearly showed the engineers that the guardrails worked, billions of taxpayer dollars were now spent on retrofitting our highways. As if that wasn't bad enough, they built the guardrails for a generation of cars that were significantly smaller than the minivans and SUVs that soon dominated the roads. The new, much larger autos simply couldn't be stopped by the short guardrails. Traffic fatalities took a slight dip, but then quickly returned to and even surpassed their former levels.[3]

One positive result of the Highway Safety Act was a major report published in 1966 called "Accidental Death and Disability: The Neglected Disease of Modern Society." This report is what started the development of prehospital emergency medical services for car-related injuries in America. Prior to that, if you were in a serious accident, you'd simply have to hope there was a nearby hospital and that you could get there in time.[4]

In 1946 C. Hunter Shelden worked as a neurologist in Pasadena. He was appalled by the number of head injuries he was seeing in his emergency room due to car crashes. He came up with the idea of putting retractable seat belts in cars to keep drivers from being smashed to pieces. He built one and it worked. When he offered it to Big Car, they shooed him out of the room. Nobody wanted it. For the next three years, Big Car was less than interested in the new device Dr. Shelden had come up with.

ENTER NASH MOTORS

Charles Nash described himself as "the most common cuss that lived." After his parents abandoned him when he was six, he worked as an indentured servant farmhand. Although Nash had virtually no schooling, he had amassed a fortune worth over fifty million dollars (more than $650 million in today's dollars) when he died in 1948. The way Mr. Nash did this was by being incredibly good at whatever he did and rising to the top of organizations. He was president of General Motors while still a young man, but turned down an offer of a million-dollar annual salary to start his own car company called Nash Motors. It became one of the most successful American middle-class automobile manufacturers in history. His slogan was "Give the customer more than he has paid for," and that's just what he did.

Nash also pulled off the largest merger that America had ever seen between companies not in the same business when Nash Motors and Kelvinator merged. In no time Kelvinator was supplying Nash's cars with the first car heaters in automotive history; air conditioning soon followed. Nash also put a "Bed-In-A-Car" into his autos. This feature let you create an opening between the passenger compartment and the trunk to allow what Nash called the "airliner reclining seats" to fold down into a somewhat comfortable two-person bed. A grateful generation of teenagers thanked him.[5]

The reason I bring up Charles Nash's company is that in 1949, a year after his death, Nash Motors became the first American company to include seat belts in its cars. The result was a colossal failure: the company had put 40,000 seat belts into their new cars, and customers didn't want them. Nash had to remove 39,000 of them to sell the cars.[6]

Why such strong resistance to a such a basic auto safety measure? There are two fundamental reasons for this, both relating to basic human psychology. First, Americans (indeed, most people) don't like being told what to do. This is true even when it concerns health and safety. Here in the United States, we have a well-documented history of forceful and often divisive resistance to public health measures. During the COVID-19 pandemic, there was intense resistance to mask and vaccine mandates in the U.S., just as there had been during the Spanish flu pandemic a century earlier. We are also witnessing a similar

FIGURE 12.1 A seatbelt apparatus with a crash test dummy.

Source: National Institute of Standards and Technology. https://commons.wikimedia
.org/wiki/File:Seatbelt_testing_apparatus.jpg

resurgence in the historical resistance to fluoridation in municipal drinking water. Fluoridation of U.S. municipal water sources
began in the 1940s. By the late 1950s, the John Birch Society,
described by some as the "birth mother" of the American right,
had mobilized such effective opposition to saving kids' teeth that
the only way the U.S. Food and Drug Administration was able
to finally allow the use of fluoride in such products as toothpaste
and mouthwash was to label it for cosmetic use.

These examples show how effectively U.S. social conserva-
tism, propped up by anti-communism and libertarianism, have
harnessed this resistance and become a force to be reckoned with.
Their opposition to seat belts, abetted by Big Car, helped keep

seat belts out of cars for almost a decade. As a further illustration of their extreme views, they also claimed that Earth Day was a Communist plot. Their proof? Why else would its first celebration fall on the 100th anniversary of Vladimir Lenin's birth?

The second psychological factor militating against the adoption of seat belts in cars is that most of us are rather lazy. After years of just sliding into the driver's seat and starting the engine, people simply were not willing to tolerate what they saw as the unbearable inconvenience of putting on a seat belt. Imagine—having to reach down, pull a belt across your lap, and then go to the enormous trouble of clicking it into place. Who had time for that?

In 1956, Ford offered seat belts to new car buyers. It cost an extra twenty-seven bucks. Ninety-eight percent of their customers said no. Streetcars had lap belts for years, but riders hardly ever used them; it was seen as too much trouble, and streetcars rarely crashed. As Ralph Nader was known to observe, "We're not much of a cognitive species."

People have always been difficult to reason with when it comes to following scientific arguments versus their own gut feelings. A lot of citizens would rather fall back on what to them is common sense when they must make a decision. The arguments most often heard about why one shouldn't wear this new safety product included:

"Seat belts cause your innards to explode."

"What if the car goes off a bridge and you are underwater? Now you got a seat belt holding you in the car and you're going to drown!"

"As long as the life risked is his own, I believe the individual should decide whether or not the use of seat belts is wise."

And my favorite survey response: "F*** off! It's none of your damn business!"[7]

In 1959 a new three-point seat belt was introduced. This one protected the whole body, not just the abdomen. People still refused to use them, resulting in all kinds of cat-and-mouse games between drivers, car manufacturers, and law enforcement. The automakers had designed it so the car wouldn't start unless the seat belt was engaged; people would simply click their seat belts together on the seat, climb onto it, and hit the road. Next, manufacturers implemented the most annoying ringing sound they could find to let drivers know that the seat belt wasn't properly engaged; people figured out how to deactivate the alert. The game continues today. Two years ago, Chevrolet added a wonderful new feature to their cars: The automobile would not shift out of park if the seat belt wasn't engaged within twenty seconds. They called it "the teen driver mode."

For years, Americans continued to argue about seat belts. Many politicians pandered to the anti-seat belt crowd, insisting they would not be tied to the cross of the seat belt, as it were.

Big Car became conflicted about what to do. They weren't thrilled about the extra cost of putting seat belts into every car. However, seat belts were still infinitely better than the far more expensive idea that was looming on the horizon: airbags.

Finally, the statistics showing the efficacy of seat belts could no longer be denied. By the 1980s, Big Car and the United States Congress agreed on mandatory seat belts for America. People went nuts. A Gallup poll in 1984 showed that almost seven out of ten Americans opposed mandatory seat belt laws. The general feeling among drivers was that the belts were inconvenient, uncomfortable, and most of all, ineffective. Many still argued that it was much safer to be thrown clear of a crashed car than to be trapped inside of it.

In 1987, the *Chicago Tribune* published an editorial stating: "In this country, saving freedom is more important than trying to regulate lives." Better to have crashed and died in freedom than to have submitted to mandatory seat belt laws.

In the end, our better angels prevailed, and eventually, almost everyone was finally using seat belts. It is estimated that over a million American lives have been saved over the last forty years because of the use of seat belts.[8] Today, when committed libertarians get into their cars on their way to march against wearing masks, or having to take vaccines, the first thing these great Americans do is put on their seat belts.

13

LEAD HERRING (PART THREE)

One should never underestimate the power of the revenge of the nerds. Rather than feeling sorry for himself, Clair Patterson—our intrepid Cal Tech professor investigating the effects of lead pollution in the environment—redoubled his efforts.

Robert Kehoe, the nefarious scientist who had hidden all his research on lead additives, continued to attack Patterson, saying that his facts about lead were just blatantly incorrect and that his conclusions were mere "rabble-rousing."

Patterson, while still in self-exile from Cal Tech, continued to do his research in one of the most remote places in California, the top of the vast mountain chain of Lake Tahoe. He took innumerable soil samples. He then carefully examined his samples to see if any of them contained lead contamination. They all did!

Clair Patterson had found his smoking gun. If the lead from car exhausts had drifted over 300 miles to this remote mountaintop, how bad must it be in big cities? What was it doing to the people who lived there?

Patterson came down off his mountain and went back into his lab. He continued to test for lead contamination in human artifacts. It was everywhere he looked, including all aspects of the human food chain. This was serious.

Again, Big Car tried to silence him. No reputable journal would publish his work. Kehoe called his research nothing more than a "lead herring."[1] He declared that Ethyl Corporation's tetraethyl lead additive had saved the American economy billions of dollars. He boasted that our entire car-centric lifestyle was only possible because of the additive. He warned that if people listened to Patterson the level of octane in gas would plummet, and people would have to use far more gasoline. He boldly stated that those who wanted to get rid of lead in our gasoline were doing nothing less than taking money out of people's pockets and burning it.

Meanwhile, Patterson now knew that the amount of lead contamination in his fellow Americans was over six hundred times that of their ancestors.[2]

In 1962, Rachel Carson's *Silent Spring* had successfully shown the world that another contaminant, DDT, was a dangerous carcinogen. Congress had held hearings; America, the media, and even our elected officials suddenly were interested in the subject. Around the same time, U.S. Secretary of the Interior Stewart Udall (under two presidents, Kennedy and Johnson), an early pioneer in the environmental movement, published *The Quiet Crisis: A History of Environmental Conservation in the USA.*

Enter Edmund Muskie. Muskie had held a wide variety of elected positions in government at both the state and national levels. He was first elected to the state assembly in his home state of Maine; he had then been elected governor of the state, and then after that, its U.S. senator. In 1968 he became the Democratic vice-presidential candidate. (His party lost.) Muskie was the grandfather of modern environmental legislation. As a senator, he sponsored both the Clean Air Act and the Clean Water

Act. These two bills fundamentally established the federal government as a player in helping preserve and protect America's environment.[3]

Meanwhile, unable to get the scientific community to listen to him, Patterson traveled to Washington. He went to see Senator Muskie, then-chairman of the Subcommittee on Air and Water Pollution, and showed him the evidence he'd found that even small levels of lead would harm children. He told him about Ethyl Corporation and that Dr. Kehoe's threshold for safe levels of lead in the human body was a lie. He showed him proof that the amount of lead being spewed into the atmosphere by car exhaust was poisoning the American people.

It worked. Muskie was willing to hold hearings.

Meanwhile, Ethyl Corporation continued to grow, although now only a fraction of its profits came from leaded gas. Annual sales had risen from $227 million to almost two billion in no time— a sevenfold increase. Dividends paid out to shareholders were generous and lucrative.

Ethyl Corporation, of course, was invited to the hearing held in Washington on June 15, 1966, about the so-called dangers of lead. Patterson's testimony emphasized that most officials were accepting bad science, either because they were too lazy to do real research or because they were making too much money from Big Car to want to disrupt things.[4] Patterson patiently explained that those who oversaw the public health and safety of America had either ignored or failed to understand the difference between "natural" and "normal" lead burden in humans. The incorrect data given to them was based on tests done on humans who had lived before the start of the Industrial Revolution. He also explained that lead was now everywhere. He presented the results of the samples that showed that lead was even in the most remote fringes of the Earth's poles. Finally, he pointed out that it was absurd to allow the very industry that was putting lead poison in the air be in charge of determining if lead poisoning in the air was a danger to the public. He showed them his results from Lake Tahoe. His data was incontrovertible—there was lead everywhere. He showed them the "smoking gun."

It made no difference. Ethyl Corporation had quickly presented to Muskie's committee a "who's who" of the scientific and medical establishment to reject Patterson's assertions. Using Kehoe's inaccurate data, they confidently pronounced the ethyl additive to be as safe as regular gasoline—even more so in that it caused engines to perform better and get more mileage, hence produce less exhaust. The committee found nothing wrong with the product, and there was no further adverse publicity. Patterson was completely ignored, and lead contamination dramatically increased over the next few years.

The problem with recognizing the harmful effects of lead is that the contamination occurred so gradually. The millions of tons of lead released into the air were indeed making people sick, but the process was so slow that it went largely unnoticed.

Another reason nobody noticed was that Kehoe and Ethyl Corporation had pulled off a brilliant, although unethical, feat. They had a monopoly on all scientific information related to the hazards of lead in gasoline. They were, apart from Clair Patterson, able to restrict all information published about their product. In fact, scientists now needed Kehoe's approval to publish any articles about lead written without Kehoe.[5] The result was that all relevant lead studies published up until the early 1970s were overwhelmingly favorable to Ethyl.

It seemed as if we'd have lead pumped into our environment for the rest of our lifetimes. Then, on January 28, 1969, workers were pulling pipe out of a freshly drilled oil well off the coast of Santa Barbara, California, when a torrent of gassy, gray mud shot out with a deafening roar, showering the men with slime. Unable to plug the hole, they activated a device that crushed the pipe and sealed off the well. The blowout seemed over—until bubbles of gas started roiling the water nearby. Pressurized oil and gas tapped by the drilling were now flowing across the ocean floor and rising to the ocean's surface.

Oil leaked out at an estimated rate of 210,000 gallons a day, creating a heavy slick across much of the ocean channel. A few days later, horrified Santa Barbara residents woke to find their beaches befouled with tar and dotted with dead and dying oil-drenched birds.

Then-President Richard Nixon was not, by nature, an environmentalist, except when it came to winning votes. So Nixon decided to come to Santa Barbara, which was then a Republican stronghold, and get some green on.

FIGURE 13.1 Nixon in Santa Barbara.

Source: U.S. National Archives and Records Administration. https://commons.wikimedia
.org/wiki/File:Santa_Barbara,_Calif,_oil_slick_area_-_NARA_-_194617.tif

He showed up with a large media crowd and boldly proclaimed, "I don't think we've paid enough attention to this . . . We're going to do a better job than we have done in the past."[6] This coming from a man who truly believed the adage "If two wrongs don't make a right, find a third one."

The Santa Barbara spill and the president's reaction are seen by some as the true start of the environmental revolution. Dying loons on the beach, covered in petroleum, were just too powerful an image to be ignored.

Nixon was not about to let Muskie, an almost surefire favorite to run against him in 1972, steal this important new voting block from him. Nixon and his people quickly wrapped themselves up in the environmental movement. In 1970, in his State of the Union address to Congress, he made it a centerpiece of his speech, saying, "Restoring nature to its natural state is a cause beyond party and beyond factions. It has become a common cause of all the people of this country."[8] He received a standing ovation.

Muskie knew Nixon didn't give a hoot about the environment and told the press that Nixon was all talk and no action. Nixon

Nixon really hated being green. On one occasion, he told leaders of the Ford Motor Company that environmentalists and consumer advocates wanted Americans to "go back and live like a bunch of damned animals. They're a group of people that aren't really one damn bit interested in safety or clean air. What they're interested in is destroying the system." In public, though, he maintained a consistently positive stance on environmental issues. Out of the public eye, however, when told that his domestic-policy successes on the environment were something he'd be remembered for, he replied, "For God's sake, I hope that's not true."[7]

brilliantly continued to use his bully pulpit to champion the environmental cause. He rapidly proposed new regulations for auto emissions and pledged to spend billions of dollars of federal money to take care of the problem. At this very same moment, his administration was fighting to keep DDT on crops and earmarking federal funds to build the Alaskan pipeline.

Suddenly Richard Nixon was America's new green president. Every environmental group in the country shook their heads in amazement but quickly jumped onto his "go green" bandwagon. Muskie could do nothing but watch. In the words of White House correspondent Dan Rather, it was as if "[Nixon's] caught the Democrats bathing and he's walked away with their clothes." (Nixon had a lavish signing ceremony to put Muskie's 1970 Clear Air Act into law. He not only failed to invite Senator Muskie to the signing, but also failed to mention his name even once.)

The centerpiece of Nixon's new strategy was to create the Environmental Protection Agency (EPA). It was pure Nixon. When he'd first run for the presidency only about 1 percent of the country thought that pollution was a national problem. By 1970 the figure had jumped to 70 percent. Adlai Stevenson, who twice ran against Nixon—and whose friend and law partner, Willard Wertz, once said, "If the Electoral College ever gives an honorary degree, it should go to Adlai Stevenson"[9]—described Richard Nixon in a campaign speech as "the kind of politician who would cut down a redwood tree, then mount the stump to give a speech about conservation."[10]

A freeze-frame of America's neglect of the environment at this time would have shown that we were belching over two hundred million tons of pollution into the atmosphere. Over a hundred million used automobile tires were relegated to dumps that were, in effect, small mountains of rubber.[11]

Suddenly there was a new sheriff in town. Ethyl Corporation and Big Car were going to have to answer to the EPA.

The EPA got right to work. They decided to set standards for air quality and pollution. They would have teams of bright, energized people measuring levels of environmental pollution so they could enforce emission standards. They would take over pollution control from the state governments. It was Ethyl Corporation's worst nightmare.[12]

But the fight was far from over. Ethyl Corporation undertook a multifaceted strategy built around lawsuits and other delaying tactics to try and keep their leaded products in gas stations. The EPA was afraid of using Dr. Patterson's studies. They knew that Patterson's studies were sure to be challenged in court, and worried that if any part of his findings were disputed and then proven wrong (nothing was), the EPA would lose legal proceedings against Ethyl.[13]

Ethyl was able to drag their court case out for another five years. Finally, the courts found that lead was indeed a health hazard and must be removed from our gas tanks. The case made its way all the way to the Supreme Court, which upheld the lower court ruling and so in 1976, after over fifty years of poisoning us, lead was finally about to be removed from gasoline sold in the United States.

But the true assassin of lead was the catalytic converter. This device converts pollutants in your exhaust into less-toxic pollutants by catalyzing them. It's simply a process of increasing the rate of a chemical reaction by adding a substance called a catalyst to the mix. These catalysts are not consumed in the reaction and remain unchanged after it.[14]

When the Clean Air Act of 1970 mandated that every new car in America be equipped with a catalytic converter, Big Car was not overly concerned. That's because in 1970 not a single catalytic converter existed. The science showing the efficacy of it

FIGURE 13.2 Cutaway of a metal-core catalytic converter.

Source: Stahlkocher. https://commons.wikimedia.org/wiki/File:Aufgeschnittener
_Metall_Katalysator_f%C3%BCr_ein_Auto.jpg

did, but there was no prototype of a model that any car company could order to install in future cars.

What ensued was a mad dash by various corporations to try and build one. As the due date drew nearer and nearer, the EPA became very uneasy. If compliance with this new pollution deterrent wasn't met, they were going to look inept.

Meanwhile, Ethyl redoubled its efforts to somehow forestall the inevitable. One of their top executives said: "The whole proceedings against an industry that has made invaluable contributions to the American economy for more than fifty years is the worst example of fanaticism since the New England witch hunts." He then once again repeated Kehoe and Ethyl's big lie. "For over half a century, no person has ever been found having an identifiable toxic effect from the amount of lead in the atmosphere today." Tell that to the tens of thousands who had already died from lead poisoning.[15]

Again, never underestimate nerds; they always seem to come through. Sure enough, an operational catalytic converter was invented, tested, and approved shortly before the installation due date.

In the end, what scientists and engineers discovered while testing this new device is what killed Ethyl's ability to keep selling leaded gasoline. All cars with newly installed converters ran well on regular gasoline. But as soon as leaded gas was added to a car with a converter it simply died. The lead poisoned the converter by covering the working surface of the device with so much lead that it simply killed the engine.

Ethyl Corporation and the oil companies who had millions of gallons of leaded gas still in stock tried desperately to get rid of as much of it as they could. For a few years, gas stations all over the country offered both leaded and unleaded gas at their pumps. Unleaded gas was priced much lower than leaded to keep people from putting leaded gas into their new cars. The configuration of the nozzles on the gas pumps had to be changed so that they wouldn't fit into new cars' gas tanks and kill their engines.

Finally, after most of the leaded inventory had been exhausted and as more people transitioned to cars that couldn't use it, leaded gasoline was phased out. However, its impact on human health had already been devastating. Exposure to lead, worldwide, has caused over nine hundred thousand premature deaths a year.[16]

Globally, the phaseout of leaded gasoline is estimated to have saved 1.2 million lives a year.[17] The United Nations has stated that the elimination of leaded petrol is an immense achievement on a par with the global elimination of major deadly diseases. Lead had caused almost as many deaths as the HIV/AIDS virus had. It still kills more people each year than malaria, war, terrorism, or natural disasters.[18]

In an ironic twist that shows pollution knows no bounds, it turns out that the production of catalytic converters is an environmental nightmare. To make a converter you need certain precious metals. One of these metals is in abundant supply in Norilsk, Russia, which has now become of one the most polluted places on the planet.[19]

One last problem with every car needing a converter is that they became a gold mine for thieves. Again, the culprit was precious metals—in this case, a metal called rhodium. It takes a thief less than a minute to get under a car and easily remove the bolted-on converter. Pickup trucks and SUVs, because of how high off the ground they are, are especially easy targets.

A thief quickly removes the converter, and sells it to a middleman, often at a junkyard, for $500—a lucrative payout for one minute's work. The middleman then takes it to yet another player and sells it to that person for $1,000, doubling their money. These people are experts on how to extract rhodium, a precious metal, from the converter. The price of rhodium shot up from about six hundred dollars an ounce in 2016 to almost thirty thousand dollars an ounce in 2021—about double the price of gold. (It fell back down to under five thousand dollars an ounce in 2024.) The manufacturers who rely on this precious metal for building converters end up saving a fortune by purchasing it from criminal extractors. It's a vicious circle and only getting worse.[20]

Clair Patterson was finally able to go back to his lab at Cal Tech. In 1978 he was appointed to a National Research Council panel, the same group that had shunned him earlier. His recommendation that lead be immediately reduced in all areas in which it interacts with humans, including gasoline, food, containers, paint, and water distribution pipes, is a major reason that millions of humans are still alive today.

He was honored by the National Academy of Sciences, the Geological Society, and many other centers of scientific research. He is one of the great unknown champions of the twentieth century. He died at his home in California, at the age of 73, in 1995.

An asteroid (2511 Patterson) is named in his honor.

14

THE FUTURE OF MOBILITY

Not all the people who work with and run Big Car are "bad people." We all interact with them socially and often politically. The problem is that when the collected numbers and might of Big Car are strategically combined, they're hard to resist. We can't say no to their products, we can't possibly compete with their place in our nation's centers of political power, and there is almost no organization with sufficient political clout or resources to stand up to them.

Still, a few brave communities are rising up in rebellion against Big Car. They are all part of a concept called Mobility as a Service (MaaS) that has gained traction worldwide. National Councils convene; people come together to share ideas, hopes, and dreams; and efforts are made to secure venture capital to bring these visions to life. Anyway, it's a great idea. Please take a moment to familiarize yourself with it. MaaS is the most advanced and organized anti–Big Car organization around. It has not yet found the voice, device, political leader, or easily understood message to become a mass movement. But it's still young. The realization of what Big Car is doing to us is beginning to spread. With massive traffic jams stealing time from our lives and increasingly frequent natural disasters dominating headlines over politics and crime, it's only a matter of time before the public begins to seek answers.

I hope we'll have the collective smarts, will, and popular support to find an alternative to Big Car. The MaaS movement has a lot of potential. Let's take a look at the ways it's being implemented around the world.

WEST PALM BEACH

Juan Ponce de Leon was a sixteenth-century Spanish conquistador. He's also the first known European to have made landfall in a region of North America that he named *La Florida* in honor of the lush greenery of the area. This is often referred to as the first settlement in North America. The larger geographical region would eventually become the State of Florida, known today for its wealthy coastal towns. West Palm Beach, approximately three hundred miles south of Ponce de Leon's landing home, is one such city.

Most of the early history of West Palm Beach is that of a tropical fruit oasis. Then, two things changed. The first was the tourist industry. Everyone living in the frigid climes of the North liked the idea of heading South and basking in the sun. Second, air conditioning was invented, which meant that people could now live in Florida year-round. By the middle of the twentieth century, West Palm Beach had experienced a land boom. Its population quadrupled. New homes, businesses, and public services grew with the city. "Buy in the Path of Progress" was the town motto.

At the end of the twentieth century, like so many other American cities toward the end of the twentieth century, West Palm Beach was falling apart. The problem was that too many of its white residents had left the city. The downtown area was plagued with a vast number of empty, often burnt-out buildings. Crime was at an all-time high. Urban flight had resulted in urban blight. Nobody wanted to be out after dark in downtown West Palm Beach in the 1980s. United States Senator Lawton Chiles referred to it as a "war zone." *Crack USA*, a documentary film about the crack epidemic in America, was filmed in West Palm Beach.[1]

Enter urban renewal and the War on Poverty. Urban renewal was a mid-century idea intended to address urban decay in our cities. Coupled with the Housing and Urban Development Act of 1968, it guaranteed financing for private entrepreneurs who were willing to invest in downtown properties. Although its goal was to clear away slums and build better housing and businesses, many urban renewal projects undertaken under its auspices were abject failures. (James Baldwin called urban renewal "Negro Removal.")[2]

In West Palm Beach, almost $400 million was put into a project called City Place. The ambitious plan called for restaurants, upscale stores, spacious apartments, and office buildings. There were even plans for a 24-screen movie theater complex. It was subsequently renamed "Rosemary Square" and another half billion was poured in for a mixed-use luxury residential tower. For reasons unknown, the name Rosemary was ditched, and the area simply became known as The Square.[3]

The good people of West Palm Beach decided to see what an urban environment such as the Square would look like and how it would function if they simply removed most of the traffic signals and road markings. It was a radical idea and challenged the traffic engineers' traditional approach to street design.

The center point of the idea was to try and put pedestrians into closer contact with cars. The planners were willing to gamble that closer proximity between people and cars would cause both to be more attentive. They were right!

The results were astounding: traffic slowed down, there were significantly fewer accidents, and the amount of time it took to get places was vastly reduced. It was soon called an urban renaissance.[4]

The idea was to redesign the city by expanding green areas, putting in ample outdoor dining venues, and adding new shops. The real genius of the idea was to get rid of traffic. They were able to transform what had been simple mall shopping into a dynamic urban neighborhood.

As curbs were removed, gray and white pavers in a new pattern gave visitors the feeling that they were in an enlarged town square. The streets were oriented toward people, not cars. It encouraged those who came to The Square to leave their cars behind and go on foot.

The core of the new space was a dense grid of narrow streets. These streets had one lane going in each direction and the maximum speed limit was 12 miles per hour. The middle of the street was for bicycle parking to support a newly instituted bike share program called SkyBike. The Square's plan for mobility was dominated by protected bike lanes.

In addition, a program called Ride West Palm Beach provided easily identifiable vans, carts, and even Tesla sedans, each with large signs on them saying "FREE RIDE." There were 15 stops throughout the Square. Circuit, a free and easily downloaded app, was made available to everyone in West Palm Beach to schedule rides.[5]

Big Car had met its match. Nobody needed a car once in The Square. It's a model that many other municipalities are replicating and shows what one town can do when they want to join the Mobility as a Service movement.

DUBAI

There is only one city on the planet with more five-star hotels than Dubai. Let's just say that one night at any of these fine establishments costs the equivalent of most people's weekly paycheck. (London has the most five-star hotels, but they have been sucking up wealth much longer.)

Dubai also now has the tallest building on the planet and the three tallest hotels.

The name Dubai is said to come from an Arabic proverb meaning "They came with a lot of money." Dubai's first oil field was named "Fateh" or "good fortune."

Dubai is the home away from home for hundreds of Russian oligarchs. (There goes the neighborhood.) Dubai is also known as a "gangster's paradise" because it is home to countless major crime syndicates. (There are said to be money-laundering machines on nearly every street corner.)[6]

Rashid bin Saeed Al Maktoum was the second prime minister of the United Arab Emirates and ruled Dubai for 32 years until he died in 1990. He is responsible for what Dubai is today. He realized that the staggering tidal wave of money that oil was bringing in would eventually wash back into the sea. He observed, "My grandfather rode a camel; my father rode a camel. I drive a Mercedes, my son drives a Land Rover, his son will drive a Land Rover, but his son will ride a camel."[7]

Rashid was succeeded by his son Maktoum bin Rashid Al Maktoum. Upon Maktoum's death in 2006, his brother Mohammed took over and Dubai subsequently witnessed one of the greatest economic explosions of wealth ever seen on the planet. Just as miners flocked to the gold fields of California and Alaska, money miners amassed in one of the hottest spots on earth, and they did well.

Little did they know that they were also helping to prop up the greatest threat to a post-Big Car world.

Mohammed began to build "smart cities"—locales where traditional services such as transportation, shopping, internet, healthcare, and manufacturing are digitized for efficiency. When Mohammed unveiled his vision for Dubai over a decade ago, one could not help but appreciate the anti–Big Car initiative at the heart of the plan.

Dubai has earned international acclaim for several initiatives in the decade since Mohammed's "smart cities" proclamation. The Dubai Autonomous Transportation Strategy calls for 25 percent of all transportation to be driverless by 2030. Instead of bumper-to-bumper traffic, Dubai will have networked autonomous ground and air taxis—yes, air taxis—that will move people around efficiently. The hyperloop transportation technology, still in testing, will eventually connect Dubai to Abu Dhabi in 12 minutes, reaching speeds of up to 650 miles per hour. Another critical technology in development is solar-powered self-driving pods that will provide last-mile transportation around Dubai's new Sustainable City, another one of Al Maktoum's "smart cities." UAE has garnered several international awards and recognition for its obsessive rapid urban sustainable development.

Dubai very well could be one of the first places of wealth that experiments with a non-car-reliant system of transportation.

On November 1, 2018, as part of the Road and Transport Authority's Public Transport Day, the most diverse human chain of hands was formed in a Dubai metro train at the Etisalat station. The record was acknowledged by Guinness World Records. The chain was formed by people from 96 countries from all over the globe.[8]

It's ironic that the so-called "hometown" of global crime has one of the lowest homicide rates in the world. Equally ironic is that a kingdom that made its wealth from working with Big Car might be the one to bring it down.

HONG KONG

Franklin Delano Roosevelt's grandfather, Warren Delano, Jr., is one of the men most responsible for Hong Kong's existence. He was one of the key men in charge of bringing China a "century of humiliation." How did this happen?

In the middle of the nineteenth century, Europe, and England in particular, developed an obsession with all things Chinese. With the explosion of cargo shipping taking place between Europe and China, the Middle Kingdom was enjoying a trade surplus of momentous proportions. Londoners couldn't get enough porcelain, silk, and tea. The problem was that they had to pay for these goods with silver. The result was a massive trade deficit with China. The Brits desperately needed something they could sell to the Chinese population. Enter Delano, Jr.

He and his cohorts finally found something the Chinese would pay handsomely for: opium, a crop they could harvest in India and quickly sell to Chinese users.

Before long, in gathering places such as tea shops, close to 25 percent of adult Chinese males were consuming 40,000 pounds of opium yearly. It was destroying the country. The Chinese tried to stop drugs from pouring in, but they were helpless against Western gunboats. Two brief wars were fought and when the dust settled, men like Delano, Jr. were the proud owners of Hong Kong. By the time Mao Zedong came to power and finally was able to eradicate opium, tens of millions of opium addicts faced a stark choice: get clean or face execution. Opium virtually disappeared from Chinese life.[9]

The result of the Opium Wars was that Hong Kong became a British colony. It also became the "clown car" of the Orient with a seemingly impossible number of people squeezed onto its various islands. (Despite having the largest number of skyscrapers on the planet, housing in Hong Kong is a nightmare.)[10]

With its vast number of people so densely jammed together, a public transit system was a vital necessity. Hong Kong developed a transport system that made public transport usage the highest in the world, with over 90 percent of the population using it.

Railways, trams, ferries, and even a vast system of moving pavements and escalators covered the islands. The Mass Transit Railway system tied together close to a hundred metro stations. Millions used it every day and it was the acceptable way to get around the territories.

Given the efficiency of Hong Kong's public transit system (they have an on-time rate of almost 100 percent), and with every station accessible from street level, the system is cheap and fast—and gets people where they want to go. The stations have clean restrooms, breastfeeding rooms, and free Wi-Fi, and cost less than a dollar to use.

Watching the vast public transport system, packed with cyclists, trains, and buses, is like watching a well-conducted symphony orchestra. Each piece seems to know exactly when and where to come in.

As a reminder of their British colonial past, a massive fleet of double-decker buses is the most prevalent form of transportation.

First known as "carriages" (they were pulled by horses), they've been around since the middle of the seventeenth century. Originally they transported only the well-to-do through city streets. Soldiers and other working-class folks were barred

FIGURE 14.1 Kowloon Motor Bus double-decker.

Source: N509FZ. https://en.wikipedia.org/wiki/File:V6B1_at_Jordan,_West_Kowloon
Station(20190322100306).jpg

from riding in them. Nothing was more important than assuring the greatest comfort and freedom of the bourgeois in those days, and the penalty for trying to ride a bus was a public whipping. It was to no avail, because soon too many of the proletarian public were hopping on to these horse-buses. It became the most efficient way to navigate crowded, and often filthy, public streets.

A typical bus of the time was simply two wooden benches facing each other inside of the passenger cabin. The driver sat on a bench atop the horse-drawn vehicle. Soon, some genius decided to put a second deck of longitudinal benches on top of the first cabin, and the double-decker bus was created.

What was unique about these vehicles was that, unlike a stagecoach, no prior booking was required. Riders could simply jump on and off whenever it was convenient for them.

FIGURE 14.2 Examples of a horse-drawn omnibus.

Source: George Grantham Bain Collection, Library of Congress. https://commons
.wikimedia.org/wiki/File:London,_England_-_London_buses
_LCCN2002715708.jpg

By the middle of the twentieth century, over a thousand double-decker buses, most with Mercedes Benz engines and many with air-conditioning, had become the accepted mode of transport for most of the population.

Today, many fully electric buses, featuring a saloon-like floor plan, continue to provide a viable alternative to Big Car. It is a model that many other communities can learn from.

TAIPEI

One of the worst jokes to spread through Taipei in the last few years is a result of a bicycle-sharing service. Chinese citizens, showing off their knowledge of America, point to their transportation and say, "Me Tarzan, YouBike."

The YouBike is the product du jour for millions of Taiwanese citizens and has replaced cars as the primary means of getting around Taipei City.

To understand why, we first must understand what BOT means. BOT stands for build-operate-transfer and allows a private company that gets the okay from the public sector to build, operate, and run a company—in this case, a very ingenious and successful bike-sharing service.

Each bike is used by riders dozens of times each day. The public-private partnership has resulted in a massive decline in cars clogging the downtown streets of Taiwan's capital city.

The parent company of YouBike, Giant, posted another 5 to 10 percent revenue growth in 2023 and forecasts sales growth of another 10 percent in 2024. They sell millions of the bikes at $300 a pop. Three years ago, they shipped over two million bikes; last year they shipped an additional two and a half million bikes, and this year they plan to distribute over six million bikes worldwide. That's a lot of "pedal power."[11]

Add to this a rapid transit system that is fast and efficient and includes countless other mass transportation facilities, and one can see how Taipei has made non-automobile mobility a science.

The glue that holds this system together, however, is YouBike. It's a rental service that enables users to lease and return bikes to many, many rental stations within the greater Taipei area. Users rent a YouBike with an iPASS card and then can use their bikes to go anywhere in the city.

In addition, civilian transport in the city is enhanced by the extensive use of scooters, which are used twice as much as cars in Taipei.

Finally, the city has built one of the safest cycling infrastructures in the world. Smack dab in the middle of one of the busiest cities in the world, one can ride for miles alongside lush green mangroves and enjoy beautiful scenic views on bike paths built along the city's rivers.

Bike lanes have seamlessly been laid through urban parks and gardens. The routes for bikes are protected and set apart from cars with cement barriers, trees, and elevated cycle lanes and bridges over highways. They are also dotted with rest stops that include bike repair facilities, water stations, vending machines, easy bike parking areas, and even clean restrooms. By investing in this infrastructure, Taipei has made it much easier and smarter for its mobile population not to have to ever use a car.

New technologies have made the YouBike rental service extremely easy to use. Their electronic managerial system allows a user to rent a bike in one place and return it in another. A user can then ride the Taipei Mass Rapid Transit Metro system and travel to any of hundreds of stations. At any of these stations, the user can then pick up another YouBike and continue his or her journey.

All the Metro systems list the exact time their trains are due to arrive and depart, so a user can easily plan a travel schedule.

The result is that, over the last few years, Taipei has transformed from a traffic nightmare into an easily traversable metropolis.

Many other cities have carefully examined the Taipei model and we'll soon be seeing more uses of this wonderful idea throughout the world.

COPENHAGEN

Jan Gehl is a Danish architect and urban designer. Born in Copenhagen, he has transformed his hometown over the last half-century from a car-dominated city to one in which pedestrians now rule.

Strongly influenced by the works of the urban activist Jane Jacobs, he has brought back the human side of architecture to city planners and landscape architects throughout the world. He has done this by making Copenhagen an example of how a major urban center can function without cars by reorienting itself towards pedestrians and cyclists. He believes that moving at slower speeds can help people get in touch with their five senses and appreciate where they are.

It all began forty years ago with the creation of a car-free zone in the center of the city. It was nothing short of a living lab that Gehl and the City of Copenhagen implemented to prove that pedestrian walkways and bike zones were just as effective as cars in getting people to utilize city streets. Today it is one of the longest pedestrian shopping areas in the world.

Copenhagen is also among the most bicycle-friendly cities in the world. Almost half of its population commutes to university, school, and work by bike. The city is lined with countless well-used bike paths and cycle tracks. The result is that Copenhagen, like Taipei, has shown that an urbanized environment with high-quality public transportation services can get people to stop using private cars.

TEMPE

Tempe is Phoenix's hot stepsister. It is the location of the main campus of Arizona State University and is bordered by the city of Guadalupe on the west. It is also one of the first cities to establish a "car-free" zone.

Phoenix has long been characterized as a concrete nightmare. It has had the distinction of being named the world's least sustainable city and a suburban wasteland. The satirical daily newspaper,

The Onion, said Phoenix is "a monument to man's arrogance" and predicted that by the middle of this century, most of America's land mass would be swallowed by Phoenix's encroaching exurbs. It's been said that trying to walk in Phoenix is like a slog through a desert interrupted by an occasional McDonald's.[12]

One brief side note: Until the 1960s, Tempe was one of the last remaining "sundown towns" in America. A sundown town's rules stipulated that "colored people" were allowed to come into the city to work during the day but then had to leave after sunset or be subject to harassment, imprisonment, and even lynching. Signs posted throughout these places informed nonwhites that they had to leave the city limits by dusk, or they would be picked up by the police. These cities were not just in the South—they included places like Levittown, New York and Glendale, California.[13]

It was not until the late 1960s that Black people were able to buy a home in Tempe.

From this troubled past comes the amazing fact that Tempe has now developed the nation's first zero-driving community.

The almost–$200 million development is called Culdesac Tempe. It contains over seven hundred apartments and 16,000 square feet of retail stores. Built on a once-vacant seventeen-acre lot, Culdesac is a direct challenge to Big Car.

Anyone wanting to live in the community is contractually forbidden from parking a vehicle within a quarter-mile radius of Culdesac. Public transportation is included in each Culdesac unit's monthly rent.

The idea of building the first car-free city in the U.S. is catching on. Culdesac is almost full, and its investors hope to expand to over 10,000 residents soon.[14]

The people funding and building the city are trying to create a walkable environment in Arizona as a reaction to the urban sprawl that has taken over Phoenix.

By providing mobility benefits through ride-sharing services and public transit agencies, the people behind Culdesac hope to prove that privately owned cars are no longer necessary. By incorporating green spaces such as courtyards, gardens, and other community gathering spots, they believe they can make a city that is walkable and livable without the congestion, noise, and danger that cars bring to our roadways.

It's a bold idea taking root in the desert, and we'll see how it grows.

SALT LAKE CITY

Salt Lake City's City Creek Center defies the logic of American malls by refusing to conform to typical mall standards. It is a place built for people rather than for cars. The mall uses its space not to store cars but to provide a slower, more scenic, and generally more appealing experience. Thus, emphasis is given to the Center's physical—not retail—experience. Now you can have nature next to you while you're consuming. It offers the same stores, and shoppers spend the same amount of money, but it's all done without you having to use your automobile. It seems to calm people down and make them smile more.

Situated over a few blocks in Utah's largest city, the City Creek Center features acres of fountains, green space, and even a mile-long stream. It has more than seven hundred thousand feet of mixed-use residential, office, and, of course, retail space. A pedestrian skyway links the two city blocks of the mall. The mall has its own light rail station. It has pocket parks and roof gardens, and gives the shopper a sense of being someplace special. It also has an underground parking lot that can accommodate

5,600 vehicles—unlike most malls, where parking structures waste entire buildings.

On a beautiful clear day, pedestrians can enjoy the sun. But the center is also designed with a retractable rooftop that encloses the entire mall space during inclement weather. The rooftop is not simply a remarkable feature; it's a radical rethinking of how open-air malls can be built in areas that are not just sensitive to bad weather but *known* for it.[15]

The rooftop is an ingenious solution and reduces pedestrians' inclination to rush back to their vehicles when the weather turns inclement. The retractable rooftop also reduces energy consumption by up to 50 percent compared to closed structures, as temperatures can be better calibrated throughout the year. Plus, it's fun to watch it going up.

The end result is a shopping destination not necessarily designed just for shopping. Instead, it represents a rethinking of the American mall. City Creek Center's design philosophy—to be both an open-air pedestrian streetscape and a suburban-style covered mall to encourage all-season shopping—represents an innovation in recent American history where the key in retail design is consumer and local space rather than connecting cars to shopping. Through its design, City Creek Center reimagines the mall by emphasizing walkability, embracing nature, and reducing energy waste.

How did this happen? City Creek Center is the unique brainchild of the Church of Jesus Christ of Latter-day Saints and a bunch of very creative engineering minds. It became part of an almost $5 billion sustainable design program to revitalize downtown Salt Lake City. (City Creek Center's share of the cut was about a billion and a half dollars; it's nice to have friends in high places.)[16]

It also helped to have a fellow named Jon Magnusson on board, who just happened to have built T-Mobile Park, home of the Seattle Mariners baseball team; Levi's Stadium, home of the San Francisco 49ers football team; and for good measure, the Seattle Central Library. The T-Mobile Arena also boasts a retractable roof, while Levi's Stadium is built to help withstand earthquakes (a common occurrence in the great state of California), and the Seattle Central Library is built over an entire city block, with open spaces for users and an irrigation system that uses rainwater onsite.

Magnusson was the one who posited the idea of a retractable roof over an open-air mall to reduce energy consumption by allowing for better environmental control. His genius was to think of a mall as a sports stadium where a bi-parting vaulted skylight on rails would retract and swing out of sight from the concourse below. If more than 100,000 people packed inside a stadium can handle a rooftop opening and closing, why not 5,000 families a day?

Through its design of being an all-season, partially open-air mall, City Creek Center represents innovation in redefining malls as walkable spaces—free from the noise and fumes of cars and designed in harmony with the environment.

So the next time a well-dressed couple comes to your door to tell you about the Book of Mormon, ask them about their mall.

CHICAGO

Phil Pagano liked to go on vacations. His job as executive director of Chicago's largest public transit line, Metra, afforded him a great deal of opportunity to travel throughout the world to see how other municipalities were handling their mass transit systems. The problem was that travel had become a tad expensive for Phil. So, he took an unauthorized $56,000 bonus to his already generous salary. Alas for poor Mr. Pagano, this opened an investigation into his vacation pay and it was found that Mr. Pagano had improperly taken another $475,000 for various sojourns and other activities. The day that he was scheduled to face the music before his Metra agency board, he instead went to a local Metra station and stepped in front of an oncoming Metra train.[17]

I mention this because now, a decade and a half later, Metra is one of the most successful mass transit systems in America.[18]

Metra is the lifeblood of Chicago, connecting the Midwest metropolis to its suburbs. Outside of New York City (which boasts five times the population of Chicago), Metra is the largest and busiest commuter rail system in the United States. Its ridership numbers are staggering: roughly 24 million passengers flowed through a system with only 500 miles of track.[19]

Metra was originally founded in 1974 as the Regional Transportation Authority to bring some order to what had become a chaotic commuting rail system with too many regional private train operators. This fragmentation made it almost impossible to create a cohesive train schedule for passengers. After several of these private train operators went bankrupt, Metra unified all regional commuter rail lines under a single system.

Metra's history of cleaning up Chicago's rail system meant they also had to bring order to their own system. After a turbulent history of financial misdoings by CEOs, current CEO and executive director Jim Derwinski has provided a sense of stability—and also innovative thinking—to Metra since 2017. An electrician by training, Derwinski worked his way up Metra's ladder. Now that he's at the top, he realizes that the future of public transport is far more problematic than simply buying new stock to keep everything running the same way it always has— nothing stays the same.

Since COVID-19, for example, the way people go to work has changed dramatically. Imagine you're a recent college graduate. Years ago, you'd have had plenty of options to go to and from work and would live in cheaper parts of town. Now, you work remotely but may have to come into the office once or twice a week—and you still want to be somewhat close to the big city for the occasional date or Cubs game. You don't take the train Monday through Friday during "normal work hours" but instead commute sporadically throughout the week. How do we accommodate this seemingly growing crowd?

Such a change in work habits, contextualized around public transport, changes the conversation around how urban planners, engineers, and architects think about urban public transportation planning: If people are not going to work in downtown areas and are instead working from home, what does that mean for "peak" hours of public transport, and how can we address the shift in transport preferences—and do it sustainably?

To provide more frequent and reliable but sustainable service, under Derwinski's tenure, Metra has looked to Europe for its new fleet of train cars. They are battery-operated, which makes them more sustainable and better for the environment. The new Metra trains will run more frequently but will be smaller and require less maintenance than diesel-operated trains, and several of the local stops will have charging stations so that the trains always have enough juice. The result will be a new way of transport that will run more frequently during the day, be more cost-effective, and, for our purposes, be another thorn in Big Car's side.

Over the past three decades, Metra has invested more than $5 billion into its infrastructure. One result is a nifty system called "Train Tracker" that provides information about where your train currently is and when it is expected to depart from your station. They've managed to make riding mass transit very consumer friendly.

What Chicago has been able to do is create an easy-to-understand and even easier-to-use system to allow any traveler in their town to get the information necessary to know when and where they need to go. Your various devices connect you in a way that you can now find out in real time when you're going to get to your desired destination.

In October 2023, Metra received a $170 million federal grant for zero-emission trainsets, and soon, Metra will be among the first and indeed the most extensive domestic rail system to operate on an enormous scale with this green technology.[20]

Today in Chicago, you no longer must sit in traffic, search for a place to park, or suffer any of the other tortures that Big Car often subjects us to. Other big cities such as New York and Los Angeles will eventually begin to move over to such systems. It is yet another weapon in our arsenal for stopping Big Car.

PORTLAND, OREGON

Today, Portland is known as a city where young people go to retire. It wasn't always like that.

Originally just called "The Clearing," two gents—one from Boston and the other from Portland, Maine—had a coin flip to settle on a name. Portland won.

Early Portland was a wide-open city. Bootlegging, gambling, prostitution, and unsanitary sewers and gutters caused its hometown paper, *The Oregonian*, to call it "the most filthy city in the Northern States."[21]

Today Portland is rated as the fourth most expensive place to live in America.[22]

Like so many other cities, as traffic became intolerable, Portland searched for solutions. Their answer was the bike. Portland has a bicycle network that connects all parts of the city. Its strong bike culture dominates the city's transportation system. In the last two decades, cycle usage has increased fourfold. What's amazing about that statistic is that the number of bike mishaps has remained the same. They're doing something right. Let's take a closer look.

Now known as America's "biking capital," it is America's Taipei. With over 150 miles of bike lanes and over seven thousand publicly installed bike racks, it is a biker's paradise. Also, biking in Portland is not a class affair; people of all income levels traverse the many bike paths in the city, and groups such as the Multnomah Wheelmen, a biking club formed in the late 1800s, reflect the long-established and fast-growing biking community of the city.

Portland's government-funded "Bicycle Plans" have been supplemented by privatized projects that reflect the bike-crazed city's desire to break free of Big Car. For example, an organization called The Street Trust is one of the most effective cycling advocacy groups in the U.S. The Trust's first project was to petition Portland's regional public transportation authority to allow bikes on trains and buses. Today the Street Trust actively helps support local legislation that expands bike lanes and enhances the city's identity as a biking capital.

Another more recent project has involved a collaboration between Motivate, a local private digital company, and Nike, arguably Portland's most globally successful home-grown business. In 2016, Motivate launched BIKETOWN, a system with over 1,000 GPS-enabled smart bikes. Ten million dollars were invested in the project, and over 100 stations covering an almost ten-mile square radius, mostly in downtown Portland, were put into operation. Nike is now a primary sponsor of the program. Through the apparel giant, interested cyclists can register for memberships that give access to great perks, such as reduced biking fees and rideshare benefits from companies such as Lyft. Last year, BIKETOWN added over 500 new electric bikes to their already vast fleet of over 2,000 bikes. (All of the new bikes are being built from recycled footwear scraps and rubber.)[23]

Portland is a prime example of what can be done when government and big business unite to take on Big Car.

HELSINKI

Sisu is a Finnish word that has no equivalent word in English. It's best described as a stoic determination that refuses to give up. I guess you could call it grit.

Sampo Hietanen is the exemplar of Finnish *sisu*. A handsome, middle-aged Helsinki resident, he is one of the godfathers of the Mobility as a Service (MaaS) movement. Sampo has worked most of his adult life to try and get rid of urban congestion by giving people the option of freedom from car ownership. A tireless proselytizer, Sampo has given several thousand worldwide talks on the subject. His message is simple and clear: "Get rid of your car and all of our lives will be better."

When he first started telling people his idea he was ridiculed, shunned, and told to shut up. But as congestion in Helsinki continued to worsen, people finally began to pay attention. By 2015, there was enough public support to pass the Finnish Transportation Act, which opened up all data on travel in Finland and gave Sampo the tools necessary to start experimenting with ideas about how to get rid of cars in the city.

Sampo's big idea was to start a subscriber-based system that would, for a monthly fee, give users an app that would seamlessly consolidate information about the existing Helsinki travel infrastructure. By simply downloading an app, users would know where every train, tram, bus, bike rental, taxi, and electric scooter was in real time. It also allowed people to use their smartphones to pay for any transportation service they wished to use—no need for tickets.

It was a big idea, but like I said, Sampo has *sisu*.

He started a company called MaaS Global to sell his Whim app, raised tens of millions of dollars, and launched the idea in Helsinki and several other cities. As the concept began to take hold, everyone agreed it was a brilliant idea. Transportation experts from around the world traveled to Helsinki to learn from the program. Sampo was going to turn Whim into the Netflix of transportation. One simple fee and all the services would be provided.

At Sampo's corporate headquarters in downtown Helsinki, he put a display board up in the center of the room that counted the number of travelers using the Whim service. On July 2018, the scoreboard hit the one million user mark. The people of Finland were embracing Whim. Within a couple of months, it was up to two million. The experiment to build a complete ecosystem was working. It was a wonderful first step in changing not only Finland's but eventually the world's relationship with Big Car.

At the same time, the MaaS movement was spreading throughout the world. An organization call MaaS Alliance was established in Brussels and soon had thousands of members. Within a year there were MaaS programs throughout Europe. Programs began in Australia, Canada, New Zealand, and even the United Arab Emirates.

Sampo's idea wasn't just working, it was scaling. And then Covid hit and the world closed down.

This may have been one of the great tragedies of the epidemic. Just as Sampo and Whim were gaining the necessary momentum to show that the app worked, people stopped traveling.

MaaS Global finally fell into the financial morass created by the pandemic. However, his team's brilliant programming has produced an app that any city will be able to use. In a world where the shared global mobility market is projected to be close to $240 billion dollars in the next five years with 15 percent annual growth, we've not heard the last of Sampo's idea![24]

CONCLUSION

We are on the brink of crossing a threshold beyond which globally catastrophic climate events will occur. Each slight increase in atmospheric warming will expose tens of millions more of us to horrific futures, including unthinkable food shortages and water scarcity. Millions more will be subjected to coastal flooding. We can also say farewell to millions of insects, birds, plants, and even mammals that will be gone forever because of the slow increase in global temperatures.

Distracted world leaders continue to deal only with the problems directly affecting their populations today. Poorer nations and low-lying countries will need international funds to survive. America, Europe, and China will be unable to help them because they will have to deal with the staggering costs of their own ecological disasters.

Unless we decarbonize our world now, we will eventually become part of the 99 percent of all other species on the planet that have gone extinct.

In the Spring of 2025, President Trump's new head of the EPA, Lee Zeldin, announced the federal government was about to have the most significant deregulatory action in American history. He said, "We are driving a dagger straight into the heart of climate change religion. We will now lower American families' living costs and unleash American energy to bring auto jobs back to the United States." At the same time, the World Health Organization announced that five and a half million deaths had occurred the previous year due to lead poisoning. Approximately 85 percent of the total lead consumption that killed these millions came from "Big Car."

Not a single person from any of these "Big Car" companies has been held accountable for these premature deaths or the tens of millions of other human beings killed by their products' usage over the last century. There will probably never be a Nuremberg court–type trial for those responsible for those millions killed, and even more deaths continue today as we subject our species to the pain and sorrow of corporate profits.

According to the International Energy Agency, we will hit peak fossil fuel usage within five years. By the end of this decade, America will drill for more oil and gas than ever in our history. According to a recent United Nations report, fossil fuel production this decade will be twice the amount allowed for by nearly all critical global warming thresholds. Emissions from burning these fuels are the main drivers of global warming and have already caused massive intensification of storms, flooding, heat waves, wildfires, and droughts—in short, climate chaos. The combined level of fossil fuel production planned by the ten largest countries alone will warm the world beyond what is safe for human existence.[1]

In the United States, fossil fuel subsidies and tax breaks are a significant cause of the increase in production. According to the International Monetary Fund, over $7 trillion in subsidies were paid out to companies in the fossil fuel business. Mike Johnson, the current House speaker, still opposes clean energy legislation and received more campaign contributions from the oil and gas companies than from any other industry last year. Representative Johnson's district includes Shreveport, which is an oil-dependent community. The Independent Petroleum Association of America recently stated that Speaker Johnson represents a quantum leap over the former speaker.[2]

In 2023, at the United Nations climate summit, it was announced that Big Car will introduce roughly 36.6 billion tons of planet-warming carbon dioxide into our environment. That's about 1 percent more than last year.[3]

Today, there are many brilliant minds in the world who are now aware of the dangers facing us. We're good at it when we put our minds and resources toward solving problems. For example, cancer deaths in America have fallen by nearly one-third over the last decade. It's still the second leading cause of death after heart disease, but in this short time span, we have used science and common sense to extend the lives of almost four million Americans.

We must start thinking of Big Car as if it were a cancer trying to destroy us. A century of regulatory history shows that Big Car has long ago captured our governmental agencies and won't protect us. Congress and the amount of funding it receives from Big Car continue to shape the public interest.

Big Car is a complex, coordinated group of companies that extract, assemble, and market how we can travel. They dominate our economic process. Their accumulation of power and influence has almost reached the point where we can no longer control it. Big Car's driving force has never been about ways to bind humanity together. Instead, it's been about finding ways to maximize quarterly profits. Big Car has now seriously endangered our ability to survive as a species.

We have to act before it's too late. Over four million Americans had to leave their homes in the last few years because of climate change disasters. Of those who had to flee, about 12 percent couldn't return for over half a year. An additional 16 percent still haven't returned home.[4]

One of the most troubling aspects about all of this is that our tax dollars are funding it. The International Monetary Fund pointed out that in 2023, Big Car was subsidized by over $4 trillion.[5] That translates into millions being given every minute to those who would destroy our homes and planet.

In my first book, published in 1972, we showed what people were willing to do in the name of profit. Sadly, those who own and run Big Car today remain just as irresponsible as their predecessors of half a century ago.

We must find each other and discover ways to work together to break free of the Big Car stranglehold. We must all "laugh or weep at the folly of humans," as William Gibbon wrote in *The Decline and Fall of the Roman Empire*. Let us hope that by finding ways to work together, we can somehow laugh our way into our children's and grandchildren's future.

Because if we don't end Big Car, Big Car will end us.

ACKNOWLEDGMENTS

A few years ago, while stuck in a horrendous traffic jam, I sat wondering how it was possible that for the seventy-plus years I'd lived in Los Angeles we still hadn't come up with a solution for something as basic and necessary as being able to drive across our city without wasting hours of our time and polluting our environment.

As a much younger man, I had done investigative journalism. A friend and I won a Pulitzer Prize for our work. I decided I would try to find out the root causes of this problem. This book is a result of what I've discovered.

I am grateful to my wife of many years, Jane Gottlieb, for always being there. Her keen insights helped me make sense of what I was learning. Her patience was limitless. Her ability to let me try and explain what I'd learned kept me focused. And her love and friendship made every day I worked on the manuscript a pleasure. To have a life partner who is also one's best friend is perhaps the greatest blessing any human can possess. This work, as well as my life, is dedicated to her.

This book would not have been possible without several special people.

First and foremost is my dear friend, Myles Thompson, of Columbia University Business School Press. Myles, like a brilliant sculptor, spent the last few years taking my ideas and forming them into a book. His endless patience, attention, and spot-on suggestions resulted in my reworking the book until it made sense to both of us. I could not have possibly done this work without his guidance and enthusiasm.

Janice Willett, my extremely capable editor, helped translate my manuscript back into English. She also forced me to provide primary source material in the many footnotes included in the work. Her tireless devotion to making the complex topic of this work into something understandable is beyond appreciated.

Mo Muzammal was a great help in finding and helping me put together the information on cities that are building sustainable travel futures.

Bill and Laurie Benenson, life-long friends and brilliant filmmakers, helped get me started on this book and have been there for me every step of the way.

Carla and Jonathan Sanger were also wildly enthusiastic early readers. Their suggestions and encouragement also helped keep me going.

Jena Pincott, my life editor and brilliant author, helped translate what Myles was trying to tell me and helped keep me sane.

My dear friends Charlie and Pattie Firestone sat patiently through innumerable brunches with Jane and me and let me go on and on about my book. Thanks.

To my dear "old geezers lunch group" of Dr. David Bearman, Dr. Daniel Fishbein, and Judge Roger Winkelman, many thanks for your many insights, information, and support.

I'd like to thank my talented son, Oly, for his wonderful support and enthusiasm for this book. Any project is always easier if your kids believe in it.

Dr. Carol Schweiger, a battle-hardened veteran of the transportation wars, was my mother hen. Carol kept me concentrated on what major issues needed to be examined and then pointed me to where I might find answers.

Likewise, Tom Radulovich, former Director of BART and also an expert in transportation matters, has been a wise and willing counselor in helping me understand the weird world of cars.

A special thanks to both Marianne Partridge, publisher of the *Santa Barbara Independent*, who has kept me writing all these years, and my sister-in-law from heaven, Lynn Kirk, for making me finish this thing.

This book originally began in Helsinki, Finland, where I went to visit an amazing company, MaaS Global, who were the pioneers in providing real-time data for transportation users. Their founder, Sampo Hietanen, is one of the early heroes of the Mobility as a Service (MaaS) movement. One of his top aides, Esra Ozbay, was invaluable in helping me navigate my way through the complex world of transportation. Also, at MaaS Global, Sohail Rashid was a great expert to be able to bounce ideas off. Sampo, Esra, Sohail, and others will be instrumental in the future crusade against Big Car.

Finally, I'd like to thank our dog, Pepper, who day after day sat next to my desk waiting for me to finish writing so we could go outside and play with her frisbee. Her slow but steady love, like all the people above, made this book possible.

NOTES

INTRODUCTION

1. Lydia DePillis, "How the Costs of Car Ownership Add Up," interactive report, prod. Rebecca Lieberman and Christa Chapman, *New York Times*, October 6, 2023, https://www.nytimes.com/interactive/2023/10/07/business/car-ownership-costs.html.

1. LEAD HERRING (PART ONE)

1. Lucas Reilly, "The Most Important Scientist You've Never Heard Of," Mental Floss, May 17, 2017, https://www.mentalfloss.com/article/94569/clair-patterson-scientist-who-determined-age-earth-and-then-saved-it.
2. Robert Kehoe, "Experimental Studies on the Inhalation of Lead by Human Subjects," *Pure and Applied Chemistry* 3, nos. 1–2 (1961): 129.
3. Dan Vahaba, "Lead Exposure in Last Century Shrank IQ Scores of Half of Americans," Duke Today, March 7, 2022, https://today.duke.edu/2022/03/lead-exposure-last-century-shrunk-iq-scores-half-americans. According to a study, half of the U.S. population has been exposed to substantially detrimental lead levels in early childhood—mainly from car exhaust, whose lead pollution peaked in the 1970s and caused widespread loss in cognitive ability. Many estimate that close to thirty thousand lives a year are still being lost to lead poisoning.

2. WHAT IS "BIG CAR"?

1. A. O. Brungardt, "Book Review: *The Automobile Industry: Its Economic and Commercial Development,*" *Journal of Business of the University of Chicago* 1, no. 3 (1928): 390–92.

2. I'm not sure if they are the people who invented the cartwheel.

3. In 2004 the bank headquarters were raided, and twenty-six thousand pounds sterling were stolen. Nobody has ever gone to jail for the heist.

4. Mort Schultz, "Tires: A Century of Progress," *Popular Mechanics* (June 1985), 64.

5. Peter Morris, "Rubber," in *Berkshire Encyclopedia of World History*, 2nd ed. (Berkshire Publishing, 2010), 2218.

6. Arthur Herman, *Freedom's Forge: How American Business Produced Victory in World War II* (Random House, 2012), 146–50.

7. T. Wenzel, "Analysis of national pay-as-you-drive insurance systems and other variable driving changes," Energy Analysis Program, Lawrence Berkeley National Laboratory, University of California, 1995.

8. Roger L. Miller and Alan D. Stafford, *Economic Education for Consumers* (Cengage Learning, 2009).

9. Kashmir Hill, "How G.M. Tricked Car Buyers on Data," *New York Times*, April 23, 2024, updated April 24, 2024, https://www.nytimes.com/2024/04/23/technology/general-motors-spying-driver-data-consent.html.

10. Geoffrey Jones, *Beauty Imagined: A History of the Global Beauty Industry* (Oxford University Press, 2010), 81.

11. "What's So Bad About Gasoline?" Coltura: Moving Beyond Gasoline, October 27, 2018, updated October 2024, https://coltura.org/gasfacts/.

12. "Carbon Dioxide Now More Than 50 Percent Higher Than Pre-Industrial Levels," National Oceanic and Atmospheric Administration website, June 3, 2022, https://www.noaa.gov/news-release/carbon-dioxide-now-more-than-50-higher-than-pre-industrial-levels.

13. Rebecca Elliot, "Oil Firm to Pay $242 Million in Settlement with E.P.A.," *New York Times*, July 13, 2024.

14. Michael Schneider, "Think Bigger: Going Electric Just Locks in the Ills of Car Culture," *Los Angeles Times*, September 15, 2022, p. A13.

15. Immanuel Ness. *Encyclopedia of Interest Groups and Lobbyists in the United States* (Routledge, 2000).

16. Pilita Clark, "The New Politics of Climate Change," *Financial Times*, book review, February 23, 2021, https://www.ft.com/content/b6bdc4b1 -d41f-49f0-a3df-61614cc1a2b7.

17. Clark, "The New Politics of Climate Change."

18. Kip Hill, "From Kettle Falls to the Capitol, Rep. Cathy McMorris Rodgers Used Conservative Bona Fides to Rise Through Ranks," *The Spokesman-Review*, October 10, 2018, https://www.spokesman.com/stories/2018/oct /10/from-kettle-falls-to-the-capitol-rep-cathy-mcmorri/.

19. "Oil and Gas Top Contributors, 2021–2022," Open Secrets, May 2022, https://www.opensecrets.org/industries/contrib?cycle=2022&ind=E01.

20. "Oil and Gas Top Contributors, 2021–2022."

21. Andrew E. Dessler, *Introduction to Modern Climate Change* (Cambridge University Press, 2021). See also the award-winning series by Neela Banerjee et al., "Exxon's Own Research Confirmed Fossil Fuels' Role in Global Warming Decades Ago," *InsideClimate News*, September 21, 2015, archived October 13, 2015, retrieved October 14, 2015, https://inside climatenews.org/news/16092015/exxons-own-research-confirmed-fossil -fuels-role-in-global-warming/. Exxon helped to found and lead the Global Climate Coalition, an alliance of some of the world's largest companies seeking to halt government efforts to curb fossil fuel emissions.

22. Spencer R. Weart, "Global Warming Becomes a Political Issue," The Discovery of Global Warming, Center for the History of Physics, American Institute of Physics, 2010, https://web.archive.org/web/20160629213628 /https://www.aip.org/history/climate/Govt.htm#S7. Weart writes: "In 1981 Ronald Reagan's administration openly scorned environmental concerns. His presidency was a high point for the backlash against the environmental movements. Conservatives denied global warming even existed. They lumped all such concerns together as rants of business-hating liberals and called the environmentalists nothing more than a Trojan Horse for government regulation."

23. "The Climate Denial Machine: How the Fossil Fuel Industry Blocks Climate Action," Climate Reality Project, September 5, 2019, https:// www.climaterealityproject.org/blog/climate-denial-machine-how-fos-sil-fuel-industry-blocks-climate-action.

24. Paul Krugman, "The Bad Economics of Fossil Fuel Defenders," New York Times, opinion, August 16, 2021, https://www.nytimes. com/2021/08/16/opinion/climate-change-republicans-economy.html.

25. Anthony Zurcher, "Does Trump Still Think It's All a Hoax?" BBC News, opinion, June 2, 2017, https://www.bbc.com/news/world-us-canada -40128034.

26. Suzanne Goldenberg, "Secret Funding Helped Build a Vast Network of Climate Denial Think Tanks." *The Guardian*, February 14, 2013, https://www.theguardian.com/environment/2013/feb/14/funding -climate-change-denial-thinktanks-network.

27. Katie Jennings et al., "How Exxon Went from Leader to Skeptic on Climate Change Research," *Los Angeles Times*, October 23, 2015, https:// graphics.latimes.com/exxon-research/.

28. Jennings et al., "How Exxon Went from Leader to Skeptic on Climate Change Research."

29. Suzanne Goldenberg, "Conservative groups spend up to $1bn a year to fight action on climate change," *The Guardian*, December 20, 2013, https://www.theguardian.com/environment/2013/dec/20/conservative -groups-1bn-against-climate-change.

30. Goldenberg, "Conservative groups spend up to $1bn a year."

31. Paul Krugman, "Krugman: Climate Denial and the Party That Ruined the Planet," *Austin American-Statesman*, December 16, 2019, https:// www.statesman.com/story/opinion/columns/more-voices/2019/12/16 /krugman-climate-denial-and-party-that-ruined-planet/2075968007/

32. Paige Bennett, "High-Income Nations Are on Track Now to Meet $100 Billion Climate Pledges, but They're Late," Ecowatch, May 2, 2023, accessed May 10, 2023, https://www.ecowatch.com/wealthy-countries -climate-change-reparations.html.

33. Ibsen Chivata Cardenas, "Mitigation of Climate Change. Increased Consideration of Risk and Uncertainty," in M. Brito et al., eds., *European Safety and Reliability Association: Proceedings of the 33rd European Safety and Reliability Conference* (ESREL 2023), 2760–61, https://www .rpsonline.com.sg/proceedings/esrel2023/html/P586.html.

3. HOW BIG CAR TOOK OVER
THE WORLD (PART ONE)

1. Peter Firchow, *Aldous Huxley, Satirist and Novelist* (University of Minnesota Press, 1972).

2. Steven Watts, *The People's Tycoon: Henry Ford and the American Century* (Vintage Books, 2005)

3. On the Model T, see Douglas Brinkley, "Prime Mover," *American Heritage* 54, no. 3 (2003): 44–53.

4. Bruce Pietrykowski, "Fordism at Ford: Spatial Decentralization and Labor Segmentation at the Ford Motor Company, 1920–1950," *Economic Geography* 71, no. 4 (1995): 383–401.

5. Mike Jones, "History of the Cadillac Motor Car," February 2002, https://www.modifiedcadillac.org/articles/History%20of%20the%20 Cadillac%20Motor%20Car.html.

6. "The Stanley Steamer, Why the Fascination?" www.stanleymotorcarriage .com, http://www.stanleymotorcarriage.com/GeneralTechnical/GeneralInfo .htm.

7. Karel Williams, Colin Haslam, and John Williams, "Ford versus 'Fordism': The Beginning of Mass Production?" *Work, Employment & Society* 6, no. 4 (1992): 517–55.

8. Henry Ford, "Why I Favor Five Days' Work with Six Days' Pay," interview by Samuel Crowther, *World's Work* 52 (1926): 613–16; reprinted in *Monthly Labor Review* 23 (1926): 1162–66.

9. Ford, "Five Days' Work."

10. Williams et al., "Ford versus 'Fordism.'"

11. Allan Nevins and Frank Ernest Hill, *Ford: The Times, The Man, The Company* (Charles Scribner's Sons, 1954).

12. Michael Alexander, "Henry Ford and the Jews: The Mass Production of Hate," *Jewish Quarterly Review* 94, no. 4 (2004): 716–18.

13. Bill McGraw, "Henry Ford and the Jews, the Story Dearborn Didn't Want Told," Bridge Michigan, February 4, 2019, https://www.bridgemi .com/michigan-government/henry-ford-and-jews-story-dearborn -didnt-want-told.

14. McGraw, "Henry Ford and the Jews."

15. Michael H. Kater, *Hitler Youth* (Harvard University Press, 2009).

16. Kater, *Hitler Youth*.

17. Kater, *Hitler Youth*.

18. "A Brief History of Volkswagen," www.hillsideimports.com, January 6, 2014, https://web.archive.org/web/20150310221809/http://www.hillside imports.com/vw-history/brief-history-volkswagen.

19. "Mercedes-Benz History," www.edmunds.com, archived March 1, 2009, https://web.archive.org/web/20090301042155/http://www.edmunds.com/mercedesbenz/history.html.

20. "A Brief History of Volkswagen."

4. HOW BIG CAR TOOK OVER
THE WORLD (PART TWO)

1. David Temple, *The Cars of Harley Earl: Features GM's Revolutionary Concept and Production Cars* (CarTech Inc., 2016).

2. *Design for Dreaming*, short film released as part of series "Motorama: Vision of the Future," produced and directed by Victor D. Solow, sponsored by General Motors Corporation, 1956, 10 mins. If you're enough of a nerd to actually read footnotes, then you MUST go and watch this film. It can be watched online and even downloaded for free via multiple film archives, including via the Library of Congress (permalink at https://www.loc.gov/item/2024601046/), and it will greatly enhance your understanding of the power "Big Car" has held over our country.

3. Jerry Burton, "Corvette: A Pop Culture Classic," *Automotive News*, October 31, 2011, https://www.autonews.com/article/20111031/CHEVY100/310319966/corvette-a-pop-culture-classic/.

4. William Manchester, *Disturber of the Peace: The Life of H. L. Mencken* (Harper & Row, 1951).

5. "General Motors," *Encyclopedia Britannica*, updated January 9, 2025, https://www.britannica.com/money/General-Motors-Corporation.

5. THE ROAD

1. Maxwell G. Lay, *Ways of the World: A History of the World's Roads and of the Vehicles That Used Them* (Rutgers University Press, 1992).

2. Ann Faulds et al., "The Definition of a Road?," chap. 4 in *Scottish Roads Law*, 2nd ed. (Tottel, 2008).

3. "John Loudon MacAdam," Electric Scotland, https://electricscotland.com/history/other/macadam_john.htm.

4. Colin R. Gagg, "Cement and Concrete as an Engineering Material: An Historic Appraisal and Case Study Analysis," *Engineering Failure Analysis* 40 (2014): 114–40, https://doi.org/10.1016/j.engfailanal.2014.02.004

5. McGraw-Hill, "Highway Engineering," *McGraw-Hill Concise Encyclopedia of Science and Technology*, 4th ed. (McGraw–Hill, 2005).

6. Raymond Forsyth and Joseph Hagwood, *One Hundred Years of Progress* (California Transportation Foundation, 1996).

7. See Frank Monaghan, *Official Guidebook of the New York World's Fair, 1939* (Exposition Publications, 1939). The futurama highway system was supported within a one-acre animated model of a projected America containing more than 500,000 individually designed buildings, a million trees of 13 different species, and approximately 50,000 cars, 10,000 of which traveled along a 14-lane multi-speed interstate highway.

8. Federal Highway Administration, "History of the Interstate Highway System," Highway History, U.S. Department of Transportation, updated December 20, 2024, https://www.fhwa.dot.gov/interstate/history.cfm.

9. Richard Wingroff, "Federal-Aid Highway Act of 1956: Creating the Interstate System," *Public Roads* 60, no. 1 (1996): 60; available online at https://highways.dot.gov/public-roads/summer-1996/federal-aid-highway-act-1956-creating-interstate-system.

10. A. Boyle and Coleman O'Flaherty, *Highways: The Location, Design, Construction and Maintenance of Road Pavements*, 4th ed. (Elsevier, 2002).

11. McGraw-Hill, "Highway Engineering."

12. Zamira Rahim, "Here's How Much Sitting in Traffic Is Costing You," Money.com, February 21, 2017, https://money.com/traffic-los-angeles-driving/.

13. Rachel Carson, *Silent Spring* (Houghton Mifflin, 1962).

14. Oliver Milman, "Shifting Gears: Why U.S. Cities Are Falling Out of Love with the Parking Lot," *The Guardian*, December 26, 2022, https://www.theguardian.com/us-news/2022/dec/26/us-cities-parking-lots-climate-walkability.

15. Ben Goldfarb, *Crossings: How Road Ecology Is Shaping the Future of Our Planet* (Norton, 2024).

6. CAR DREAMS

1. Ford Motor Company, "Innovative Marketing and PR Helped Build the Mustang Legend," Ford Motor Company Media, Ford.com, archived

June 11, 2009, https://web.archive.org/web/20090611100027/http://media
.ford.com/article_display.cfm?article_id=18037.

2. Kerry Segrave, *Drive-In Theaters: A History from Their Inception in 1933.*
(McFarland & Co., 2006).

3. Robin Reid, "The History of the Drive-In Movie Theater," *Smithsonian Magazine*, May 28, 2008, https://www.smithsonianmag.com/arts
-culture/the-history-of-the-drive-in-movie-theater-51331221/.

4. *Los Angeles Times*, April 2, 2024, A8.

5. Kevin Bartley, "Big Data Statistics: How Much Data Is There in the
World?" Rivery, August 27, 2023, updated December 11, 2024, https://
rivery.io/blog/big-data-statistics-how-much-data-is-there-in-the-world/.

6. Scott Calvert, "Rate of Crash Deaths on U.S. Roads Rose During
Coronavirus Pandemic," *The Wall Street Journal*, October 1, 2020, https://
www.wsj.com/articles/coronavirus-increased-rate-of-crash-deaths-on
-u-s-roads-11601582215.

7. Virginia Tech, *"New data from Virginia Tech Transportation Institute
provides insight into cell phone use and driving distraction,"* news.vt.edu,
July 29, 2009, https://news.vt.edu/articles/2009/07/2009-571.html.

8. John Baxter, *King Vidor* (Simon & Schuster, 1976).

9. Baxter, *King Vidor.*

10. John Jakie and Keith A. Sculle, *Fast Food: Roadside Restaurants in the
Automobile Age* (Johns Hopkins University Press, 1999).

11. Henry Samuel, "McDonald's Restaurants to Open at the Louvre," *The
Telegraph*, October 4, 2009, https://www.telegraph.co.uk/news/world
news/europe/france/6259044/McDonalds-restaurants-to-open-at-the
-Louvre.html#:~:text=McDonald's%20confirmed%20that%20a%20
restaurant%20will%20open,Louvre%2C%20known%20as%20the%20
Carrousel%20du%20Louvre.

12. Marion Nestle, *Food Politics: How the Food Industry Influences Nutrition
and Health* (University of California Press, 2002).

13. Andrew F. Smith, *Fast Food and Junk Food: An Encyclopedia of What We
Love to Eat* (Greenwood, 2012).

14. Thomas L. Friedman, "Foreign Affairs Big Mac I," editorial, *The New
York Times*, December 8, 1996, sec. 4, p. 15.

15. Heather McGregor, "Everything You Need To Know About The Wienermobile," WKFR 103.3, May 20, 2019, https://wkfr.com/everything
-you-need-to-know-about-the-wienermobile/.

16. Derek Scally, "World's First Bicycle Ride Took Place 200 Years Ago" *The Irish Times*, June 10, 2017, https://www.irishtimes.com/culture/heritage /world-s-first-bicycle-ride-took-place-200-years-ago-1.3112354.

17. Beth L. Bailey, *From Front Porch to Back Seat: Courtship in Twentieth-Century America* (Johns Hopkins University Press, 1989).

18. John A. Jakle et al., *The Motel in America* (Johns Hopkins University Press, 1996).

19. Christopher Setterlund, "The History of Howard Johnson's Restaurant," CapeCod.com, February 2, 2022, https://www.capecod.com/lifestyle/the -history-of-howard-johnsons-restaurant/.

20. Dylan Tweney, "Aug. 12, 1888: Road Trip! Bertha Takes the Benz," *Wired*, August 12, 2010, https://www.wired.com/2010/08/0812berta-benz-first -road-trip/.

21. Andrew Sheldon, "The History of the Car Wash Industry," Your AAA Today, *AAA Northeast Magazine*, June 16, 2022, https://magazine .northeast.aaa.com/daily/life/cars-trucks/auto-history/history-of-the -car-wash/.

22. Ericson, Makishima, and Berger. (January 1975) "Chemical and Physical Properties of Obsidian: A Naturally Occurring Glass," *Journal of Non-Crystalline Solids* 17, no. 1 (1975): 129–42.

23. Mark Byrnes, "Victor Gruen Wanted to Make Our Suburbs More Urban. Instead, He Invented the Mall," *Bloomberg*, July 18, 2013, https:// www.bloomberg.com/news/articles/2013-07-18/victor-gruen-wanted -to-make-our-suburbs-more-urban-instead-he-invented-the-mall.

24. Alexandra Lange, *Meet Me by the Fountain: An Inside History of the Mall* (Bloomsbury, 2022).

7. LEAD HERRING (PART TWO)

1. See Benjamin Ross and Steven Amter, *The Polluters: The Making of Our Chemically Altered Environment* (Oxford University Press, 2010).

   Our same Dr. Kehoe had been asked by the U.S. military to investigate reports that the chemical benzidine might cause bladder cancer. Showing the same regard for humanity that he would display in his disgraceful cover up of the dangers of lead toxicity, Kehoe indeed found overwhelming evidence that Benzidine was highly toxic for humans. However, one of his clients, DuPont made benzidine, so instead of letting American workers at their plants know about the risks they were facing Kehoe instead stuffed the facts into a file and hid it. Years later his moldy records were discovered when countless DuPont employees, having contracted cancer because of their exposure to benzidine, sued.

2. Kat Eschner, "One Man Invented Two of the Deadliest Substances of the 20th Century," *Smithsonian Magazine*, special report, May 18, 2017, available at SmithsonianMag.com, https://www.smithsonianmag.com/smart-news/one-man-two-deadly-substances-20th-century-180963269/.

3. Eschner, "One Man."

4. David Rosner and Gerald Markowitz, "A 'Gift of God'? The Public Health Controversy Over Leaded Gasoline During the 1920s," *American Journal of Public Health* 75, no. 4 (1985): 344–52, https://doi.org/10.2105/ajph.75.4.344.

5. Joseph C. Robert, *Ethyl: A History of the Corporation and the People Who Made It* (University Press of Virginia, 1983).

6. Robert, *Ethyl.*

7. Dan Vahaba, "Lead Exposure in the Last Century Shrunk IQ Scores of Half of Americans," *Duke Today*, March 7, 2022, https://today.duke.edu/2022/03/lead-exposure-last-century-shrunk-iq-scores-half-americans.

8. L. D. Grant, "Lead and Compounds," in *Environmental Toxicants: Human Exposures and Their Health Effects*, ed. Morton Lippmann and George D. Leikauf, 3rd ed. (Wiley-Interscience, 2009), 757–809.

9. Gemma Tarlach, "Lead in Ancient Rome's Water Was 100 Times Natural Levels," Discover, April 21, 2014, archived January 14, 2016, https://web.archive.org/web/20160114092050/http://blogs.discovermagazine.com/d-brief/2014/04/21/ancient-romes-water-100-times-lead-local-spring-water/#.Vpdojy_P32c.

10. Geoffrey Lean, "Pollution: Triumph of the Inconvenient Truth—Derek Bryce-Smith's Warnings About Lead in Petrol Made Him a Public Health Hero," *The Telegraph*, July 29, 2011.

11. Lydia Denworth, *Toxic Truth: A Scientist, A Doctor, and the Battle over Lead* (Beacon Press, 2009).

12. Lucas Reilly, "The Most Important Scientist You've Never Heard Of," MentalFloss.com, May 17, 2017, https://www.mentalfloss.com/article

/94569/clair-patterson-scientist-who-determined-age-earth-and
-then-saved-it?curator=MediaREDEF.

8. THE CORVAIR

1. Paul Sabin, *Public Citizens: The Attack on Big Government and the Remaking of American Liberalism* (Norton, 2021).
2. David Borgenicht, Sesame Street Unpaved: Scripts, Stories, Secrets, and Songs (Hyperion, 1998).
3. Motor Trend, "Bar Talk: 1960 Car of the Year—Making You an Instant Expert on the Chevrolet Corvair," MotorTrend.com., December 2009, https://www.motortrend.com/legacy/112-1001-1960-car-of-the-year/.

9. CAR NIGHTMARES

1. Millions of people each year will spend long weeks in hospitals after severe crashes, and many will never be able to work or play as they used to. Current efforts to address road safety are minimal in comparison to the increase in human suffering. See Margie Peden et al., *World Report on Road Traffic Injury Prevention* (World Health Organization, 2004), 44. PDF at https://iris.who.int/bitstream/handle/10665/42871/9241562609.pdf.
2. "Keeping You Safe—Safercar". National Highway Traffic Safety Administration. Archived from the original on September 1, 2006, retrieved May 27, 2017, https://web.archive.org/web/20060901201917/http://www-odi.nhtsa.dot.gov/cars/problems/recalls/childseat.cfm
3. David Leonhardt, "The Rise in U.S. Traffic Deaths: What's Behind America's Unique Problem with Vehicle Crashes?," *New York Times*, Morning Newsletter, December 11, 2023, https://www.nytimes.com/2023/12/11/briefing/us-traffic-deaths.html.
4. Leonhardt, "The Rise in U.S. Traffic Deaths."
5. Isabelle Fallon and Desmond O'Neill, "The World's First Automobile Fatality," *Accident Analysis and Prevention* 37, no. 4 (July 2005): 37.
6. "Finn's Speed Fine Is a Bit Rich," BBC News, news.bbc.co.uk, http://news.bbc.co.uk/2/hi/business/3477285.stm.
7. "Colonel Post Dies, Auto, Air Pioneer," *New York Times*, October 5, 1952,

8. "Colonel Post Dies."
9. "Our History," American Automobile Association (AAA) Official Site, https://mwg.aaa.com/about-us/our-history.
10. Peter Moore, "Almost Everyone Jaywalks, but Many Still Want It to Be Illegal," YouGov.com, September 25, 2014, https://today.yougov.com /society/articles/10571-almost-everyone-jaywalks.
11. "Tribute to the American Automobile Association School Safety Patrols," 104 Cong. Rec. E1757 (daily ed. Sept. 12, 1995) (statement of Rep. Mica).
12. "J. C. Furnas, Wry Historian Of American Life, Dies at 95." *New York Times*, June 12, 2001, https://www.nytimes.com/2001/06/12/arts/j-c -furnas-wry-historian-of-american-life-dies-at-95.html
13. The Highway Users Federation was formed by the merger of the Automotive Safety Foundation (ASF), the National Highway Users Conference (NHUC), and the Auto Industries Highway Safety Committee.
14. Mary Roach, "I was a human crash test dummy." *Salon*, November 19, 1999, archived March 11, 2006, retrieved November 29, 2007, https:// web.archive.org/web/20060311013317/http://archive.salon.com/health /col/roac/1999/11/19/crash_test/print.html.
15. Keir Martin, "Robert McNamara and the limits of 'bean counting,'" *Anthropology Today* 26, no. 3 (June 2010): 16–19.
16. Michael Schneider. "L.A. resolved to end traffic deaths. So why have they almost doubled?," *Los Angeles Times*, January 25, 2024.
17. Maxwell Lay, *Ways of the World: A History of the World's Roads and of the Vehicles That Used Them* (Rutgers University Press, 1992).
18. R. Dale Grinder, "The United States Department of Transportation: A Brief History," U.S. Department of Transportation, https://transportation .libguides.com/c.php?g=1154894&p=8441208
19. Tom Standage, *A Brief History of Motion: From the Wheel, to the Car, to What Comes Next* (Bloomsbury, 2021),
20. Peter D. Norton, *Fighting Traffic: The Dawn of the Motor Age in the American City* (MIT Press).
21. Lawrence Ulrich, "Hybrid Cars Enjoy a Renaissance as All-Electric Sales Slow," *New York Times*, June 19, 2024, https://www.nytimes.com /2024/01/17/business/hybrid-cars-electric-vehicles.html

22. Paul Barter, "'Cars are parked 95 percent of the time.' Let's check!" Reinventing Parking, February 22, 2013, https://www.reinventingparking .org/2013/02/cars-are-parked-95-of-time-lets-check.html.

23. Adolf D. May, *Traffic Flow Fundamentals* (Prentice Hall, 1990).

24. United States National Research Council, *Urban Stormwater Management in the United States* (The National Academies Press, 2008), https:// doi.org/10.17226/12465, 5.

25. "Coin-in-Slot Parking Meter Brings Revenue to City," *Popular Mechanics*, October 1935.

26. Hal Burton, *The Morro Castle: Tragedy at Sea* (Viking Press, 1973).

27. United States Census Bureau, "Commuting (Journey to Work)," information portal, updated May 19, 2023, https://www.census.gov/topics /employment/commuting.html.

28. United States Census Bureau, "Commuting."

29. Los Angeles County Metropolitan Transportation Authority, "Metro Facts At A Glance," updated February 22, 2023, archived March 19, 2023, https://web.archive.org/web/20230319120952/https://www.metro.net /about/facts-glance/.

30. One newspaper article of the era offered this explanation of smog: "It is really not fog at all, but a cloud of pure white mist, warmer and much less wetting than a 'Scotch Mist,' not differing entirely from the true British fog, facetiously spelled 'smog' because always colored and strongly impregnated with smoke, a mixture as unwholesome as it is unpleasant." See "The Morning Fog," *Santa Cruz Weekly Sentinel*, July 3, 1880, 3.

31. Elizabeth T. Jacobs et al., "The Donora Smog Revisited: 70 Years After the Event That Inspired the Clean Air Act," *American Journal of Public Health* 108, suppl. 2 (2018): S85–S88, https://pmc.ncbi.nlm.nih.gov/articles /PMC5922205/.

32. Damian Carrington, "Global Pollution Kills 9m a Year and Threatens 'Survival of Human Societies,'" *The Guardian*, October 20, 2017, https:// www.theguardian.com/environment/2017/oct/19/global-pollution-kills -millions-threatens-survival-human-societies.

33. T. J. Bouchard, Jr., "Genetic and Environmental Influences on Adult Intelligence and Special Mental Abilities," *Human Biology* 70, no. 2 (1998): 257–79, PubMed, https://pubmed.ncbi.nlm.nih.gov/9549239/.

34. Doug Stanglin, "Global Pollution Is the World's Biggest Killer and a Threat to Survival of Mankind, Study Finds," *USA Today*, October 20, 2017, https://www.usatoday.com/story/news/2017/10/20/study-global -pollution-worlds-biggest-killer-and-threat-survival-mankind/783321001/.

35. Alejandra Borunda, "Natural Gas Is a Much 'Dirtier' Energy Source, Carbon-Wise, Than We Thought," NationalGeographic.com, February 19, 2020, https://www.nationalgeographic.com/science/article/super -potent-methane-in-atmosphere-oil-gas-drilling-ice-cores.

36. Issam Ahmed, "Current Carbon Dioxide Levels Last Seen 14 Million Years Ago," Phys.org, December 9, 2023, https://phys.org/news/2023-12 -current-carbon-dioxide-million-years.html.

37. National Oceanic and Atmospheric Administration (NOAA), "Carbon Dioxide Now More Than 50 Percent Higher Than Pre-Industrial Levels," NOAA.gov, June 3, 2022, https://www.noaa.gov/news-release /carbon-dioxide-now-more-than-50-higher-than-pre-industrial-levels.

38. NOAA, "Carbon Dioxide Now More Than 50 Percent Higher Than Pre-Industrial Levels."

39. National Records of Scotland, "Thomas Telford: 1757–1834," NRScotland. gov.uk, https://webarchive.nrscotland.gov.uk/20200618051621/https://www .nrscotland.gov.uk/print/2609.

40. Engineers' Council for Professional Development, *Criteria for Accrediting Programs in Engineering in the United States: Including Objectives and Procedures* (Engineers' Council for Professional Development, 1976).

41. National Society of Professional Engineers (NSPE), "NSPE Code of Ethics for Engineers," revised July 2019, accessed March 19, 2025, https://www.nspe.org/career-growth/nspe-code-ethics-engineers.

42. Jeffrey L. Meikle, *Twentieth Century Limited: Industrial Design in America, 1925–1939* (Temple University Press, 1979), 206–7.

43. Peter D. Norton, *Fighting Traffic: The Dawn of the Motor Age in the American City* (MIT Press, 2008).

44. Laura Pulido, "Rethinking Environmental Racism: White Privilege and Urban Development in Southern California," *Annals of the Association of American Geographers* 90, no. 1 (2000): 12–40.

45. Richard Rothstein, *The Color of Law: A Forgotten History of How Our Government Segregated America* (Liveright/Norton, 2017).

46. Kenneth T. Jackson, *Crabgrass Frontier: The Suburbanization of the United States* (Oxford University Press, 1985).

47. Finesse Moreno-Rivera, "Police Kill Far Too Many People During Traffic Stops: We Must Change Why Stops Are Made," *USA Today*, November 20, 2022, https://www.usatoday.com/story/opinion/policing/2022/11/20/police-killings-no-decline-despite-reforms-george-floyd/10648861002/.

48. Malcolm X, *Malcolm X Speaks: Selected Speeches and Statements*, ed. G. Breitman and Ibram X. Kendi (Grove Press, 1990).

49. AAA National Magazine, 1998.

50. "Mary Anderson: Windshield Wipers," https://lemelson.mit.edu/resources/mary-anderson, accessed March 20, 2025.

51. Jessica Gross, "Who Made That?: Who Made That Turn Signal?" *New York Times Magazine*, July 14, 2013.

52. For statistics on alcohol-related car accidents in the U.S. in 2023, see "2023 SafeTREC Traffic Safety Facts: Alcohol-Impaired and Alcohol-Involved Driving," Safe Transportation Research and Education Center, UC Berkeley, accessed March 19, 2025, https://safetrec.berkeley.edu/2023-safetrec-traffic-safety-facts-alcohol-impaired-and-alcohol-involved-driving. For the 2022 statistics, see National Highway Traffic Safety Administration (NHTSA), "Alcohol-Impaired Driving," August 2024 (revised), DOT HS 813 578.

53. National Highway Traffic Safety Administration (NHTSA), "Alcohol-Impaired Driving."

54. J.-F. Payne, "Anstie, Francis Edmund (1833–1874), Physician," *Dictionary of National Biography*, vol. 2 (Smith, Elder & Co, 1885).

55. Stacey D. Stewart, "Mothers Against Drunk Driving's (MADD) 43rd Anniversary," (September 8, 2023). MADD.org, September 8, 2023, https://madd.org/43rd-anniversary/.

56. Stewart, "Mothers Against Drunk Driving's (MADD) 43rd Anniversary."

10. THE EDSEL

1. Robert Daines, *Edsel: The Motor Industry's Titanic*, (Academy Books, 1994).

2. Chris Perkins, "The Edsel Proved Why You Should Never Design a Car by Committee," *Road and Track*, January 23, 2017, https://www.roadandtrack.com/car-culture/classic-cars/a32380/ford-edsel-history/.

11. OUR CONTINUED LOVE AFFAIR WITH BIG CAR

1. David Leonhardt, "The Rise in U.S. Traffic Deaths: What's Behind America's Unique Problem with Vehicle Crashes?" *New York Times*, Morning Newsletter, December 11, 2023, https://www.nytimes.com/2023/12/11/briefing/us-traffic-deaths.html.
2. Julia Kollewe, "The History of General Motors," *The Guardian*, April 30, 2009, https://www.theguardian.com/business/2009/apr/30/general-motors-gm-history.
3. Tom Standage, *A Brief History of Motion: From the Wheel, to the Car, to What Comes Next* (Bloomsbury, 2021).
4. Kollewe, "The History of General Motors."

12. ROAD SAFETY

1. Jim Hinckley and Jon G. Robinson, *The Big Book of Car Culture: The Armchair Guide to Automotive Americana* (MotorBooks, 2005).
2. John M. Vincent, "The IIHS Announces 2023 Top Safety Pick Winners," *U.S. News & World Report*, February 23, 2023.
3. David Shepardson, "U.S. Traffic Deaths Jump 10.5 Percent in 2021 to Highest Number Since 2005," *Reuters*, May 17, 2022, https://www.reuters.com/world/us/us-traffic-deaths-jump-105-2021-highest-number-since-2005-2022-05-17/.
4. John M. Howard, "Historical Background to Accidental Death and Disability: The Neglected Disease of Modern Society, *Prehospital Emergency Care* 4, no. 4 (2000): 285–89.
5. "Early History of AMC, American Motor Cars," Southernclassic.tripod.com, https://southernclassic.tripod.com/id1.html.
6. "Early History of AMC."
7. Daniel Ackerman, "Before face masks, Americans went to war against seat belts," *Business Insider*, MSN.com, May 26, 2020, https://www.businessinsider.com/when-americans-went-to-war-against-seat-belts-2020-5.
8. Larry Ronan, "Seatbelts: 1949–1956," U.S. Department of Transportation, National Highway Safety Administration, April 1, 1979, DOT-HS-803-911, DOT-TSC-NHTSA-79-01, https://rosap.ntl.bts.gov/view/dot/11828.

13. LEAD HERRING (PART THREE)

1. Jerome O. Nriagu, "Clair Patterson and Robert Kehoe's Paradigm of 'Show Me the Data' on Environmental Lead Poisoning," *Environmental Research* 78, no. 2 (August 1998): 71–78.

2. Herbert L. Needleman, "Clair Patterson and Robert Kehoe: Two Views on Lead Toxicity," *Environmental Research* 78, no. 2 (August 1998): 79–85.

3. Clean Air Amendments of 1970, Pub. L. No. No. 91–604, 1676, Stat. 84 (1970).

4. Lucas Reilly, "The Most Important Scientist You've Never Heard Of," MentalFloss, May 17, 2017, https://www.mentalfloss.com/article/94569 /clair-patterson-scientist-who-determined-age-earth-and-then-saved-it.

5. Reilly, "The Most Important Scientist."

6. Meir Rinde, "Richard Nixon and the Rise of American Environmentalism," *Distillations Magazine*, June 2, 2017, ScienceHistory.org, https://www.sciencehistory.org/stories/magazine/richard-nixon-and -the-rise-of-american-environmentalism/.

7. Rinde, "Richard Nixon."

8. Rinde, "Richard Nixon."

9. See John Bartlow Martin's two studies: *Adlai Stevenson of Illinois: The Life of Adlai E. Stevenson* (Anchor Press/Doubleday, 1976); and *Adlai Stevenson and the World: The Life of Adlai E. Stevenson* (Anchor Press/ Doubleday, 1978).

10. William Manchester, *The Glory and the Dream: A Narrative History of America, 1932–1972* (Bantam, 1974).

11. Jennifer Leman, "Car Tires and Brake Pads Produce Harmful Microplastics," *Science News*, November 12, 2018, https://www.sciencenews.org /article/car-tires-and-brake-pads-produce-harmful-microplastics.

12. United States Environmental Protection Agency (EPA), "The Plain English Guide to the Clean Air Act," April 2007, https://www.epa.gov /sites/default/files/2015-08/documents/peg.pdf.

13. David Demortain, *The Science of Bureaucracy: Risk Decision Making and the US Environmental Protection Agency* (MIT Press, 2020).

14. Petersen Publishing Company and Erwin M. Rosen, "The Catalytic Converter," in *The Petersen Automotive Troubleshooting and Repair Manual* (Grosset & Dunlap, 1975), 493.

15. Peter Brimblecombe, "History of Air Pollution," in *Composition, Chemistry, and Climate of the Atmosphere*, ed. H. B. Singh (Van Nostrand Reinhold, 1995), 1–18.

16. Agency for Toxic Substances and Disease Registry (ATSDR), "Toxicological Profile for Lead," Centers for Disease Control and Prevention, August 2020, 20. Document accessible online at https://www.atsdr.cdc.gov/toxprofiles/tp13.pdf.

17. United Nations International Children's Emergency Fund (UNICEF), "Revealed: A Third of World's Children Poisoned by Lead, UNICEF Analysis Finds," *UN News*, July 29, 2020, https://news.un.org/en/story/2020/07/1069251.

18. The Associated Press, "Biden Administration Proposes Strictest Lead Pipe Rules in More Than Three Decades," WUSF.org, November 30, 2023, https://www.wusf.org/2023-11-30/biden-administration-proposes-strictest-lead-pipe-rules-in-more-than-three-decades.

19. Bryan Walsh, "The World's Most Polluted Places: Norilsk, Russia," *Time* Magazine, September 12, 2007, https://content.time.com/time/specials/2007/article/0,28804,1661031_1661028_1661022,00.html.

20. Caelyn Pender, "Why Do People Steal Catalytic Converters?" *KRON4*, August 9, 2022, https://www.kron4.com/news/why-do-people-steal-catalytic-converters/.

14. THE FUTURE OF MOBILITY

1. "Crack USA: County Under Siege," *New York Times*, June 25, 2011, http://movies.nytimes.com/movie/300539/Crack-USA-Country-Under-Siege/details.

2. James Campbell, *Talking at the Gates: A Life of James Baldwin* (University of California Press, 2021).

3. Joel Engelhardt, "It'll Be One of the Great Areas in America," Palm Beach Post, October 27, 2000, p. 8A.

4. Tony Doris, "New Name, Features, as CityPlace Transforms From Mall to Urban Neighborhood," *Palm Beach Post*, April 8, 2019, updated April 10, 2019, https://www.palmbeachpost.com/story/news/local/2019/04/08/new-name-features-as-cityplace-transforms-from-mall-to-urban-neighborhood/5274232007/.

5. American Public Transportation Association (APTA), "Transit Ridership Report Fourth Quarter 2023," March 4, 2024, https://www.apta.com/wp-content/uploads/2023-Q4-Ridership-APTA-Update-1.pdf.

6. Christian Baghai, 'How Dubai Became a Safe Haven for Europe's Most Wanted Criminals', Medium, December 27, 2023, https://christianbaghai.medium.com/how-dubai-became-a-safe-haven-for-europes-most-wanted-criminals-5fed2392108d.

7. Ron Gluckman, "Hong Kong of the Desert?" Ron Gluckman's Reporting Pages, Gluckman.com, accessed March 20, 2025, https://www.gluckman.com/DubaiBiz.html.

8. "Most nationalities in a human chain," Guinness World Records, accessed March 14, 2025, https://www.guinnessworldrecords.com/world-records/106292-most-nationalities-in-a-human-chain

9. Frank Dikötter et al., *Narcotic Culture: A History of Drugs in China* (University of Chicago Press, 2004).

10. Council on Tall Buildings and Urban Habitat, "Hong Kong," The Skyscraper Center, accessed March 20, 2025, https://www.skyscrapercenter.com/city/hong-kong.

11. Sam Challis, "Size Matters: How Giant Became the Biggest Bike Maker in the World," *Cyclist*, January 18, 2021, updated November 12, 2024, https://www.cyclist.co.uk/in-depth/size-matters-how-giant-became-the-biggest-bike-maker-in-the-world.

12. Andrew Needham, Power Lines: Phoenix and the Making of the Modern Southwest (Princeton University Press, 2015).

13. Joseph T. Durham, "Sundown Towns: A Hidden Dimension of American Racism," Negro Educational Review 57, nos. 1–2 (Spring 2006): 137–40.

14. Conor Dougherty, "The Capital of Sprawl Gets a Radically Car-Free Neighborhood," *New York Times*, October 31, 2020, https://www.nytimes.com/2020/10/31/business/culdesac-tempe-phoenix-sprawl.html.

15. "More than a Prayer: Salt Lake's City Creek Inspires Lofty Expectations," Durability and Design Technology Publishing, March 23, 2012, https://web.archive.org/web/20120327112624/http://www.durabilityanddesign.com/news/?fuseaction=view&id=7415.

16. Jasen Lee, "$1.5B City Creek Center on Schedule for March 22 Opening," *Deseret News*, January 27, 2012, https://www.deseret.com

/2012/1/28/20392081/1-5b-city-creek-center-on-schedule-for-march-22
-opening/.

17. Greg Hinz, "FBI File on Metra's Phil Pagano Offers Sad Lessons," *Crain's Chicago Business*, April 2, 2014, https://www.chicagobusiness.com/article
/20140402/BLOGS02/140409939/fbi-file-on-metra-s-phil-pagano
-disclosed.

18. APTA, "Transit Ridership Report Fourth Quarter 2023."

19. APTA, "Transit Ridership."

20. "Metra Wins Federal Grant to Acquire Battery-Powered Trains," *Progressive Railroading*, October 17, 2023, https://www.progressiverailroading.com/passenger_rail/news/Metra-wins-federal-grant-to-acquire-battery
-powered-trains--70433.

21. E. Kimbark MacColl, The Shaping of a City: Business and Politics in Portland, Oregon, 1885–1915 (The Georgian Press, 1976).

22. Elliot Njus, "Zillow: Portland Area Leads Nation in Home-Price Increases, Second in Rent Hikes," *The Oregonian* and *OregonianLive.com*, January 19, 2017, https://www.oregonlive.com/front-porch/2017/01
/zillow_portland_area_leads_nat.html.

23. Jayati Ramakrishnan, "Portland to Expand BikeTown Fleet as Ridership Hits Record," *The* Oregonian and OregonLive.com, April 21, 2023, https://www.oregonlive.com/commuting/2023/04/portland-to-expand
-biketown-fleet-as-ridership-hits-record.html.

24. "Green Transport: How Countries Can Grow Their Mobility Infrastructure Sustainably. World Economic Forum, Nov 27, 2024, https://
www.weforum.org/stories/2024/11/green-mobility-sustainable
-transport-infrastructure/

CONCLUSION

1. National Oceanographic and Atmospheric Administration (NOAA), *The NOAA Annual Greenhouse Gas Index (AGGI)*, NOAA.gov. National Oceanographic and Atmospheric Administration (NOAA), Spring 2023, https://gml.noaa.gov/aggi/aggi.html.

2. NOAA, *Greenhouse Gas Index* (2023).

3. Brad Plumer and Max Bearak, "In a First, Nations at Climate Summit Agree to Move Away from Fossil Fuels," *New York Times*, December 13, 2023.

4. Lee Ying Shan, "The Climate Crisis Has a Price—and It's $391 Million a Day," CNBC.com, October 23, 2023, https://www.cnbc.com/2023/10/24/the-climate-crisis-has-a-price-and-its-391-million-a-day.html.

5. Lisa Friedman, "The Zombies of the U.S. Tax Code: Why Fossil Fuels Subsidies Seem Impossible to Kill," *New York Times*, March 15, 2024, updated March 20, 2024, https://www.nytimes.com/2024/03/15/climate/tax-breaks-oil-gas-us.html.

BIBLIOGRAPHY

Ackermann, Malte. *Mobility-as-a-Service: The Convergence of Automotive and Mobility Industries.* Springer, 2021.

Agency for Toxic Substances and Disease Registry (ATSDR), "Toxicological Profile for Lead," Centers for Disease Control and Prevention, August 2020.

Alexander, Michael. "Henry Ford and the Jews: The Mass Production of Hate," *Jewish Quarterly Review* 94, no. 4 (2004): 716–18.

Appleyard, Bryon. *The Car: The Rise and Fall of the Machine That Made the Modern World.* Pegasus, 2022.

Bailey, Beth L. *From Front Porch to Back Seat: Courtship in Twentieth-Century America.* Johns Hopkins University Press, 1989.

Baxter, John. *King Vidor.* Simon & Schuster, 1976.

John Boederman. *The Cambridge Ancient History.* Cambridge University Press, 1997.

Borgenicht, David. Sesame Street Unpaved: Scripts, Stories, Secrets, and Songs. Hyperion, 1998.

Bowen, Galo. *Mobility 2040: Exploring the Emerging Trends Radically Transforming Transportation Systems in the U.S.* New Degree Press, 2021.

Brimblecombe, Peter. "History of Air Pollution." In *Composition, Chemistry, and Climate of the Atmosphere*, ed. H. B. Singh. Van Nostrand Reinhold, 1995.

Brinkley, Douglas. "Prime Mover." *American Heritage* 54, no. 3 (2003): 44–53.

Brungardt, A. O. "Book Review: *The Automobile Industry: Its Economic and Commercial Development.*" *Journal of Business of the University of Chicago* 1, no. 3 (1928): 390–92.

Buchanan, Brenda J. "McAdam, John Loudon (1756–1838), Builder and Administrator of Roads." In *Oxford Dictionary of National Biography*. Oxford University Press, 2004.

Campbell, James. *Talking at the Gates: A Life of James Baldwin.* University of California Press, 2021.

Carson, Rachel. *Silent Spring.* Houghton Mifflin, 1962.

Clean Air Amendments of 1970. Pub. L. No. No. 91–604, 1676, Stat. 84 (1970).

Cohen, Larry J. *The Quirky World of Parking: Four Decades of Observations, One Parking Space at a Time.* CAPP, 2021.

Daines, Robert. *Edsel: The Motor Industry's Titanic.* Academy Books, 1994.

Demortain, David. *The Science of Bureaucracy: Risk Decision Making and the US Environmental Protection Agency.* MIT Press, 2020.

Denworth, Lydia. *Toxic Truth: A Scientist, a Doctor, and the Battle Over Lead.* Beacon, 2008.

Dessler, Andrew E. *Introduction to Modern Climate Change.* Cambridge University Press, 2021.

Dikötter, Frank, Lars Peter Laamann, and Xun Zhou. *Narcotic Culture: A History of Drugs in China.* University of Chicago Press, 2004.

Durgnat, Raymond E., and Scott Simmon. *King Vidor, American.* University of California Press, 2023.

Durham, Joseph T. "Sundown Towns: A Hidden Dimension of American Racism." *Negro Educational Review* 57, nos. 1–2 (Spring 2006): 137–40.

Ericson, J. E., A. Makishima, R. Berger, and J.D. Mackenzie. "Chemical and Physical Properties of Obsidian: A Naturally Occurring Glass." *Journal of Non-Crystalline Solids* 17, no. 1 (1975): 129–42.

Fallon, Isabelle, and Desmond O'Neill. "The World's First Automobile Fatality." *Accident Analysis and Prevention* 37, no. 4 (July 2005): 601–603.

Faulds, Ann, Trudi Craggs, and John Saunders. "The Definition of a Road?" In *Scottish Roads Law*, 2nd ed. Tottel, 2008.

Firchow, Peter. *Aldous Huxley, Satirist and Novelist.* University of Minnesota Press, 1972.

Ford, Henry. "Why I Favor Five Days' Work with Six Days' Pay." Interview by Samuel Crowther. *World's Work* 52 (1926): 613–16. Reprinted in *Monthly Labor Review* 23 (1926): 1162–66.

Forsyth, Raymond, and Joseph Hagwood. *One Hundred Years of Progress.* California Transportation Foundation, 1996.

Gagg, Colin R. "Cement and Concrete as an Engineering Material: An Historic Appraisal and Case Study Analysis." *Engineering Failure Analysis* 40 (2014): 114–40.

Goldfarb, Ben. *Crossings: How Road Ecology Is Shaping the Future of Our Planet.* Norton, 2024.

Grant, L. D. "Lead and Compounds." In *Environmental Toxicants: Human Exposures and Their Health Effects,* ed. Morton Lippmann and George D. Leikauf. 3rd ed. Wiley-Interscience, 2009.

Halberstam, David. *The Fifties.* Villard, 1996.

Heitmann, John Alfred. *The Automobile and American Life.* 2nd ed. McFarland & Company, 2018.

Herman, Arthur. *Freedom's Forge: How American Business Produced Victory in World War II.* Random House, 2012.

Hinckley, Jim, and Jon G. Robinson. *The Big Book of Car Culture: The Armchair Guide to Automotive Americana.* MotorBooks, 2005.

Howard, John M. "Historical Background to Accidental Death and Disability: The Neglected Disease of Modern Society. *Prehospital Emergency Care* 4, no. 4 (2000): 285–89.

Jakle, John A., and Keith A. Sculle. *Fast Food: Roadside Restaurants in the Automobile Age.* Johns Hopkins University Press, 1999.

Jones, Geoffrey. *Beauty Imagined: A History of the Global Beauty Industry.* Oxford University Press, 2010.

Kater, Michael H. *Hitler Youth.* Harvard University Press, 2009.

Kehoe, Robert A. "Experimental Studies on the Inhalation of Lead by Human Subjects." *Pure and Applied Chemistry* 3, nos. 1–2 (1961): 129–44.

Ladd, Brian. *Autophobia: Love and Hate in the Automotive Age.* University of Chicago Press, 2008.

Lange, Alexandra. *Meet Me by the Fountain: An Inside History of the Mall.* Bloomsbury, 2022.

Lay, Maxwell G. *Ways of the World: A History of the World's Roads and of the Vehicles That Used Them.* Rutgers University Press, 1992.

Litman, Todd. *New Mobilities: Smart Planning for Emerging Transportation Technologies.* Island Press, 2021.

MacColl, E. Kimbark. *The Shaping of a City: Business and Politics in Portland, Oregon, 1885–1915.* Georgian Press, 1976.

William Manchester, *Disturber of the Peace: The Life of H. L. Mencken.* Harper & Row, 1951.

—. *The Glory and the Dream: A Narrative History of America, 1932–1972.* Little, Brown and Company, 1974.

Marohn, Charles L. *Confessions of a Recovering Engineer: Transportation for a Strong Town.* Wiley, 2021.

Martin, John Bartlow. *Adlai Stevenson and the World: The Life of Adlai E. Stevenson.* Anchor Press/Doubleday, 1978.

—. *Adlai Stevenson of Illinois: The Life of Adlai E. Stevenson.* Anchor Press/Doubleday, 1976.

McGraw-Hill, "Highway Engineering." *McGraw-Hill Concise Encyclopedia of Science and Technology.* 5th ed. McGraw–Hill, 2005.

Miller, Roger L., and Alan D. Stafford, *Economic Education for Consumers.* Cengage Learning, 2009.

Monaghan, Frank. *Official Guidebook of the New York World's Fair, 1939.* Exposition Publications, 1939.

Morris, Peter. "Rubber." In *Berkshire Encyclopedia of World History.* 2nd ed. Berkshire, 2010.

Needham, Andrew. *Power Lines: Phoenix and the Making of the Modern Southwest.* Princeton University Press, 2015.

Needleman, Herbert L. "Clair Patterson and Robert Kehoe: Two Views on Lead Toxicity," *Environmental Research* 78, no. 2 (August 1998): 79–85.

Nelson, Walter Henry. *Small Wonder: The Amazing Story of the Volkswagen.* Rev. ed. Little, Brown, 1970.

Nestle, Marion. *Food Politics: How the Food Industry Influences Nutrition and Health.* University of California Press, 2002.

Nevins, Allan, and Frank Ernest Hill, *Ford: The Times, The Man, The Company.* Charles Scribner's Sons, 1954.

Newman, Peter, and Jeffrey R. Kenworthy. *The End of Automotive Dependence: How Cities Are Moving Beyond Car-Based Planning.* Island Press, 2015.

Norton, Peter D. *Fighting Traffic: The Dawn of the Motor Age in the American City.* MIT Press, 2008.

Nriagu, Jerome O. "Clair Patterson and Robert Kehoe's Paradigm of 'Show Me the Data' on Environmental Lead Poisoning." *Environmental Research* 78, no. 2 (August 1998): 71–78.

Parissien, Steven. *The Life of the Automobile: The Complete History of the Motor Car.* Atlantic Books, 2013.

Peden, Margie et al. *World Report on Road Traffic Injury Prevention*. World Health Organization, 2004. https://iris.who.int/bitstream/handle/10665 /42871/9241562609.pdf.

Petersen Publishing Company, and Erwin M. Rosen. "The Catalytic Converter." In *The Petersen Automotive Troubleshooting and Repair Manual*. Grosset & Dunlap, 1975.

Pietrykowski, Bruce. "Fordism at Ford: Spatial Decentralization and Labor Segmentation at the Ford Motor Company, 1920–1950." *Economic Geography* 71, no. 4 (1995): 383–401.

Robert, Joseph C. *Ethyl: A History of the Corporation and the People Who Made It*. University Press of Virginia, 1983.

Ronan, Larry. "Seatbelts: 1949–1956." U.S. Department of Transportation, National Highway Safety Administration. April 1, 1979. DOT-HS-803-911, DOT-TSC-NHTSA-79-01, https://rosap.ntl.bts.gov/view/dot/11828.

Rosner, David, and Gerald Markowitz. "A 'Gift of God'? The Public Health Controversy Over Leaded Gasoline During the 1920s." *American Journal of Public Health* 75, no. 4 (1985): 344–52, https://doi.org/10.2105/ajph.75 .4.344.

Ross, Benjamin, and Steven Amter. *The Polluters: The Making of Our Chemically Altered Environment*. Oxford University Press, 2010.

Sabin, Paul. *Public Citizens: The Attack on Big Government and the Remaking of American Liberalism*. Norton, 2021.

Segrave, Kerry. *Drive-In Theaters: A History from Their Inception in 1933*. McFarland, 2006.

Sloan, Alfred P., and Boyden Sparkes. *Adventures of a White-Collar Man*. Doubleday, 1941.

Smith, Andrew. *Fast Food and Junk Food: An Encyclopedia of What We Love to Eat*. Greenwood, 2012.

Solow, Victor D, dir. "Design for Dreaming." Part of series *Motorama: Vision of the Future*. General Motors Corporation, 1956. 10 mins.

Standage, Thomas. *A Brief History of Motion: From the Wheel, to the Car, to What Comes Next*. Bloomsbury, 2021.

Temple, David. *The Cars of Harley Earl: Features GM's Revolutionary Concept and Production Cars*. CarTech Inc., 2016.

Watts, Steven. *The People's Tycoon: Henry Ford and the American Century*. Vintage/Random House, 2005.

Wenzel, T. Analysis of National Pay-As-You-Drive Insurance Systems and Other Variable Driving Charges. Energy Analysis Program, Lawrence Berkeley National Laboratory. University of California, 1995.

Williams, Karel, Colin Haslam, and John Williams. "Ford versus 'Fordism': The Beginning of Mass Production?" *Work, Employment & Society* 6, no. 4 (1992): 517–55.

Wingroff, Richard. "Federal-Aid Highway Act of 1956: Creating the Interstate System," *Public Roads* 60, no. 1 (1996).

INDEX